LEADING THE REVO·LUTION

GARY HAMEL
LEADING THE REVO·LUTION

HARVARD BUSINESS SCHOOL PRESS
BOSTON, MASSACHUSETTS

Library of Congress Cataloging-in-Publication Data

Hamel, Gary

    Leading the revolution/Gary Hamel.

        p. cm.

    Includes bibliographical references and index.

    ISBN 1-57851-189-5 (alk. paper)

    1. Creative ability in business. 2. Strategic planning. I. Title.

HD53 .H353 2000

658.4'012--dc21   00-038920

The paper used in this publication meets the requirements of the American
National Standard for Permanence of Paper for Publications and Documents in
Libraries and Archives Z39.48-1992.

This book is dedicated to Professor Paul Hamel.

There is no one who has taught me more.

There is no one I hold in higher regard.

It is my greatest fortune to be his son.

LEADING THE REVO· LUTION

CONTENTS

PREFACE

If you are about to embark on a journey through this book, you deserve to know something about its provenance and purpose. Its origins go back as far as 1983, when I left the University of Michigan to start my teaching career at the London Business School. Shortly before my departure, a well-meaning professor took me aside and gave me some advice: "Gary, if you want to get ahead in the world of academia, spend the first few years of your career extending an already well-developed theory. Find a generally accepted paradigm and apply it in some new context." He went on: "The next step is to write a string of articles for refereed journals." This, he assured me, was the surest route to tenure. "When you've accumulated enough gray hair, then you can strike off into new territory. By then you will have earned the right to create new theory."

Wise counsel—if my ambition had been limited to getting tenure. But I wanted to do something more: I wanted to challenge the deterministic view of strategy that prevailed at the time, a view that had no place for passion, ambition, creativity, and serendipity. In the mid-1980s industrial economists dominated the field of business strategy. To them, competition took place within well-defined industry boundaries. Industry combatants were assumed to be more alike than different. They competed at the margin in an endless game of thrust and parry. Coca-Cola versus Pepsi in the soft drink industry, Kodak versus Fuji in photographic film, Kimberly-Clark versus Procter & Gamble in disposable diapers—these were the cases that dominated the strategy curriculum in most business schools at the time. Yet it was apparent to me that a sterile and deterministic view of strategy was incomplete, if not outdated. Deregulation, globalization, privatization, and new technology were making industry boundaries as meaningless as borders in the Balkans. Moreover, I was dubious that competitive outcomes could be fully explained by a company's initial market position or its existing competitive advantages. As I began to dig deeper, I found that the most successful companies weren't obsessed with their competitors; instead they were following the polestar of some truly noble aspiration. What counted was not so much how they positioned themselves against long-standing rivals, but how creatively they used their core competencies to create entirely new markets.

So I rejected my professor's advice. And I rejected the economists' bloodless and deterministic view of competitive success and failure. And if I have had any success as a management thinker and author, it is because I did. If I had spent a decade elaborating old theories, *Competing for the Future* would never have been written. *Strategic intent, core competence,* and *industry foresight* would never have become part of the management lexicon. Yes, I've written a few articles in narrowly academic journals. But most of my energies went into writing for the *Harvard Business Review*—a magazine aimed at managers, not academicians. I didn't want to build on someone else's concepts, I wanted to create new concepts, and useful ones at that. This is a dangerous course for a young assistant professor. But one I was compelled to follow.

In 1993, in the midst of writing *Competing for the Future*, with C. K. Prahalad, I moved to the heart of the Silicon Valley. While I didn't abandon academia entirely (I became a visiting professor at the London Business School and later took a part-time research position at the Harvard Business School), I reduced my business school responsibilities to about a dozen days a year. I had grown frustrated with the long lead times between concept development and practical application. Sure, a lot of people read the *Harvard Business Review*, but do they *do* anything as a result? Do they feel compelled to *act*? And would they know where to start? I was becoming less and less interested in writing intriguing articles and more and more interested in helping companies invent the new management practices that would be critical to success in the new economy. My heroes were no longer Peter Drucker, Tom Peters, Michael Porter, and other management gurus, though I am continually awed by their profound insights. Instead my heroes had become Joseph Juran and W. Edwards Deming, the pioneers of the quality movement. These men were more than gurus—they were builders. They invented the tools and methods that turned quality into a ubiquitous capability. I loved teaching M.B.A. students and reveled in the intellectual stimulation of the business school environment. But I knew that if I was really going to help companies build radical new capabilities, I would have to become more than an armchair theorist. And so, in the summer of 1993, I flew home to America after 10 years in Britain so that I could devote all of my energies to helping companies invent and build the new capabilities that would allow them to thrive in the post-industrial economy. My goal, immodest to be sure, was to do for innovation what Deming and Juran had done for quality—to turn it from a hit-or-miss kind of thing into a deeply embedded capability.

Silicon Valley has given me a ringside seat for the birth of the digital age, and Strategos, a company I founded in 1994 with a few equally zealous souls, became the vehicle for developing the new tools and methods, the metrics and processes that would allow companies to become habitual innovators. Over the past six years, I and my colleagues at Strategos have been lucky enough to work with dozens of world-class companies, from Internet start-ups to the biggest multinationals on earth, that have all shared a single passion: to make radical innovation a deeply embedded capability.

Leading the Revolution is the product of that experience. Like *Competing for the Future*, it aims to overturn comfortable management nostrums. Many believe that there is an unbridgeable chasm between the old economy and the new economy. The very different fortunes of the Dow Jones Industrial Average and the NASDAQ over the past few years suggest to some that unless a company is a dot-com start-up, it has no chance of being an outstanding wealth creator, much less a company filled with passion and missionary zeal. Even *Fortune* magazine has occasionally made a blunt distinction between "old farts" and "upstarts." Of course there is a dividing line between companies that venerate the past and those that invent the future. But that line is not between the old economy and the new economy, it is between those that are capable of profound innovation and those that are not. The Home Depot, Gap, Virgin Atlantic Airways, Sephora, and Starbucks—these companies have been every bit as innovative as eBay, Amazon, Yahoo!, priceline.com, or any other Silicon Valley darling.

Indeed, the real story of Silicon Valley is not "e," but "i," not electronic commerce but innovation and imagination. What distinguishes many of the dot-com companies is not their technical prowess (you won't find any billion-dollar R&D budgets), but their imagination. They are young, hungry, and totally devoid of tradition. It is the power of "i," rather than "e," that separates the winners from the losers in the twenty-first-century economy.

Moreover, companies like Nokia, Enron, and Charles Schwab have shown themselves capable of continually reinventing themselves and their industries. Yet there are those who continue to maintain that "large companies can't innovate." But they can, and a few of them do. And in this book I'll tell you how. On the other hand, there are many who believe that small companies are inherently more creative. Some start-ups are creative, but most are not—that's why there's a 90 percent mortality rate for new companies. And even those that have been buoyed up by a tidal wave of e-phoria will find themselves washed up on the rocks of irrelevance if they don't learn how to reinvent themselves again and again. This book is as much for them as for the geriatric survivors of the industrial age.

This is a book about innovation—not in the usual sense of new products and new technologies, but in the sense of radical new business models. It begins by laying out the revolutionary imperative: we've reached the end of incrementalism, and only those companies that are capable of creating industry revolutions will prosper in the new economy. It then provides a detailed blueprint of what *you* can do to get the revolution started in your own company. Finally, it describes in detail an agenda for making innovation as ubiquitous a capability as quality or customer service. Indeed, my central argument is that radical innovation is *the* competitive advantage for the new millennium.

This is a book for those who want to make a difference—in their world and in their organization. It is a manifesto *and* a manual. It is a book for those who refuse to surrender to Dilbert–style cynicism. It is a book for those who believe the future is something you create, not something that happens to you. It is a book for those who believe passion is just as important as profits. It is a book for those who believe industrial age management practices are a liability in a post–industrial world. It's a book for those who refuse to believe that incumbents can't innovate. This is a book for those who are tired of playing it safe. It is a book for those who are unwilling to sacrifice their dreams on the altar of accepted wisdom. It is a book for those who care so much about their customers, their colleagues, and their own legacy that they simply can't imagine not leading the revolution.

ACKNOWLEDGMENTS

Whatever the shortcomings of this book, they are mine; whatever its strengths, they owe much to the generous contributions of others. In large part, this book is the product of what I and my colleagues at Strategos have learned from the thousands of individuals we have had the privilege of working with in our worldwide innovation practice.

Linda Yates, my co–founder at Strategos, deserves credit for encouraging me to write a book that would speak not only to vice presidents and corporate mavens, but to anyone, in any organization, who harbored a creative mind and a restless spirit.

Peter Skarzynski, Strategos's CEO, shouldered a disproportionate share of executive burdens as I took time off to write this book. For this, I thank him. I also thank him and his colleagues for demonstrating so conclusively that the principles laid out in this book really *can* ignite revolutionary passions and spawn rule–breaking strategies in companies of every size and shape.

Professor Peter Williamson of INSEAD, founder of the Strategos Institute, played an important role in helping to develop several of the key conceptual themes of this book. Mark Bonchek and Robert Chapman Wood, part of the original Institute research team, deserve credit for helping to crystallize the idea of "innovation styles," and for illuminating many of the impediments to innovation that exist in large companies. Pierre Loewe and David Crosswhite also made a significant contribution to the development of the Institute's point of view on innovation and, thereby, my own understanding. Peter Birkeland spent a year as my personal research associate, navigating through an ocean of financial data in order to better document the diminishing returns achieved by cost-cutting, reengineering, and other incremental improvement programs. Michael Hickcox, an extraordinarily capable researcher, worked to develop much of the anecdotal evidence used throughout the book.

Liisa Valikangas and Amy Muller, also of the Strategos Institute, informed and challenged me in countless ways. Their success in developing tools and methods for "strategy activists" further strengthened my belief that so-called ordinary employees can indeed re-vector even the largest and most hidebound of companies. Ellen Pruyne, a researcher at the Harvard Business School, helped me identify the important parallels between political and corporate activism.

Erick Schonfeld took a six-month leave of absence from his responsibilities as a writer at *Fortune* to help me prepare key sections of the manuscript. As research partner, sounding board, and writer, he played a critical role in documenting the successes of real-world corporate activists and in describing the practices of companies that seem to have found the secret of perpetual innovation. His enthusiasm, diligence, and professionalism were a blessing.

There are many who let me interrupt their busy lives so that I might better understand the challenge of building revolutionary strategies. Faith Popcorn, Jim Barksdale, Andy Bechtolsheim, Jim Clark, John Seely Brown, Marc Andreessen, Bill Gross, Alan Kay, John Naisbitt, Nick Negroponte, and Jim Taylor helped me better understand what it takes to be a seer, a heretic, and a serial revolutionary. Courageous activists like John Patrick, David Grossman, Ken Kutaragi, and Georges Dupont-Roc took the time to teach me about what it takes to change large, complicated organizations when you're *not* the CEO. And executives at Cisco, GE Capital, Charles Schwab, Enron, Disney, Virgin, and Shell helped me uncover some of the secrets of perpetual innovation.

Marjorie Williams, of the Harvard Business School Press, exercised an extraordinarily deft hand in her role as editor. She strengthened the manuscript in countless ways. At the beginning of this project, I asked the HBS Press team to help me produce a book that wouldn't look like a typical, turgid business tome. To the extent we have succeeded in this, much of the credit must go the superb design and art program created by Mike Fender and Anton Marc. Thanks also to Carol Franco, Director of the HBS Press, who committed the Press so enthusiastically and completely to the success of this book. Suffice to say, I count it as an enormous privilege to have worked with the remarkable HBSP team, including Chuck Dresner, Genoveva Llosa, Katie Mascaro, Sarah McConville, Greg Mroczek, Barbara Roth, Gayle Treadwell, and Leslie Zheutlin.

More than anyone else, though, it is Grace Reim who made this book possible. In addition to her substantial duties within the Strategos Institute, she voluntarily took on the task of project manager for what turned out to be a two-year, globe-spanning enterprise. Her contributions have been legion—from taking a myriad of tasks off my plate so I could devote time to research and writing, to arranging countless interviews, to negotiating with agents and publishers, to cajoling me when I got distracted and encouraging me when the task seemed overwhelming. Her spectacular competence and unflagging dedication made this book possible. I will be forever in her debt.

LEADING THE REVO·LUTION

1

THE END
OF PROGRESS

THE AGE OF PROGRESS IS OVER.
It was born in the Renaissance, achieved its
exuberant adolescence during the Enlightenment,
reached a robust maturity in the industrial age, and
died with the dawn of the twenty–first century. For
countless millennia there was no progress, only
cycles. Seasons turned. Generations came and went.
Life didn't get better, it simply repeated itself in an
endlessly familiar pattern. There was no future, for
the future was indistinguishable from the past.

Then came the unshakable belief that progress
was not only possible, it was inevitable. Life spans
would increase. Material comforts would multiply.
Knowledge would grow. There was nothing that
could not be improved upon. The discipline of
reason and the deductive routines of science could
be applied to every problem, from designing a more
perfect political union to unpacking the atom to
producing semiconductors of mind–boggling
complexity and unerring quality.

Throughout the last century progress was not simply honored, it was worshiped. A chicken in every pot? Hah! How about two SUVs in every garage? Yet progress is not quite so alluring as it once was. There is a gnawing sense that while humankind continues to improve its means, it does not always improve its purposes. Two world wars made infinitely more brutal by modern weaponry, the threat of biological and nuclear terrorism, dead rivers and butchered forests, mega–cities teeming with displaced peasants, workaholics from Tokyo to San Jose who have sacrificed health and family on the altar of prosperity: progress has exacted a price. The age of progress began in hope—it is ending in anxiety. Life is no

The age of progress began in

longer defined by the gentle meandering of the seasons, but by the pell-mell pace of "Internet time," where life's passing is measured in dog years.

The age of progress has been a stern taskmaster—and never more so than in recent times. Employees around the world have been strapped to the wheel of continuous improvement. With eyes glazed, they have repeated the mantra: faster, better, cheaper. Employees have found themselves working harder and harder to achieve less and less. That's the reward for surviving the downsizing, outsourcing, and restructuring that have so dramatically thinned the ranks of industrial–age companies. No wonder *Dilbert's Management Principles* is the best-selling business book of all time. Humor cloaks anxiety and gives voice to cynicism.

And the late twentieth–century version of progress has made us cynical. We were promised relief from tedium; we got the white–collar factory. We were promised a degree of autonomy; we got binders full of corporate policy. We were promised a sense of true purpose; we got the tyranny of quarterly returns. We were promised the chance to contribute; we got endless meetings where form regularly beat substance to a pulp. We were promised an outlet for our creativity; we got reengineering. We were often called "associates," but were as expendable as worn-out machines. Yeah, our backs were straighter—the age of progress lightened the physical load—but our minds were numb and our spirits were anywhere but at work.

THE AGE OF REVOLUTION

We now stand on the threshold of a new age—the age of revolution. In our minds, we know the new age has already arrived; in our bellies, we're not sure we like it. For we know it is going to be an age of upheaval, of tumult, of fortunes made and unmade at head-snapping speed. For change has changed. No longer is it additive. No longer does it move in a straight line. In the twenty-first century, change is discontinuous, abrupt, seditious. In a single generation, the cost of decoding a human gene has dropped from millions of dollars to around a hundred bucks. The cost of storing a megabyte of data has dropped from hundreds of dollars to essentially nothing. Global capital flows have become a raging torrent, eroding national economic sovereignty. The ubiquity of the Internet has rendered geography meaningless. Bare-knuckled capitalism has vanquished all competing ideologies and a tsunami of deregulation and privatization has swept the globe.

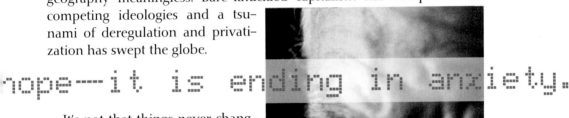

hope---it is ending in anxiety.

It's not that things never changed in the age of progress; they did. Old companies faded away—remember American Motors and Eastern Airlines?—and new companies emerged. But to use a metaphor from biological evolution, it was a world of punctuated equilibrium, where change happened by degrees and seldom spawned entirely new life forms. Today we live in a world that is all punctuation and no equilibrium. We are witnessing a Cambrian explosion of new competitive life forms. In this new age, a company that is evolving slowly is already on its way to extinction.

THE NEW INDUSTRIAL ORDER

Out of the age of progress came a world of industrial giants: Mitsubishi, ABB, Citigroup, General Electric, DaimlerChrysler, DuPont, and their peers. These companies harnessed the disciplines of progress: rigorous planning, continuous improvement, statistical process control, six sigma, reengineering, and enterprise resource planning. Decade after decade they focused single-mindedly on getting better. If they happened to miss something that was changing in the environment, there was plenty of time to catch up. The advantages of incumbency—global distribution, respected brands, a deep pool of talent, cash flow—granted them the luxury of time. For instance, although Apple Computer got an early start in the microcomputer business, IBM quickly reversed Apple's lead when it threw its worldwide distribution might behind the PC. But in a world of discontinuous change, a company that misses a critical bend in the road may never catch up. Consider these examples:

- Between 1994 and 1999, the number of mobile phones sold each year exploded from 26 million to nearly 300 million. At the same time, the technology changed from analog to digital. Motorola, the world leader in the cellular telephone business until 1997, missed the shift to digital wireless technology by just a year or two. In that sliver of time, Nokia, a hitherto unknown company, perched on the edge of the Arctic circle, became the world's new number one. A decade earlier Nokia had been making snow tires and rubber boots; suddenly it was one of Europe's fastest growing high-tech companies. For Motorola, regaining its top spot will be a Herculean task.

- Want to build a great Internet portal site? Sorry, too late. If you're an incumbent like Sony or Bertelsmann and you want to grab a few million online eyeballs, you're going to have to write a check for a zillion dollars or so and give it to a twenty-something kid who's managing a company that is hemorrhaging cash. Or maybe you'll get lucky and Yahoo! will buy you.

- In recent years Nike has learned a painful lesson about the attention span of 14-year-olds. They're no longer badgering their parents to lay down 100 bucks for a pair of Air Jordans. To them, Michael Jordan's just an old guy leading a second-rate basketball team. Their sneakers of choice—at least for the moment—are Vans and Airwalks.

NEVER HAS INCUMBENCY BEEN WORTH LESS.

- In the 1990s, SAP, based in Waldorf, Germany, proved that a European company could compete successfully with the likes of Oracle and Computer Associates in the market for enterprise software. Indeed, thousands of companies installed SAP's R/3 software to help them integrate internal operations like purchasing, accounting, and manufacturing. But when companies started using the Web to link up with suppliers and customers, SAP was nowhere to be seen. In the space of a few months, Ariba, i2 Technologies, Siebel Systems, and a bunch of new B2B specialists zoomed by SAP to stake out leadership positions in computerdom's hottest new software market.

In the age of revolution, opportunities come and go at light speed—blink and you've missed a billion-dollar bonanza.

Never has incumbency been worth less. Schumpeter's gale of creative destruction has become a hurricane. New winds are battering down the fortifications that once protected the status quo. Economic integration has blown open protected markets. Deregulation has destroyed comfortable monopolies. The Internet has turned bricks and mortar into millstones. And venture capitalists pour millions of dollars into terrorist training camps for industry insurgents.

Compaq, Novell, Westinghouse, DEC, TWA, Kodak, Kmart, Nissan—these and a hundred other incumbents have found themselves struggling to stay relevant in a topsy-turvy world. Just as the Age of Reason undermined the authority of organized religion in matters secular, the age of revolution will undermine the authority of the world's industrial incumbents in matters commercial.

Consider some evidence. If you're an American over the age of 40, you may remember Main Street—that humble row of shops operated by neighborly souls who knew your kids by name and catered to your every need. All that is gone now, replaced decades ago by look-alike shopping malls with Sears at one end, J. C. Penney at the other, and a row of specialty shops such as B. Dalton and KB Toys in between. Then, when you weren't looking, those suburban malls started down the long road toward retail irrelevance. Category killers like Toys "R" Us, The Home Depot, and Staples slowly crushed many of the specialty retailers that once made the malls work, and Wal-Mart displaced Sears as America's biggest retailer. But what's the chance that the retailing revolution stops with Wal-Mart and Toys "R" Us? None. Consumers aren't going to spend the rest of their lives wandering the soulless canyons of Wal-Mart to save a couple of bucks on a hammer. Woolworth never escaped Main Street. Sears got stuck in the mall. And all those "big box" retailers afloat in a sea of asphalt will one day find themselves on the wrong side of the Internet-enabled revolution. With only one or two exceptions, there is not a single market leader in the offline retailing world that leads its category online. Most of the old-line companies just didn't move quickly enough. They weren't revolution-ready.

The experience of AOL in the United Kingdom demonstrates that even companies which grew up in Internet time are vulnerable to revolutionary new business concepts. Freeserve, an offshoot of Dixons, Britain's leading electronics retailer, launched a free Internet access service in September 1998. Fifteen months later it had won 1.5 million users and had displaced AOL UK as the largest Internet access provider in Britain.

Freeserve's innovation was to provide surfers free Internet access, taking instead a small percentage of the revenue generated by each user's phone connection charges. (In the United Kingdom, even local calls are billed by the minute.) At the end of its first day as a publicly listed company, Freeserve was valued at £2.07 billion, and it was worth more than £8 billion by February of 2000, around two and

FIRST
THE REVOLUTIONARIES WILL TAKE YOUR
MARKETS AND YOUR CUSTOMERS.

a half times British Airways. Having questioned the sustainability of the Freeserve model, AOL was forced to follow suit, and announced it too would offer a free Internet access service.[1] Whether Freeserve actually lives up to its valuation is quite beside the point. What is indisputable is that revolutionaries like AOL are just as vulnerable to radical new business models as flabby geriatrics, and that speed is no substitute for rule-breaking new business concepts. If your company is more than a day old, it's already an incumbent!

You can call it the "new economy," or the "digital economy," or the "post-industrial economy," but it's more than that. The collapse of communism gave us a new *world* order. The collapse of incumbency is giving us a new *industrial* order. In the new industrial order, the battle lines don't run between regions and countries. It's no longer Japan versus the United States versus the European Union versus the developing world. Today it's the insurgents versus the incumbents, the revolutionaries versus the landed gentry. Hundred-year-old companies with venerated brands are as vulnerable as yesterday's Internet darlings.

Royal Dutch/Shell is one of the world's premier oil companies, with a history as old as the industry. Yet one day Shell awoke to find that a supermarket, Tesco, had become the largest retailer of "petrol" in Britain, one of Shell's home markets. How do you handle that? You've spent hundreds of millions of pounds over several decades trying to convince consumers that your brand of petrol is better than the next guy's, and suddenly it's being sold as a loss leader along with milk and eggs.

Starbucks has become America's premier coffee brand and has the most loyal clientele of any retailer in the United States. The average Starbucks customer visits a store 18 times a month! (You'll have to find your own legal drug to sell—caffeine's already taken.) So picture all the brand managers sitting at Nestlé headquarters in Vevey, Switzerland, running Nescafé, the best-selling coffee in the world. Do you think they ever wondered how they could entice bus drivers and schoolteachers to line up five deep to pay three bucks for a latte? No? What were they worrying about? What color cans to put on supermarket shelves? How to beat Procter & Gamble?

Industry incumbents often mistake historical rivals for the enemy. Go to any large telecommunications company. Find its strategic plan from 1990. Look for any reference to Qwest, WorldCom, Level 3, Global Crossing, Cisco, Williams, or Enron. You won't find any. But by 2000 there were 3,000 registered telecom carriers in the United States. There had only been 200 a decade before—*worldwide!*[2] Go to any grocery retailer and ask to see its strategic plan from a few years back. I'll bet there's no mention of Bechtel as a potential competitor. Yet

NEXT THEY'LL TAKE YOUR BEST EMPLOYEES.

the world's largest construction company is helping Webvan, a start-up, build a new distribution infrastructure that will support the home delivery of groceries ordered online. Know this: whoever you think your competitors are, they aren't.

Industry revolutionaries will exploit any protective urge, any hesitancy on the part of the oligarchy. Any attempt to hunker down, to fall back and regroup, or to disengage will be seized as an opportunity to claim more ground. First the revolutionaries will take your markets and your customers. Southwest Airlines might have started in Texas, but it's not just serving the southwest any more. Amazon.com may have started as a bookstore, but now it will sell you everything from toys to tools. Next

FINALLY, THEY'LL TAKE YOUR ASSETS.

they'll take your best employees. The number of Silicon Valley execs who used to work at AT&T, Apple, Xerox, Andersen Consulting, and other venerable but stodgy companies is in the thousands. And don't expect to hire many of those bright, young Harvard Business School grads. In a recent class of 880 M.B.A.'s, 340 expected to launch start-ups or join the world of venture capital, a figure that has trebled in four years.[3] Tomorrow's competitors are already hiring the best people. Finally, they'll take your assets. How unexpected that eBay, the Internet auction firm, acquires the third largest auction house in the United States, Butterfield & Butterfield. How surprising that Vodafone, still in its teens, buys Mannesmann, one of Germany's oldest and proudest companies. How weird that AOL, the company that made the Internet safe for technophobes, would create a "merger of equals" with Time Warner, a company with revenues five times those of AOL. The barbarians are no longer banging on the gate—they're eating off of your best china. This is the old guard versus the vanguard. The oligarchy versus the revolutionaries. The power of incumbency versus the power of imagination. You know which way to bet.

Simply put, never has it been a better time to be a rebellious newcomer, eager to upend industry dogma. Softbank, Ariba, Starbucks, Level 3, Amazon.com, Freeserve, IKEA—these and a hundred others are the new revolutionaries. Not all of them will survive, but their success thus far is a testament to the vulnerability of incumbents.

LIMITED ONLY BY IMAGINATION

Every age brings its own blend of promise and peril, and the age of revolution has plenty of both. But there is reason to be more hopeful than fearful, for the age of revolution is presenting us with an opportunity never before available to humankind. For the first time in history we can work backward from our imagination rather than forward from our past. For all of history, human beings have longed to explore other worlds, to reverse the ravages of aging, to transcend distance, to shape their environment, to conquer their destructive moods, to share any bit of knowledge that might exist on the planet. With the Mars Pathfinder, tissue farming, videoconferencing, virtual reality, mood-altering drugs, and Internet portals, we've begun to turn each of these timeless dreams into reality. Indeed, the gap between what can be imagined and what can be accomplished has never been smaller.

We have not so much reached the end of history, as Francis Fukuyama would have it, as we have developed the capacity to interrupt history—to escape the linear extrapolation of what was. In the age of progress, the future was better than the past. In the age of revolution, the future will be different from the past and, perhaps, infinitely better. Our heritage is no longer our destiny.

Today we are limited only by our imagination. Yet those who can imagine a new reality have always been outnumbered by those who cannot. For every Leonardo da Vinci, Jonas Salk, or Charles Babbage, there are tens of thousands whose imagination cannot escape the greased grooves of history. For though there is nothing that cannot be imagined, there are few who seem able to wriggle free from the strictures of a linear world. Like a long–captive elephant that stands in place out of habit, even when un–tethered, most minds have not grasped the possibilities inherent in our escape from the treadmill of progress. Yet  individuals and organizations that are incapable of escaping the gravitational pull of the past will be foreclosed from the future.

To fully realize the promise of our new age, each of us must become a dreamer, as well as a doer. In the age of progress, dreams were often little more than fantasies. Today, as never before, they are doorways to new realities. Our collective selves—our organizations—must also learn to dream. In many organizations there has been a massive failure of collective imagination. How else can one account for the fact that so many organizations have been caught flat-footed by the future?

THRIVING IN THE AGE OF REVOLUTION

Somewhere out there is a bullet with your company's name on it. Somewhere out there is a competitor, unborn and unknown, that will render your strategy obsolete. You can't dodge the bullet—you're going to have to shoot first. You're going to have to out–innovate the innovators. Those who live by the sword will be shot by those who don't.

When Bill Gates says, "Microsoft is always two years away from failure," he's not defending himself yet again from the charge of being a monopolist. Gates understands the competitive reality of the new age. He knows that it's not only product life cycles that are shrinking; strategy life cycles are getting shorter, too. An almost stupefying pace of change ensures that any business concept, no matter how brilliant, will rapidly lose its economic efficiency. The difference between being a leader and a laggard is no longer measured in decades, but in years, and sometimes months. Today, a company must be capable of reinventing its strategy not just once a decade, in the midst of a crisis when it trades one CEO for another, but continuously, year after year.

Gates isn't the only corporate leader who understands the dynamics of the new industrial order. In a Gallup survey I authored,[4] approximately 500 CEOs were asked, "Who took best advantage of change in your industry over the past 10 years—newcomers, traditional competitors, or your own company?" The number one answer was newcomers. They were then asked whether those newcomers had won by "executing better" or "changing the rules of the game." Fully 62 percent of the CEOs said the newcomers had won by changing the rules. Despite this, how many times have you heard a CEO or divisional vice president say, "Our real problem is execution"? Or worse, they'll tell people that "strat-

In a nonlinear world, only nonlinear ideas will create new wealth.

egy is the easy part, implementation is the hard part." What rubbish! These worthless aphorisms are favored by executives afraid to admit that their strategies are seriously out of date, executives who'd prefer their people stop asking awkward questions and get back to work. Strategy is easy only if you're content to have a strategy that is a derivative of someone else's strategy. Strategy is anything but easy if your goal is to be the author of industry transformation. It is, however, immensely rewarding. What could be more gratifying than putting one's fingerprints all over the future?

One CEO put it to me this way: "I used to spend most of my time worrying about the *how*—how we did things, how we operated, how efficient we were. Now I spend much of my time worrying about the *what*—what opportunities to pursue, what partnerships to form, what technologies to back, what experiments to start." The point is simple. By the time an organization has wrung the last 5 percent of efficiency out of the *how*, someone else will have invented a new *what*. Inventing new whats—that's the key to thriving in the age of revolution.

GOING NONLINEAR

The signal accomplishment of the industrial age was the notion of continuous improvement. It remains the secular religion of most managers. Its first incarnation came in Frederick Winslow Taylor's scientific management. Its many descendents include the Japanese concept of *kaizen* and the oh-so-'90s notions of reengineering and enterprise resource planning. Taylor is the spiritual godfather of every manager and consultant who has ever sought to describe, measure, and streamline a business process.

Organizational learning and knowledge management are first cousins to continuous improvement. They are more about getting better than getting different. The final accomplishment of the age of progress was to turn knowledge into a commodity. Today you can buy knowledge by the pound—from consultants hawking best practice, from the staff you've just hired from your competitor, and from all those companies that hope you'll outsource everything. Yet in the age of revolution it is not knowledge that produces new wealth, but insight—insight into opportunities for *discontinuous* innovation. Discovery is the journey; insight is the destination. You must become your own seer.

In a nonlinear world, only nonlinear ideas will create new wealth. Most companies long ago reached the point of diminishing returns in their incremental improvement programs. Continuous improvement is an industrial-age concept, and while it is better than no improvement at all, it is of marginal value in the age of revolution. Radical, nonlinear innovation is the only way to escape the ruthless hypercompetition that has been hammering down margins in industry after industry. Nonlinear innovation requires a company to escape the shackles of precedent and imagine entirely novel solutions to customer needs.

In *Competing for the Future*, C. K. Prahalad[5] and I drew a distinction between numerator and denominator management. We took companies to task for focusing exclusively on cutting the denominator (capital, headcount, and investment) in their financial ratios—"corporate anorexia," we termed it. We argued that downsizing wasn't the only way to reap efficiency gains. If you could grow the numerator off a more-or-less fixed base of investment and headcount, you could also drive productivity higher. Well, a lot of companies got the message. Although downsizing has continued unabated, with more than 675,000 layoffs by large American companies in 1999, there aren't many CEOs who haven't been fretting about how to pump up revenues. Yet growth ain't that easy. In the summer of 1999, Procter & Gamble announced

15,000 layoffs around the world and warned investors of a potential $1.9 billion charge against earnings. This despite the fact that in 1995 P&G set itself the ambitious goal of doubling its revenues to $70 billion by 2005. This would have required a 10 percent annual growth rate. In 1999 P&G was a long way off that pace.[6] In early 2000, Unilever PLC, P&G's Anglo–Dutch competitor, announced a $5 billion restructuring that would eliminate 25,000 jobs and close as many as 100 factories. Ironically, Antony Burgmans, Unilever's co–chairman, described the massive retrenchment as "all about accelerating the rate of growth at Unilever."[7] Yeah, sure. I bet it was more about convincing Unilever's long–suffering shareholders that top management hadn't fallen asleep at the switch.

The growth problems of P&G and Unilever are not unique. It's not easy to grow the top line with a strategy that's "more of the same." For some years, McDonald's growth in the United States has been sputtering. The company introduced a new cooking system that promised made–for–you hamburgers even quicker off the grill. Will this solve McDonald's growth problem? It might, but maybe McDonald's should ask itself if Americans are already eating as many hamburgers as they're ever going to. Maybe Americans have reached their cholesterol limit. In a recent survey across 20 industries, I found that only 11 percent of companies had been able to grow revenues twice as fast as their industry over a decade, and only 7 percent had been able to grow shareholder returns at twice the industry average. The message is clear: in the absence of nonlinear innovation, industry *is* destiny!

The challenge is not numerator *versus* denominator; it's not getting bigger *versus* getting leaner. Growth is *not* the antidote to cost cutting. After all, revenues and costs play equally important roles in driving earnings. The real issue today is linear innovation versus nonlinear innovation— whether the challenge is kicking growth into high gear or taking a big chunk out of costs.

How did Dell get to the point where it was turning its inventory over five or six times faster than Compaq? This wasn't the product of reengineering; this was nonlinear innovation. Why is Internet banking inevitable? Because the estimated cost of an Internet banking transaction is 1 percent of the cost of a branch–bank, teller–assisted transaction. Whenever you take 99 percent out of the cost structure of a product or service, it's a safe bet that you're going to blow apart the industry.

If you're trying to grow revenues or slice costs with a straight–line, incremental approach, you're going to find yourself facing an "innovation gap" with competitors who have managed to break conventions and achieve step function changes. The world is increasingly divided into two kinds of organizations: those that can get no further than continuous improvement, and those who've made the jump to radical innovation.

BUSINESS CONCEPT INNOVATION

Industry revolutionaries take the entire business concept, rather than a product or service, as the starting point for innovation. Revolutionaries recognize that competition is no longer between products or services, it's between competing business concepts. A few examples:

- Internet telephony is an entirely different business concept from dedicated voice networks, requiring different assets, technologies, and pricing.
- Buying insurance via the Internet is a radically different business model from going to a physical agency. You can instantly compare policies and be sure you are getting the very lowest price.
- Over the last couple of decades, banks have lost nearly half their share of U.S. household financial assets to newcomers such as Fidelity and Charles Schwab. Bankers looked at customers as savers; the mutual fund industry knew we were investors, too.
- IKEA has a high-volume business model for selling affordable home furnishings that is quite unlike that of a traditional furniture store. For one thing, you can take the furniture home with you. For another thing, you get great design at minimalist prices.
- Hotmail's strategy for winning online eyeballs—free advertising-supported e-mail—was completely different from AOL's initial approach to capturing customers—carpeting the world with AOL sign-on diskettes. In 18 months, Hotmail went from a standing start to 10 million users; by mid-1999 it boasted 40 million accounts to AOL's 18 million. Hotmail was ultimately acquired by Microsoft.
- Searching for a job at Monster.com, which in early 2000 had more than 350,000 job listings, is nothing like perusing the help wanted section in your local newspaper. For one thing, you can search for jobs all across the country.
- Hughes' highly successful DirecTV service is built on a business model that has no parallel in the old world of network broadcasting: hundreds of channels, programming menus, pay-per-view, and more besides.
- Downloading Barenaked Ladies (that's a pop group) off the Web via MP3 is not remotely like buying music from Tower Records or a Virgin megastore. Or you can download a utility from napster.com that will

help you search the Web for any piece of music you'd like to download. With a high-speed modem, you can burn your own CDs faster than you can drive to your local music store.

- AllAdvantage.com is turning advertising on its head. Install the company's ad-laden view bar next to the browser on your computer, and you get 50 cents an hour while you surf. Watch an ad, get paid— whadda concept! In the future, all of us will expect to be compensated every time we take the trouble to view an ad.

- When you go down to the mall, you have all the purchasing power of, well, you. When you buy via mercata.com, you have the purchasing power of everyone who's buying the same stuff you are. The more folks buying, the cheaper the price. Instant buyer co-ops. Another radical new business concept.

- On the NASDAQ, traditional market makers are challenged by new "electronic communication networks," such as Instinet, that offer 24-hour trading and narrower spreads.

INDUSTRY REVOLUTIONARIES DON'T TINKER AT THEY BLOW UP OLD BUSINESS MODELS

Industry revolutionaries don't tinker at the margins; they blow up old business models and create new ones. While not all of the companies mentioned here will survive the next decade, the new business concepts they've pioneered most probably will.

Yet there are few individuals in most organizations who know how to invent entirely new business concepts or make radical adjustments to existing business concepts. In most companies, a call for "more innovation" is interpreted as a plea for new products or new features on old products. In this sense, most people possess a highly truncated view of innovation. They suffer from what I sometimes call the "Double Stuf Oreo" phenomenon. At Nabisco, innovation is when you stuff twice as much filling between two chocolate cookies as you used to. Don't get me wrong. Oreos are great cookies, and Double Stuf Oreos are even better, but that is not business concept innovation—it is linear innovation focused on a single *component* of the business model. Make no mistake, product innovation is still important. When, after years of trying, Clorox managed to create lemon-scented bleach, it drove the category into double-digit growth. And anyone who's shaved with Gillette's Mach III razor knows why it commands a price premium. Yet a product-based view of innovation is excessively narrow. I'm not sure that Starbucks coffee is better than what I can get in any gourmet food shop, but it's served up inside a very different business model—one that blends conviviality and theater with the java.

Many also view innovation as essentially technology-led, and it frequently is. Yet business concept innovation often has little to do with new technology—think of IKEA, Old Navy, Virgin Atlantic, and many other innovators that are not technology pioneers. Technology, especially information technology, is available to all. The question is whether you can apply that technology in a unique way. Most companies have been engaged in a technology arms race—each forced to match its competitors' ever-rising IT budget. The same is likely to hold true for the billions companies are now spending on Net-related technology. Most of this investment will be focused on Web-enabling old business

Most people possess a highly truncated view of innovation. They suffer from what I sometimes call the "Double Stuf Oreo" phenomenon.

HE MARGINS;
AND CREATE NEW ONES.

models, rather than on using the Internet to create radical new business models. Like Wal-Mart or FedEx in the '80s and '90s, there will be a few companies that will use the new technology to realize dramatically new business concepts, but for every Dell Computer or Amazon.com there will be hundreds of others that will spend millions playing an endless game of catch-up. To turn information technology into a *secret* weapon, you have to be able to conceive of hip, new business models—a skill possessed by few CIOs. If technology is going to become anything other than a great leveler, CIOs will have to become Chief Imagination Officers.

CEOs, CIOs, and efficiency-besotted consultants spent the '90s learning to think systematically about business processes. Initiatives aimed at supply chain integration, process reengineering, enterprise resource planning, and customer relationship management demolished functional chimneys and crisscrossed organizational boundaries. Yet they were seldom radical, and many impacted only a single component or process in the company's overall business model. Business concept innovation is both radical *and* systemic. (See the figure "Beyond Continuous Improvement.")

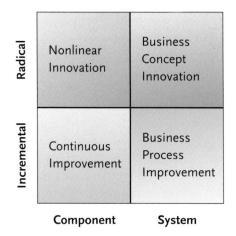

The age of revolution beckons us to expand our horizons. So much more is possible than mere product line extensions and IT-enabled business processes. The latitude for innovation has never been broader—if only our minds can stretch to it. At the heart of industry revolution are daring new business concepts. It is this type of systemic innovation that poses the greatest risk for incumbents, because a response calls for action across a broad front—action that often undermines old business concepts. Look, for example, at the failure of Compaq Computer to adapt itself to Dell's direct-sales, build-to-order business concept. While Dell was building a bold new business model, Compaq was playing grave robber, buying Digital Equipment Corporation, a nearly deceased computer maker that had once been an industry revolutionary itself. In the end, Compaq's CEO Eckhard Pfeiffer got the boot. This was the second time a Compaq CEO had been flung out the door as the company tried to negotiate a tight bend in the road to the future. What an expensive—and humiliating— way to change strategies!

Business concept innovation will be *the* defining competitive advantage in the age of revolution. Business concept innovation is the capacity to reconceive existing business models in ways that create new value for customers, rude surprises for competitors, and new wealth for investors. Business concept innovation is the only way for newcomers to succeed in the face of enormous resource disadvantages, and the only way for incumbents to renew their lease on success.

New Wealth

With every wrinkle in the fabric of history, new wealth gets created and old wealth gets destroyed. It will be no different as the age of progress gives way to the age of revolution. The question is, Who will create the new wealth and who will squander the old? The revolutionaries have already laid their hands on enough wealth to ransom all the world's potentates several times over. With a net worth that hovers around $90

WHO WILL CREATE THE NEW WEALTH AND WHO WILL SQUANDER THE OLD?

billion, Bill Gates is the richest human being in history, having used Microsoft as a giant lever with which to overturn the computer industry. Heading up a company that, in 1999, had more than twice the market cap of America's largest car maker, Michael Dell is a bigger fish on Wall Street than Jack Smith, the chairman of General Motors. Likewise, the value of Wal-Mart is more than 14 times the combined value of Sears, Roebuck and J. C. Penney.

Companies today are obsessed with satisfying shareholders. Spin-offs, de-mergers, share buybacks, tracking stocks, efficiency programs—all these things *release* wealth, but they don't create *new* wealth. Neither do mega-mergers. These strategies don't create new wealth because they don't create new markets, new customers, or new revenue streams. Industry revolutionaries are in the business of creating new wealth. You won't find them playing shell games with shareholders. Go look at growth in market valuations over the past decade for some successful revolutionaries—companies like Charles Schwab, The Home Depot, Gap Inc., Yahoo!, Amazon.com, eBay, Dell Computer, and others. Then ask yourself, Do any of your company's improvement programs, do any of its financial engineering schemes, do any of its potential acquisitions, do any of its creative earnings management techniques offer that kind of upside? Don't bother answering. I can tell you they don't. If you want to thrive in the age of revolution, you're going to have to do more than wring a bit more wealth out of yesterday's strategies. You're going to have to get everyone focused, from top to bottom, on the challenge of capturing more than your fair share of tomorrow's opportunities. Revolutionaries don't release wealth, they create it. They do more than just conserve, they build.

TOWARD CAPABILITY

At the core of business concept innovation is a capacity to create new wealth-generating strategies—strategies that are as revolutionary as the time we live in. This raises a question you may already be asking yourself: Where do new wealth-creating strategies come from? The strategy industry—all those unctuous consultants, self-proclaimed gurus, and left-brain planners—doesn't have an answer. They all know a strategy when they see one—Look! Twenty-two "profit zones"!—but they don't know where new strategies come from. They don't have a theory of strategy creation, much less any insight into how to build a deeply embedded capacity for strategy innovation. Maybe a general manager hungry for a new strategy should eat a fiery vindaloo curry at eleven o'clock at night and hope that when the inevitable indigestion strikes, it will succeed in provoking a strategy insight.

Perhaps strategies come from the annual planning process—that well-rehearsed ritual found in almost every organization. Consider the planning process in your own company. What adjectives would best describe it? Those in column A or column B? Unless your company is truly exceptional, you'll probably have to admit that the descriptors in column A are more apt than those in column B.

___ A ___		___ B ___
Procedural		Creative
Reductionist		Expansive
Extrapolative		Inventive
Elitist		Inclusive
Easy		Demanding

The notion that strategy is "easy" rests on the mistaken assumption that strategic planning has something to do with strategy making. Of course strategy appears easy when the planning process narrowly limits the scope of discovery, the breadth of involvement, and the amount of intellectual effort expended, and when the goal is something far short of revolution. The assumption that strategy is easy says more about the inadequacies of our planning processes than the challenge of creating industry revolution.

Giving planners responsibility for creating strategy is like asking a bricklayer to create Michelangelo's *Pieta*. Any company that believes planning will yield revolutionary strategies will find itself caught in a prison of incrementalism as free-thinking newcomers lead successful insurrections. If the goal is to create new strategies, you might as well dance naked round a campfire as go to one more semisacramental planning meeting.

No wonder that in many organizations, the whole notion of strategic planning has been devalued. How often has it produced any radical value-creating insights? No wonder corporate strategy has become little more than deal making. No wonder consulting companies are doing less and less "strategy" work and more and more "implementation" work.

Well then, perhaps revolutionary strategies come from "visionaries" like Bill Gates (Microsoft), Ted Turner (CNN), Anita Roddick (The Body Shop), Rupert Murdoch (News Corp), Andy Grove (Intel), Jeff Bezos (Amazon.com), Howard Schultz (Starbucks), Mickey Drexler (The Gap), and Michael Dell (Dell Computer). Many, if not most, industry revolutions have their genesis in the vision of a single individual who often ends up as CEO or chairman. Yet today's visionary is often tomorrow's intellectual straightjacket. All too often a company runs to the end of the visionary's headlights, and then crashes and burns. Just remember Apple Computer, where Steve Jobs, the poster boy for missed opportunities, resisted efforts to license the Macintosh operating system to other companies. Improbably, after having been booted from the company he helped to create, Jobs got a second chance when he took up the CEO reins again in 1997. Yet however miraculous Apple's more recent turnaround, the company will forever be a footnote in the history of the computer industry—in large part because of the myopia of the company's founder. Likewise, Dell Computer will be similarly doomed if its top management is unable to escape a PC-centric view of the computer industry. The mainframe was eclipsed by the minicomputer, which was in turn eclipsed by the personal computer. DEC became the second largest computer company in the world when IBM was slow to respond to the threat of minicomputers, and Dell became the most dynamic company in the PC business when IBM, Compaq, and others were slow to reinvent their business models. Yes, there will almost certainly be a post–PC world, there will even be a post–Windows world, and if history is any guide, Dell Computer, Microsoft, and the industry's other current leaders will be bystanders in that new world.

Visionaries don't stay visionaries forever. Few of them can put their hands on a second vision. Worse, their compatriots become dependent on the visionary's prescience, thus abdicating their own responsibility for envisioning new opportunities. More times than not, a fading visionary who is also CEO or chairman unwittingly strangles a company's capacity for radical innovation. That is why visionary companies seldom live beyond their first strategy. The Silicon Valley, fertile ground for industry

...visionary companies seldom live beyond their first strategy.

revolutionaries, is also a graveyard for one–strategy companies. There are only a handful of Valley companies—Hewlett–Packard, Intel, Applied Materials, Cisco—that have been revolutionaries more than once.

Of course most companies are not led by visionaries; they're led by administrators. No offense, but your CEO is probably more ruling–class than revolutionary. So don't sit there staring at the corporate tower hoping to be blinded by a flash of entrepreneurial brilliance. Administrators possess an exaggerated confidence in great execution, believing this is all you need to succeed in a discontinuous world. They are accountants, not seers. Visionary CEO or sober–suited *apparatchik*, neither is likely to be a font of wealth–creating strategies.

Maybe some of you have sat through a business–school case study—a 90–minute striptease where some creaky professor undresses a management principle that has been enrobed in 20 pages of colorless prose. Suppose the case being discussed concerns a hugely successful company, and the professor is in the midst of an elaborate and elegant post hoc analysis . . .

> *. . . so you see, they developed a killer application by exploiting a disruptive technology that allowed them to capture increasing returns from their unique core competencies, thereby creating a new ecosystem with a deep, new profit pool.*

In the midst of such blather did you ever think to yourself, "Wait a minute, was this success the result of some terribly incisive strategic thinking or was it pure, dumb luck?" Luck or foresight? Where does strategy come from? That's a damn good question.

Consider the genesis of three revolutionary strategies:

> *When her husband left their home in Littlehampton, England, to pursue a lifelong dream of riding horseback from Buenos Aires to New York, Anita Roddick was left to fend for herself and her daughters. To support her family, Anita opened a small cosmetics shop in nearby Brighton, filling cheap plastic bottles with goo. From this seed grew The Body Shop, a company with revenues of $1 billion in 1998.*

Just before his fifty-eighth birthday, Mike Harper, the acquisitive CEO of ConAgra Inc., suffered a heart attack. After an extended stay in intensive care, Mike left the hospital with a commitment to changing his dietary habits. The newly health-conscious CEO challenged his company to create a line of good-for-you products that would be equally great tasting. The result was Healthy Choice, a line of nutritious frozen dinners that quickly became the leader in its category. The Healthy Choice brand now spans more than 300 products—from breakfast cereals to snack foods to deli meats to ice creams—that had more than $15 billion in sales in 1999.[8]

What do Pez dispensers—those little plastic heads that dole out candy—have to do with one of the world's hottest Internet start-ups? Plenty. Just ask Pierre Omidyar. His fiancée was a committed Pez collector. How, Pierre wondered, could he help his girlfriend feed her Pez passion? The answer: an online, person-to-person trading community where Pezheads could buy and sell their weird collectibles. Pierre's idea blossomed into eBay, the Web's premier auction site, where more than 2 million members place a million bids a day. As eBay's founder, Pierre is credited with transforming everything from classified ads in small town newspapers to the pompous practices of the world's elite auction salons.[9]

Luck or foresight? Where do radical new business concepts come from? The answer is this: new business concepts are always, always, the product of lucky foresight. That's right—the essential insight doesn't come out of any *dirigiste* planning process, it comes from some cocktail of happenstance, desire, curiosity, ambition, and need. But at the end of the day, there has to be a degree of foresight—a sense of where new riches lie. So business concept innovation is always one part fortuity and one part clear-headed vision.

If the capacity of an organization to thrive in the age of revolution depends on its ability to reimagine the very essence of its purpose and destiny, and to continually create for itself new dreams and new destinations, we are left in a quandary. How do you increase the probability that radical new wealth-creating strategies emerge in *your* organization? Can we turn serendipity into capability?

The quality movement provides a useful analogy. Thirty years ago, if you had asked someone, "Where does quality come from?" they would have replied, "From the artisan" or perhaps, "From the inspector at the end of the production line." Quality came from the guy with magical hands at Rolls-Royce, who spent weeks hammering a fender around a wooden form, or from the white-coated inspectors at the end of the Mercedes-Benz production line. Then Dr. Deming came along and said, "We must institutionalize quality—it has to be everyone's job. That guy down there on the shop floor, with 10 years of formal education and grease under his fingernails, that guy is responsible for quality. " It's easy to forget how radical this idea was. In Detroit, auto execs said, "You gotta be kidding! Those guys down there are saboteurs."

It took many companies a decade or more to grasp and internalize quality as a capability. But the challenge is no longer quality. You've been there, done that, got the Baldrige. Neither is it time–to–market, supply chain management, or even e–commerce. Today the challenge is to build a deep capability for business concept innovation—a capability that produces entirely new business concepts and dramatically reinterprets old ones.

Like Deming, Juran, and the early leaders of the quality movement, we're going to have to invent *new* practice. If you had wanted to benchmark best–of–breed quality in 1955, where would you have gone? The answer's not obvious. There was no Deming prize; no ISO 9000. Yet the quality pioneers were undeterred. They invented new practice, built on a new philosophical foundation. Like them, we must aspire to more than "best practice," for most of what currently passes for best practice innovation is grounded in the age of progress; it's simply not good enough for the age of revolution.

Creating a companywide capacity for radical innovation will be no less challenging than creating an organization infused with the ethos of quality—and this time it can't take 10 years. And it won't—not if you're willing to kick off the lead boots of denial; not if you're willing to dump all that useless management theory you picked up back there in the age of progress; not if you're ready to climb over the walls of your Dilbert cell and take responsibility for something more than your "job."

ACTIVISTS RULE

Whether what you now hold in your hands is simply shelfware, or an incendiary device, depends on you. You've been told that change must start at the top—that's rubbish. How often does the revolution start with the monarchy? Nelson Mandela, Václav Havel, Thomas Paine, Mahatma Gandhi, Martin Luther King: did they possess political power? No, yet each disrupted history; and it was passion, not power, that allowed them to do so.

Most of us pour more of our life into the vessel of work than into family, faith, or community. Yet more often than not the return on emotional equity derived from work is meager. The nomadic Israelites were commanded by God to rest one day out of seven—but He didn't decree that the other six had to be empty of meaning. By what law must competitiveness come at the expense of hope? If you're going to pour out your life into something, why can't it be into a chalice rather than down a drain hole? For every one of us, it is our sense of purpose, our sense of accomplishment, our sense of making a difference that is at stake—and that is more than enough.

Never has it been a more propitious time to be an activist:

- Intranets and corporatewide e-mail are creating something close to an *information democracy*. The information boundaries that used to delineate corporate authority are more permeable than ever.

- More than ever, senior executives know they cannot command commitment, for the generation now entering the workforce is more *authority averse* than any in history.

- It is universally apparent that we are living in a world so complex and so uncertain that authoritarian, control-oriented companies are bound to fail.

- Increasingly, intellectual capital is more valuable than physical capital, and it is employees who are becoming the true "capitalists."

- Millions of employees are now shareholders as well—they are suppliers *and* owners.

Activists are changing the shape of companies around the world. At Sony, a midlevel engineer challenges top management to overcome its prejudice against the video-game business. "We don't make toys!" they protest. He badgers, plots, and schemes. Against all odds he persuades Sony to develop the PlayStation—a phenomenally successful video-game console that in 1998 accounted for more than 40 percent of Sony's profits. He keeps pushing. Finally Sony sets up a Computer Entertainment division and commits itself to making the computer more than a soulless business machine.

A Web-besotted computer scientist and a gadget-loving market planner join forces at IBM in the early 1990s. Their quixotic goal is to turn IBM into an Internet-savvy powerhouse. They establish a bootleg lab and begin building Webware. They organize an underground lobbying effort that turns a disparate and far-flung group of Webheads into a forceful community of Internet advocates. Their grassroots efforts become the foundation for IBM's emergence as the e-business company.

So don't tell me it can't be done. Only ask yourself if you have the guts to lead the revolution.

Dream, create, explore, invent, pioneer, imagine: do these words describe what *you* do? If not, you are already irrelevant, and your organization is probably becoming so. The age of revolution requires not diligent

radical new wealth-creating strategies emerge in your organization?

soldiers, throwing themselves at the enemy *en masse*, but guerilla fighters, highly motivated and mostly autonomous. So enough of Dilbert, that whining little weasel. When's the last time he stuck his head above the walls of his cubicle? When's the last time he pushed back? When's the last time he actually *fought* for an idea? He's a *wimp*. He deserves what he gets.

The age of revolution requires revolutionaries. If you act like a ward of your organization, you'll be one, and both you and your company will lose. So if you're still acting like a courtier or a consort, bending to the prejudices of top management, buffing up their outsized egos, fretting about what they *want* to hear, getting calluses on your knees—stop! You're going to rob yourself and your company of a future that's worth having. No excuses. No fear. If you're going to be an activist, these have to be more than T-shirt slogans.

In the new industrial order, the battle is not democracy versus totalitarianism or globalism versus tribalism, it is innovation versus precedent. Ralph Waldo Emerson put it perfectly when he said, "There are always two parties—the party of the past and the party of the future, the establishment and the movement."

Which side are *you* on?

THE NEW INNOVATION REGIME

In the age of revolution we will see competition not only between business models, but between innovation regimes. Big science, boffins in their labs, seemingly intractable problems, years of concentrated development, Eureka! moments, bet–the–company launches, Bell Labs, Sarnoff Labs, Watson Labs: this was the innovation regime of the industrial age. Its footsteps were measured and slow: Ready, ready, ready, ready, aim, aim, aim, fire. It gave us the compact disc, cholesterol–fighting drugs, the 747, optical fiber, speech recognition, the TGV, fuel cells, Kevlar, LCD, and so much more. It created enormous wealth for companies brave enough and rich enough to risk it all on the vagaries of scientific discovery. From the 1900s through the 1950s, big science had no rival as a mechanism for creating new wealth.

In the postwar years a second innovation regime was born—one that first created and then fed off the consumer society. Its heroes were Coca–Cola, Procter & Gamble, Unilever, Nestlé, and Kellogg. Though these companies and their many competitors invested in R&D, they

Dream, create, explore, invent, pioneer, imagine: do these words describe what you do?

were more in the business of manufacturing wants than creating scientific breakthroughs. In a world that was no longer capacity constrained, the challenge was to get consumers to buy *your* particular brand of soap powder, peanut butter, or soft drink. Here the marketers, rather than the scientists, were the innovators. They were endlessly inventive in using advertising to create the stories we wanted to tell ourselves about ourselves. Suddenly shampoo and toothpaste were sitting atop Maslow's hierarchy of needs. Thousands of look–alike products were launched each year, distinguished only by their advertising. From the 1950s to the 1990s, consumer marketing was innovation's high ground. The best and brightest no longer wanted to be scientists, they wanted to be brand managers.

The new industrial order is the product of a very different type of innovation—one built on neither the slow accretion of scientific knowledge nor the breathless hype of Madison Avenue, but instead on leaps of human imagination. Here, one's starting resource position is nearly irrelevant—innovators typically start with empty pockets. Development timescales are measured in weeks, not years. Customers are co–developers, providing real–time feedback in an endless cycle of experiment, adapt, experiment, adapt. Fire, fire, fire, fire, aim again, fire, fire, fire—there is no time for "ready." The goal is not a patent or a new ad campaign, but a radically new business concept. Here innovators are as likely to be college dropouts as Ph.D.'s and M.B.A.'s. They are neither scientists nor brand managers; they are entrepreneurs—what Charles Handy terms "the new alchemists"[10]—individuals able to produce something out of nothing. They struggle not against Nature but against the hegemony of established practice.

This is more Silicon Valley than corporate lab or customer focus group. In Silicon Valley, there is no CEO allocating resources across competing projects. There are no market researchers burrowing through reams of ethnographic data. Instead, there are thousands of novel business ideas competing in what has become an open market for business concept innovation. Those with merit attract talent and capital the way a flower captures the attention of a honeybee. While R&D and consumer marketing will forever be routes to wealth creation, they are no longer the only routes, nor even the most profitable ones. As the new millennium begins, industry revolution is the superhighway to El Dorado, and nowhere are there more revolutionaries per capita than in Silicon Valley. Yet in the new innovation regime Silicon Valley is not a place, but a metaphor for unfettered imagination, rampant experimentation, and an utter lack of nostalgia. To thrive in the age of revolution, every company will have to learn to bring the unique alchemy of Silicon Valley inside its own borders.

Big science is an elephant dragging a hardwood log up the steep incline of scientific inquiry. Consumer marketing is a trained seal—a consumer who has been taught to respond to the inducements and blandishments of clever marketers. The new innovation regime is a gazelle leaping again and again above the tall grass of precedent. Cisco, Yahoo!, Amazon.com, Sycamore Networks, Red Hat, CMGI—these and a thousand other industry revolutionaries are the children of this new regime. But if they are to succeed more than once, they must become its students as well. Gray-haired incumbents and acne-faced newcomers alike must embrace a new innovation agenda, one that builds on the two that have come before—and then goes far, far beyond them.

THE NEW INNOVATION AGENDA

Continuous improvement	*and*	Nonlinear innovation
Product and process innovation	*and*	Business concept innovation
"Releasing" wealth	*and*	Creating wealth
Serendipity	*and*	Capability
Visionaries	*and*	Activists
Scientists, marketers	*and*	Silicon Valley

Those who commit themselves to this new agenda will soon discover that the age of revolution is also the age of opportunity. Just as nineteenth-century America opened its doors to all those who believed in the possibility of a better life, the twenty-first century opens its doors to all those who believe in the possibility of new beginnings. It welcomes the dispossessed and the discontent. Just as the American Revolution sealed the end of feudalism as a political system, the age of revolution will put an end to corporate feudalism. The privileges of the industrial oligarchy, the prerogatives of brain-dead SVPs, the worshipful observance of corporate convention—all these will be swept away.

In the age of revolution it will matter not whether you're the CEO or a newly hired administrative assistant, whether you work in the hallowed halls of headquarters or in some distant backwater, whether you get a senior citizen discount or whether you're still struggling to pay off school loans. Never before has opportunity been so democratic.

Will you embrace the new innovation agenda? Do you care enough about your organization, your colleagues, and yourself to take responsibility for making your company revolution-ready? If you do, you have the chance to reverse the process of institutional entropy that robs so many organizations of their future. You can turn back the rising tide of estrangement that robs so many individuals of their sense of meaning and accomplishment. You can become the author of your own destiny. You can look the future in the eye and say:

I am no longer a captive to history.
Whatever I can imagine, I can accomplish.

I am no longer a vassal in a faceless bureaucracy.
I am an activist, not a drone.

I am no longer a foot soldier
in the march of progress.

I am a Revolutionary.

RISING EXPECTATIONS, DIMINISHING RETURNS

SHAREHOLDERS RULE.

They rule with an iron fist in America, in Britain, and, increasingly, around the world. They're hunting down complacent CEOs in Germany, France, and Italy. And you can even hear them asking rather indelicate questions of Japan's imperial corporate leaders. This isn't news. Your company is already kneeling at the altar of shareholder returns. Indeed, your company has turned itself inside out to satisfy shareholders. It's been restructured, reengineered, and delayered. It's launched programs for enterprise resource planning and customer relationship management. Your company has bought back its own shares, made a big acquisition or two, and spun off underperforming divisions. Maybe it has even launched a tracking stock to capitalize on the growth potential of an e–commerce subsidiary. Yet over the next decade it is going to have to do more, far more, to fill the gaping maw of the ever–hungry shareholder.

Maybe you're in one of those hot, young companies with millions in revenue and billions in market cap. That's cool, but you'd be foolish to mistake Internet investment fever for a rock–solid business concept. Sure the new economy demands some new math—companies *can* grow more quickly than ever before because they *are* less constrained by physical capital than ever before. But sooner or later you company's earnings performance will have to match its valuation, so you'd better be damn sure your company has a business concept that will live up to that implicit promise. If it doesn't, I'd hold off on pledging those stock options as collateral on a multi–million–dollar house.

If you're under 30, you may not remember that the personal computer industry spawned dozens of "hot" companies—Osborn, Kaypro, Commodore, and AST Research to name a few. But only one, Dell, was a wealth–creating superstar throughout the '90s, and even its share price sat on a plateau for most of 1999. So is your company going to be Kaypro or Dell? Are you going to join the ranks of Yahoo!, AOL, and Amazon.com, or get washed down the drain of companies that were unable to recognize and change a decaying business concept? Let me be clear: there are even more poorly conceived, ultimately uneconomic, me-too business concepts in the new economy than there are in the old. And even the best ones decay rapidly in the fetid environment of the Internet. If you're not extraordinarily adept at *perpetual* innovation, that e-business wave of hype your company is riding on right now is going to crash.

THE REVOLUTION OF RISING EXPECTATIONS

Every year investors raise the bar. Read an annual report from a decade ago, and you're likely to find a company chairman bragging about exceeding the prior year's performance. Back then you just had to beat yourself. Then investors began demanding more: "We don't care how you did against yourself. We want to know how you performed against your best–in–class peers." So the bar went up a few feet. Every diversified industrial company was pressed to meet the standards set by General Electric. Every retailer was expected to match the returns achieved by Wal–Mart. And every software company was measured by Microsoft's yardstick. Navel gazing was out; financial benchmarking was in.

Then the bar went up again. Investors said, "Wait a minute. You may be doing okay when compared to your peers, but what about the absolute standard of 'economic value added'? Are you actually earning more than your cost of capital?" Amazingly enough, the idea that a business should earn its cost of capital struck many executives as a new thought. Clearly more than a few had slept through Finance 101. So diligent executives across the planet began weeding out projects that couldn't promise a positive net present value. J. C. Penney, Toys "R" Us, Siemens, and dozens of other companies signed up for the EVA diet. Investors said, "Make those assets sweat."

As investors became more demanding, and less patient, CEOs felt the heat. John Akers (IBM), Kay Whitmore (Kodak), Roger Smith (General Motors), Bob Allen (AT&T), Gil Amelio (Apple Computer), Eckhard Pfeiffer (Compaq), Doug Ivester (Coca-Cola), and dozens more got the boot or slunk off into early retirement as investors grew weary of empty promises. The message of this bloodletting wasn't lost on the survivors: deliver or else.

Today's investors have an unquenchable thirst for ever higher returns. Cisco, Charles Schwab, AOL, Lucent, Amazon.com, Gap, Yahoo!, Dell, and Microsoft. None of these companies is more than a generation old. Yet their collective market cap at the beginning of 2000 was nearly $1.5 trillion, or close to 10 percent of the total market cap of all publicly listed companies in America. These companies were the stock market stars of the 1990s. But the bar is going up yet again and, if history is any guide, these companies are unlikely to repeat their superstar performance. There's a new crop of wealth creators whose eye-popping returns are once again resetting the gauge of investor expectations: CMGI, Akamai, Ariba, eBay, JDS Uniphase, COLT Telecom Group plc, and Sycamore Networks are just a few of the come-from-nowhere chart busters that started the new century with $15 billion-plus market caps. Sure, most of these companies will crash and burn, but their stratospheric returns, however temporary, have further fueled investor passions.

There are no more widows and orphans. With a new economy aborning and billions of dollars of potential wealth up for grabs, every investor wants a piece of the action. Forget the high jump, investors expect you to pole-vault. No longer are they fretting over whether or not you're earning your cost of capital. Nor do they care how you're performing against your equally underwhelming peers. Instead, they're asking whether you're likely to join the pantheon of wealth-creating superstars. Perched atop their IRA and 401(k) nest eggs, millions of investors are obsessed with beating the market. If you can deliver outstanding shareholder returns, you're a god. If you can't, you're a bum.

I can already hear you making excuses. "That's fine for Amazon.com or Cisco," you say, "but we're in a mature industry. We're not a start-up. We're not some Internet comet." I don't buy it. Wealth creators come in all sizes, can be found in all kinds of industries, and must often overcome the inertia of tradition and precedent. Scan the list of companies that delivered record-breaking returns during the 1990s, and you'll see companies such

as Gap, Harley-Davidson, SunAmerica, Clear Channel, The Home Depot, Progressive Insurance, and Merrill Lynch—hardly high-tech shooting stars.

It's not easy to become a stock market supernova, but it's even harder to stay one. At the same time that petulant investors have been demanding edge-of-the-atmosphere returns, the percentage of companies that have been delivering better-than-average returns has been steadily declining. In 1999 only 31 percent of the S&P 500 companies outperformed the S&P average—in terms of total return to shareholders. That was down from 58 percent in 1992, and the second lowest percentage in more than a decade. (In 1998, 29 percent of the S&P 500 did better than average.) Put simply, 7 out of 10 companies *underperformed* the market in 1999. By definition 50 percent of the S&P 500 outperformed the *median*, but fewer than 1 in 3 outperformed the *mean*. The discrepancy between the mean and the median is evidence that a few outstanding performers are simply outdistancing the rest of the field. Perhaps more surprisingly, only 10 percent of the stocks

There is an ever-growing population of mediocre companies and an ever-diminishing population of truly great performers.

on the NASDAQ beat the market average in 1999.

The brutal truth is this: there is an ever-growing population of mediocre companies and an ever-diminishing population of truly great performers. The explanation for the performance gap is simple. Companies that spent the past decade trying to wring the last ounce of efficiency out of tired, old business models have now reached the point of diminishing returns. Their strategies have become virtually indistinguishable from their competitors'. And with top management's attention focused internally on process and systems, they've left themselves wide open to unorthodox innovators. Only a few companies have escaped this writhing mass of mediocrity. Only a few companies have been successful in inventing entirely new business models, or in profoundly reinventing existing business models. These are the companies up there in investor heaven.

It is impossible to meet the rising expectations of shareholders without actually creating *new* wealth. To create *new* wealth you must innovate—in ways that competitors are not or cannot. You can't buy your innovation "off the shelf" from the same tired, old consulting companies your competitors are using. Cisco, The Home Depot, Pfizer, Charles Schwab, Yahoo!, and most of the other companies that have thrilled investors are true innovators. They've created new industries, new products, new services, all atop new business models.

Stewardship versus entrepreneurship, optimization versus innovation—these are fundamental dichotomies between the mediocre many and the extraordinary few. Stewards polish grandma's silver—they buff the assets and capabilities they inherited from entrepreneurs long retired or long dead. But in the new economy, investors don't want stewards; they want entrepreneurial *heroes*. Stewards are focused on "unlocking" shareholder wealth. Entrepreneurs are obsessed with the challenge of creating *new* wealth. They know you have to continually surprise investors with new wealth-creating achievements. There are no laurels.

HITTING THE WALL OF DIMINISHING RETURNS

The longest bull market in history produced extraordinary gains for shareholders and executives alike. Yet there is considerable evidence that many of the tactics used by companies in the 1990s to deliver ever-rising shareholder returns will fail to deliver the goods in the new decade. Put simply, many of the corporate programs and initiatives that pushed share prices ever higher are now reaching the point of diminishing returns. If you doubt this, ask yourself the following:

- How much more cost savings can your company wring out of its current business model? Are you and your colleagues working harder and harder for smaller and smaller efficiency gains?

- How much more revenue growth can your company squeeze out of its current business model? Is your company paying more and more for customer acquisition and market share gains?

- How much longer can your company keep propping up its share price through share buybacks, spin-offs, and other forms of financial engineering? Is top management reaching the limits of its ability to push up the share price without actually creating *new* wealth?

- How many more scale economies can your company gain from mergers and acquisitions? Are the costs of integration beginning to overwhelm the savings obtained from slashing shared overhead costs?

- How different are the strategies of the four or five largest competitors in your industry and from your company's strategy? Is it getting harder and harder to differentiate your company from its competitors?

If you answered "not much" and "yes" more than a couple of times, your company, and its business model, may be reaching the point of diminishing returns. Unless you're willing to face up to this fact, you'll have no incentive to embrace the new innovation agenda. So let's look at the evidence.

Unsustainable Cost Cutting—Getting Blood from a Stone

Over the past decade the pressure on executives to produce an escalator of steadily rising earnings has been intense. This pressure produced a myriad of initiatives aimed at cutting overhead, reducing labor and material costs, and improving capital utilization. Outsourcing, six sigma programs, reengineering, restructuring, ERP, and downsizing are all examples of efficiency–oriented programs. In the second half of the 1990s, this single-minded attack on inefficiency produced several years of double-digit earnings growth for the majority of the S&P 500. Indeed, in many cases, earnings growth far outstripped revenue growth.

For a year or two, or maybe even longer, profits can grow much faster than revenues. We often see this phenomenon in Lazarus cases such as

GROWTH IS THE SCOREBOARD, IT'S NOT THE GAME.

IBM, General Motors, and Sears, Roebuck. Corpulent companies go on a crash diet. Head count is slashed, assets are sold, and costs cut. While revenue growth remains sluggish, margins quickly improve. But there's ultimately a limit to how much profit even the best–managed, most–efficient company can squeeze out of any fixed amount of revenue.

We have to be suspicious of any company that has been growing earnings substantially faster than it's been growing revenues, especially if it has been doing so for more than a couple of years. Let's take a few examples. Between 1994 and 1999, the ratio of net income growth over revenue growth was 196 for Unisys, 53 for Adobe Systems, 39 for Eastman Kodak, 38 for Northrup-Grummer, 26 for Marriott International, 19 for AMR (the parent of American Airlines), and 10 for Xerox. Ask yourself, How long can a company grow earnings 10 times or 38 times or 52 times revenue? The answer is, Not for long. If earnings growth has been exceeding revenue growth by more than 5 to 1 in your company, for more than a few years, there's every reason to believe your core strategy is mostly dead. In such a situation, a smart CEO will be cashing in share options and looking for the exit.

While cost cutting has a way to run in Japan and continental Europe, many American and British companies have already reached the point of

diminishing returns in their efficiency programs. In 1999, the average operating margin for the nonfinancial services companies in the S&P 500
was 15.7 percent. Five years earlier, the average operating margin for these
same companies had also been 15.7 percent. Indeed, between 1994 and
1999, the average operating margin for these companies never varied by
more than 1.3 percentage points. Whatever the contribution of downsizing, ERP, and other efficiency programs to lower costs, these initiatives
haven't done much recently to fatten margins. Most of the cost savings got
passed directly to consumers, and further cost cutting, while necessary, is
unlikely to fuel earnings growth.

This doesn't mean that companies should abandon their zeal for cost
cutting, but it does suggest that there isn't much fat left in traditional business models. What these companies need is not more incremental cost
cutting, but radical innovation and new business concepts. Even the most
extensive program of corporate liposuction can't turn a sumo wrestler into
a lithe gymnast.

Unsustainable Revenue Growth—Spinning Your Wheels

Downsizing is a harrowing experience. A lot of former efficiency addicts
are now eager to grow. Growth is a worthy goal, but there is always a tendency to mistake the scoreboard for the game. Growth is the scoreboard;
it's not the game. Profitable growth is a derivative of innovation. Focusing
on growth, rather than on the challenge of business concept innovation, is
more likely to destroy wealth than to create it. The reason is simple. After
some point, trying to squeeze more revenue growth out of a moribund
business model is no easier than trying to squeeze out more costs. In the
absence of radical innovation, a blind allegiance to growth can suck a company into zero–sum market share battles or seduce it into paying exorbitant sums for customer acquisition. The result of a growth obsession is
often bigger revenues but not much traction in terms of additional profits.
This seems to be the pattern among many Internet start–ups. It is not sustainable. Let's flip our earlier ratio and look at revenue growth over earnings growth. If the ratio of revenue growth to earnings growth is more than
5 to 1, and has been so for several quarters, it suggests that a strategy melt-
down is in progress or, in the case of a start–up, a solid strategy has yet to
be found.

Between 1994 and 1999, the ratio of revenue growth over earnings
growth was 90 for Albertson's, 12 for Duke Energy, 11 for Hasbro, 10 for
Cooper Tire & Rubber, and 8 for Disney. For many companies the ratio
was actually negative. While the revenues of Compaq Computer were up
more than 250 percent over the five–year period, profits were down by 34
percent. And despite growing its top line by 140 percent, Coca–Cola

Enterprises saw its bottom line contract by 15 percent. Clearly, growth, by itself, is no substitute for radical innovation.

Companies that can grow revenue only by "giving away value" at close to zero profit are spinning their wheels—the engine's racing, but there's not much forward progress. Of course, there will be times when profits are scarce as a company "builds out" its strategy and amortizes its start-up costs. You're not going to be immensely profitable in the early years of building out a digital satellite broadcast system or a big optical telecom network or a giant online retailer. But in an extant business model, a declining ratio of earnings growth over revenue growth is a sure sign of strategy decay—the strategy may not stink yet, but it's sure dead.

On the other hand, many companies have had a reasonably balanced ratio of revenue growth to earnings growth. Between 1994 and 1999 the ratio for QUALCOMM was 1,349 percent to 1,222 percent, or 1.1. For Solectron the ratio was 476 percent to 429 percent, also 1.1. Merck's ratio was 1.2 and Wal-Mart's 0.9. While a balanced ratio isn't proof of a sound strategy, a seriously unbalanced ratio usually indicates a decrepit strategy.

Unsustainable Growth in Shareholder Returns— The Limits of Financial Engineering

It is fashionable today to talk of "unlocking" shareholder wealth. The metaphor is telling. The assumption is that the wealth is already there—it's already been created—and with a little creative financial engineering it can be set free.

To unlock shareholder wealth you get out of bad businesses—as Jack Welch did when he took over GE. You spin off companies that may command a significantly higher P/E than the parent company—witness the recent appetite for spin-offs and de-mergers at 3M (Imation), Hewlett-Packard (Agilent Technologies), AT&T (Lucent Technologies and AT&T Wireless), and other old economy companies. You try to dump inflexible and expensive capital assets onto someone else via outsourcing. Of course there's a limit to how many bad businesses a company can divest and how many of its assets it can dump. It's not surprising that after a couple of rounds of corporate restructuring, CEOs turn to share buybacks as an even easier way of plumping up share prices.

Share buybacks are one of the simplest and perhaps most simpleminded ways of unlocking shareholder wealth. Fresh out of ideas? No compelling investment opportunities? No problem! Take the cash being produced by today's business model and return it to shareholders. We shouldn't be surprised that over the last few years we've seen a record level of equity buybacks (see the graph "Share Buybacks among the S&P 500"). After all, there's nothing on this earth with a shorter time horizon than a 60-year-old CEO

SHARE BUYBACKS AMONG THE S&P 500

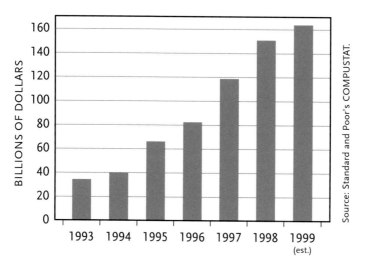

with a boatload of stock options who's racing his first coronary to the bank. And there's no way to get the share price up faster than buying back your own stock. Not surprising then that the number of share buybacks has grown apace with the number of share options held by senior executives in America's largest companies.

BUYBACK CHAMPS: CUMULATIVE ANNUAL BUYBACKS AS A PERCENTAGE OF MARKET CAPITALIZATION, 1994–1999

US Airways	66		Dow Chemical	31
Times Mirror	60		R. R. Donnelley & Sons	31
W. R. Grace & Co.	57		General Motors	30
Tandy	53		Union Carbide	30
Reebok International	44		Autodesk	30
Knight-Ridder	43		DuPont	26
Ryder System	40		AMR	26
PG&E	39		Phelps Dodge	25
ITT Industries	39		Sunoco	25
Liz Claiborne	36		Nordstrom	24
Cooper Industries	34		Deluxe	23
Adobe Systems	34		Hershey Foods	22
Hercules	33		Delta Air Lines	22
Maytag	32		Textron	22
IBM	31		Allstate	21

Source: Standard and Poor's COMPUSTAT; Strategos calculations.

If downsizing was the quick fix for corporate obesity, buybacks have become the instant cure for slow–growth syndrome. In the five years through 1999, companies as diverse as DuPont, IBM, PG&E, Maytag, The Limited, US Airways, Times Mirror, Tandy, and Bear, Stearns bought back shares worth more than 25 percent of their market capitalization (see the table "Buyback Champs"). Buybacks are a way of rewarding shareholders despite a lack of apparent growth prospects. Indeed, between 1994 and 1999 the average compound annual revenue growth rate of the top 50 buyback champs was a measly 4 percent. That rate for the S&P 500 was 13 percent, and the 50 fastest–growing companies averaged 50 percent compound annual revenue growth. "Here," buyback CEOs seem to be saying. "We don't know what to do with the cash. You take the money and go see if *you* can find some better investment opportunities." Of course this is exactly what a CEO bereft of new strategy ideas *should* do! But it's no more sustainable than selling off assets.

There are dozens and dozens of companies that have, over the past few years, delivered healthy shareholder returns, but have at the same time generated little or no growth in their overall market value. (A few are listed in the table "Growth in Shareholder Returns versus Growth in Market Capitalization.") These companies haven't created much new wealth.

GROWTH IN SHAREHOLDER RETURNS VERSUS GROWTH IN MARKET CAPITALIZATION, 1994–1999

	Shareholder Returns 1994–1999 (annualized)	Growth in Market Cap 1994–1999 (annualized)	Difference
W. R. Grace & Co.	18.3	(31.2)	49.5
Dun & Bradstreet	12.9	(15.4)	28.3
Times Mirror	27.2	(2.3)	24.9
Fortune Brands	9.2	(7.4)	16.6
Philip Morris	8.5	(6.4)	14.9

Source: Standard and Poor's COMPUSTAT.

When growth in shareholder returns significantly outpaces growth in a firm's market value (i.e., when share price is going up faster than the overall value of the firm), you can be sure there's a bit of financial legerdemain going on somewhere. No problem with that, but don't mistake financial engineering for radical innovation. A company that is relying extensively on sell–offs, spin–offs, or buybacks to drive up its share price is admitting, however inadvertently, that its strategy is headed for the abattoir.

De–mergers, spin–offs, share buybacks, and other techniques for unlocking shareholder wealth have built–in limits—at some point, there's no more wealth to "unlock." Unlocking shareholder wealth is a lesser challenge than creating *new* wealth. Stewards unlock wealth, entrepreneurs create wealth.

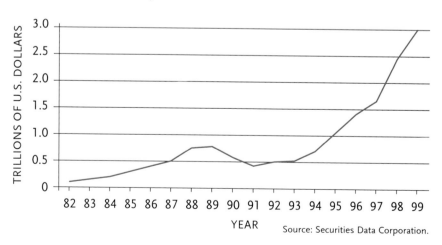

UNSUSTAINABLE CONSOLIDATION— WHEN BIGGER'S NOT ENOUGH

There is yet another option open to executives who have exhausted internal cost–cutting possibilities and are blind to opportunities for organic growth—the mega–merger. Hoping for a temporary respite from the law of diminishing returns, companies have been merging and acquiring at a record pace. The value of the mergers and acquisitions announced globally in 1998 amounted to nearly $2.5 trillion (see the graph "Value of Announced Mergers and Acquisitions Worldwide"). In the United States alone, announced M&A activity totaled more than $1.7 trillion, roughly 14 percent of the value of all publicly listed companies in America. And in 1999, 3 trillion dollars' worth of mergers were announced. Indeed, 19 out of the top 20 mergers in history, by size, were announced in the 18 months leading up to the end of the century. With virtually every com-

VALUE OF ANNOUNCED MERGERS AND ACQUISITIONS WORLDWIDE

Source: Securities Data Corporation.

Stock Options: Top Management's No–Lose Bet

More than 50 percent of the senior executives of America's largest companies derive a significant portion of their compensation from stock options. Indeed, a $100 million stock option payout is not unusual. A few executives have reaped close to half a billion dollars in a single year by exercising their accumulated share options. And these are not hot, young CEOs building new fortunes, but tenured administrators running legacy companies. While the theory was that option–owning managers would work even harder to create new wealth, the reality has been somewhat different.

With most of their assets tied up in stock options, it's difficult for top management to diversify their own shareholdings. Hence they cannot easily offset the risk of holding a large hoard of one company's equity. Thus it's not surprising that option–rich executives are likely to be even more conservative and short–sighted than the average investor who has the freedom to diversify across many companies. With so much of their net worth riding on a single stock, and retirement just a few years away, senior executives can be expected to prefer low–risk strategies for pumping up the share price. Buying back one's own shares is a safer bet than betting on novel business concepts.

Most option plans are not tied to the relative performance of a company against the S&P 500 or any other index. According to the *Wall Street Journal*, of the 209 big stock option grants made by large companies in 1998, only 36 had any type of performance trigger.[a] Thus an executive could underperform the average and still cash in, as his company's stock price was on the rise. Worse, options are frequently repriced if a stock falls below the strike price—an option not open to outside investors who may find themselves underwater thanks to management's malfeasance. Even the *Wall Street Journal*, hardly known for begrudging wealthy CEOs their due, had to conclude that "these days CEOs are assured of getting rich, however the company does."[b]

A few compensation committees do set specific stock price hurdles that must be reached before the options can be exercised. Level 3 Communications grants its top executives options that can be exercised only if the company's stock outperforms the S&P 500 stock index. General Mills requires executives to hold on to most of the shares they buy when they exercise their options.[c]

The law of unintended consequences is ever at work. Rather than getting CEOs focused on growing the long–term value of their companies, stock options have seduced many into short–term, one–shot, price–pumping schemes such as share buy–backs, spin–offs, and mega–mergers. In too many cases executives are not managing in the best long–term interests of their shareholders; they are managing in the best short–term interests of themselves.

[a] Joann S. Lublin, "Lowering the Bar," *Wall Street Journal*, 8 April 1999.

[b] Ibid.

[c] Tamar Hausman, "Predicting Pay," *Wall Street Journal*, 8 April 1999.

pany "in play," this superheated merger activity helped to buoy stock prices ever higher. But sadly, there is an in–built limit to industry consolidation. After all, at the current pace, another seven or eight years of merger mania would leave the American economy with one giant company!

Over the past few years it has been hard to pick up a financial magazine and not feel like you've just been transported to Jurassic Park. Everywhere you look there are dinosaurs mating: Exxon and Mobil, BP and Amoco, Travelers Group and Citicorp, Norwest and Wells Fargo, AT&T and TCI, Daimler–Benz and Chrysler, Bell Atlantic and GTE, SBC and Ameritech, Pharmacia and Upjohn. Hundreds of other copulating companies dot the landscape. While some of these couplings are propelled by truly strategic considerations—global market access or industry convergence—many are simply the last gasp of cost–cutting CEOs who hope that by slamming to-gether two lumbering incumbents they will be able to lop off another $1 billion or so of shared overhead.

Yet shareholders lose more often than they gain from such mergers. A 1999 study found that of the 700 largest deals completed between 1996 and 1998, more than half had actually diminished shareholder value.[1] These mergers follow a familiar course. The share price takes a bounce on expectations of future efficiencies, top management in the acquired com-pany gets a Midas–like payout, and, in the months that follow the deal, the usual postmerger turmoil and ever–escalating integration costs wipe out nearly all of the expected benefits.

A recent study in the pharmaceutical industry suggests that the most notable impact of a merger is the loss of market share by the participating companies. Furthermore, the study finds little evidence that bigger companies are any more productive at new drug discovery.[2] A significant minority of mega–deals, such as AT&T's purchase of NCR, Novell's acquisition of WordPerfect, Dow Jones & Co.'s purchase of Telerate, and Quaker Oats's acquisition of Snapple Beverage, turn out to be monumental stinkers, with the acquired company sold after an enormous write–off. Putting two drunks together doesn't make a stable person.

If there is a secondary logic to the wave of mergers sweeping the planet, it is the simple arithmetic of oligopoly. If you reduce the competitive intensity in an industry by reducing the number of independent competitors, profits are likely to go up. It's hard not to conclude that this logic has driven a number of telecom deals such as that between SBC and Ameritech. The industrial oligarchy loves an oligopoly: just enough competition to avoid direct government control, not enough to threaten a profitable sinecure.

Defending their merger plans, CEOs are often quoted as saying, "You have to be number one in your market to make any money," or "Only the biggest will survive." This rationale is largely specious. Sure there are network effects and scale economies that penalize smaller competitors. But

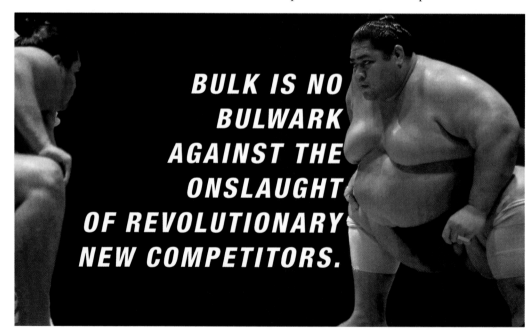

BULK IS NO BULWARK AGAINST THE ONSLAUGHT OF REVOLUTIONARY NEW COMPETITORS.

size doesn't inoculate a company from rule-busting innovation. A case in point: Despite their late start and small size, telecom newcomers such as Qwest, Williams Communications, and Level 3 have built fiber-optic networks that are as capacious as those owned by AT&T, Sprint, and MCI WorldCom, for a small fraction of the investment. Bandwidth capacity in the United States is set to multiply by up to 200 times in the first five years of the new millennium. AT&T's assets and revenues dwarf these rambunctious upstarts, but it's not clear that AT&T's size and scope make it a tougher competitor. Being an even bigger bank doesn't help you defend yourself from the likes of Charles Schwab or E*TRADE. Being the world's biggest physical bookstore doesn't protect you from the world's biggest virtual bookstore. There's no guarantee that Wal-Mart, America's biggest retailer, will become the biggest online merchant. For every action, there is an equal and opposite reaction. As incumbents seek to increase the concentration of industry power, newcomers plot ways to dilute it. While dinosaurs merge, upstarts race toward the future. Bulk is no bulwark against the onslaught of revolutionary new competitors. And it's hard to mate and run at the same time. The thinking in some merger-obsessed executive suites seems to go something like this: "If we're a really, really big dinosaur, then maybe we can survive the Ice Age." No chance. Look around you. The dinosaurs are gone.

In fact, for the top 1,000 publicly listed companies in America, the correlation between company size (as measured by average revenues over the past 3 years) and profitability (measured by average operating margins for the same period), whether measured over 3, 5, or 10 years, is no more than .004—a result that isn't statistically significant.[3] Put simply, there is no reason to expect that being bigger will make a company more profitable. Size and imagination of the sort that produces new, wealth-creating strategies are not correlated. Sure size brings advantages, but in the age of revolution those advantages are often offset by disadvantages—inflexibility, internal strife, and sloth.

A final rationale for many mega-mergers is "synergy"—a word that should send investors racing for the door. Here's what AT&T's CEO said in 1991 when his company acquired NCR: "I am absolutely confident that together AT&T and NCR will achieve a level of growth and success that we could not achieve separately. Ours will be a future of promises fulfilled." Here's what AT&T's CEO said in 1995 when the company was spun off to shareholders: "The complexity of trying to manage these different businesses began to overwhelm the advantages of integration. The world has changed. Markets have changed." No shit, Sherlock. That's the age of revolution for you—all that damn change. Well, then, be careful about loading up the balance sheet with billions of dollars of fixed assets on the basis of something as ethereal as "synergy."

Of course CEOs don't talk about synergy anymore. They've found a new word to justify imperial overstretch: "convergence." This seems to be the logic behind AT&T's shopping spree for cable television companies—and maybe investors will go to the bank this time, but it's not the way to bet.

Yeah, there are going to be a lot more mega–deals in the years ahead, particularly in Europe, where there are still dozens of subscale national champions. And yes, a well thought out program of disposals and acquisitions can play a critical role in revitalizing a company's core strategy. This has been the case for Britain's Cable & Wireless plc, a once small and stodgy telecom operator that has sold off some of its once–prized voice networks and bought its way into a burgeoning data–focused network. Yet by itself, no acquisition or merger, no matter how brilliantly conceived, will ever vault a company up into the ranks of the wealth–creating super-stars. It is interesting to note that at the end of the millennium, Nokia had become Europe's most valuable company, elbowing past BP Amoco p.l.c. While Nokia has made a string of small, targeted acquisitions and is in-volved in dozens of strategic partnerships, it has so far eschewed any mega–deals. On the other hand, it is consistently ranked as one of Europe's most innovative companies. How long Nokia retains the top spot is any-body's guess. But I challenge anyone to find a mega–merger that has pro-duced as much wealth for shareholders as Nokia has.

The central question to be asked of any merger–happy CEO is not whether the deal will bring cost savings, not whether it will yield scale ad-vantages, nor even whether it exploits "convergence." The real question is this: Where's the business concept innovation in all this, and why couldn't it be achieved through a more flexible means than a large–scale merger? In the age of revolution, deal making is no substitute for radical innova-tion. And getting bigger is no substitute for actually creating new wealth through business concept innovation. While mergers may have propped up stock markets around the globe in the '90s, it is a safe bet they are not going to be the surest route to wealth creation in the new millennium.

STRATEGY CONVERGENCE—THE LIMITS TO BEST PRACTICE

In a recent survey, funded by MCI and conducted by Gallup, I asked more than 500 CEOs whether they believed the strategies of their major competitors had been getting more alike or more dissimilar. The number one answer: more alike. This is not good news. Do you remember back to Economics 101 and the idea of "perfect competition"—when everyone in an industry followed an identical strategy and had similar resources? You probably also remember the textbook result: every company made just

ALL TOO OFTEN A SUCCESSFUL NEW BUSINESS MODEL BECOMES THE BUSINESS MODEL FOR COMPANIES NOT CREATIVE ENOUGH TO INVENT THEIR OWN.

enough profit to survive and no more. It's the business equivalent of a subsistence economy. That's the inevitable result of convergent strategies.

In nearly every industry, strategies tend to cluster around some "central tendency" of industry orthodoxy. Strategies converge because success recipes get slavishly imitated. All you computer industry executives who've been trying to imitate Dell's build–to–order business model, raise your hands! All you car company honchos who spent two decades trying to duplicate Toyota's lean manufacturing model, 'fess up! All you department store execs who've been using Wal–Mart as a case study in how to manage logistics, go ahead, admit it. Nothing wrong with imitation, of course, as long as you've achieved strategy differentiation in *other* areas of your business. But all too often a successful new business model becomes *the* business model for companies not creative enough to invent their own.

Aiding and abetting strategy convergence is an ever–growing army of eager young consultants transferring "best practice" from leaders to laggards. When some big consulting company whispers in your ear, "We have a really deep understanding of your industry," what are they saying? Simply this: "We'll infect you with the same orthodoxies we've infected everyone else with in your industry." The challenge of maintaining any sort of competitive differentiation goes up proportionately with the number of consultants moving management wisdom around the world.

Outsourcing has been another powerful force for strategy convergence. As companies outsource more and more, the scope for competitive differentiation gets narrower and narrower. There's a reason Dell Computer hasn't outsourced its core IT processes and is no friend of cookie–cutter ERP solutions. Dell's business model is based on creating unique *advantages* out of IT—that's something that can't be easily done with off-the-shelf solutions. Industrywide business–to–business exchanges, of the sort envisioned by Ford, General Motors, and DaimlerChrysler, will be another force for convergence.

Executives who spend much of their time attending the same trade shows, reading the same industry magazines, and listening to the same e–biz pundits accelerate the pace of strategy convergence. In the end, strategies converge because everyone defines the industry in the same way, uses the same segmentation criteria, sells through the same channels, adopts the same service policies, and so on. In fact, the typical definition of an "industry" is simply those companies that are all operating with the same business model.

In the airline industry the strategies of American, United, and Delta are virtually indistinguishable—at least from the perspective of a customer. If tonight, while everyone was asleep, we randomly reassigned the top 100 executives from each of these airlines to their competitors, would you expect anything substantial to change in your flying experience? Despite a vibrant economy, the U.S. airline industry's return on sales was a meager 5 percent in 1999. Come the next downturn, we'll witness a return to intra-industry cannibalism, as undifferentiated competitors try to steal each other's customers. Of course, cheapskate flyers will heartily applaud the spectacle of contestants chewing off each other's limbs, but investors may be less amused.

Or think about department stores. May Department Stores, Federated Department Stores, J. C. Penney, Sears, and Dillard's have all underper-formed the S&P 500 in recent years. And no wonder: store layout, mer-chandise selection, and service policies are boringly similar. Wal-Mart, Gap, Best Buy, and Dayton Hudson's Target stores are the standout per-formers. Each has a strategy that's distinctly different from traditional de-partment stores.

The credit card industry is another sector where strategies have been listlessly converging. Here are just a few indicators:

- Direct mail solicitations sent to U.S. households rose from 2.4 billion in 1994 to 3.4 billion in 1998, while the response rate fell from 1.6 percent to 1.2 percent.

- Price, in the form of annual fees and interest rates, has become the major promotional tool and differentiator.

- Industry ROA fell from 4.1 percent in 1993 to 2.9 percent in 1998.

- Three issuers command 48 percent of the domestic Visa card market and 10 companies control 76 percent of the market.

Quick, can you think of any breakout innovator in the credit card business over the past few years? Nope? That's why the major issuers are locked in a wasteful promotional arms race.

In general, wealth-creating champions possess highly differentiated strategies. Sure they face competitors, but they have unique capabilities, unique assets, unique value propositions, and unique market positioning. You won't mistake a flight on Virgin Atlantic for one on United. You won't mistake Old Navy for the clothing department at J. C. Penney. If a strategy ain't different, it's dead. Bernie Ebbers, the rebel who built WorldCom and then acquired MCI, detests convergence. At an analysts' meeting, he was asked whether he was going to buy up cable television properties as AT&T's Michael Armstrong had done. His reply: "We're not going to do anything that he's doing."[4]

So how do you know if your strategy is converging with everyone else's? Well, if your company's revenue growth, return on investment, operating margins, or P/E ratios are tightly clustered around the industry average, it's a good bet that strategies are converging. Have a look at the performance of the major U.S. airlines over a 10-year period (see the table "Key Financial Indicators for Selected U.S. Airlines, 1989–1999"). Who do you think has the most differentiated strategy here? Southwest's earnings grew nearly twice as fast as the industry average, as did its revenues. It also has the healthiest operating margins by far. It should be no surprise that Southwest also has the most highly differentiated strategy. Southwest said, in effect, "If we're going to treat customers like cattle, we might as well develop a business model for cattle—no reserved seating, no meals,

KEY FINANCIAL INDICATORS
FOR SELECTED U.S. AIRLINES, 1989–1999

	Average Operating Margin *1990–1999*	Compound Annual Growth in Net Income *1989–1999*	Compound Annual Growth in Revenue *1989–1999*
AMR (American Airlines)	6.1	3.7	5.4
Northwest	4.9	16.2	4.6
Delta Air Lines	4.2	9.1	6.2
UAL (United Airlines)	3.4	14.3	6.3
Southwest	**11.6**	**20.8**	**16.7**

Source: Standard and Poor's COMPUSTAT.

no fancy lounges, and no in-flight entertainment." The airline industry is not unique. Strategy convergence tends to produce margin convergence—around a relatively low average.

Without radical innovation, a company will devote a mountain of resources to achieve a molehill of differentiation. The amount spent on advertising indistinguishable soft drinks, the legion of telemarketers trying to induce customers to switch from one mediocre long-distance carrier to another, the millions of "free" miles given away by airlines to induce customers to remain "loyal" despite uniformly awful service, the marketing investment needed to get investors to pay attention to any one of the more than 3,500 mutual funds available in the United States, the resources expended in producing half a dozen look–alike television newsmagazines, the "incentives" car companies have to pay to move indistinguishable autos off dealer lots—these are just a few examples of the high–cost, low–impact futility of carbon copy strategies.

What's the ratio of competitive differentiation to investment in your company? Are you locked in an investment arms race with companies pursuing essentially equivalent strategies, or have you escaped strategy convergence and developed a "secret weapon" of competitive differentiation? Here are a few questions you might want to ask yourself:

1. **Have we let others define customer expectations?** Sears, Roebuck let Wal–Mart and Target set customer expectations for value. Target went a step further and created a shopping environment substantially more inviting than Wal–Mart's warehouse format. Target's payoff: loyal shoppers from across the entire socioeconomic spectrum.

2. **Do competitors see us more as rule takers than rule breakers?** When it introduced its "Digital One Rate" pricing plan for wireless phones, AT&T became, surprise, surprise, a rule breaker. A flat rate per minute and no long–distance charges sent the rest of the industry scrambling. When AT&T's a rule breaker, you know the rest of the industry's brain–dead.

3. **Has our strategy changed in some important way in the last two years (two months for Internet companies)?** More specifically, have we built any new competencies? Have we entered new markets? Have we created any new sources of competitive advantages? Has our revenue or profit mix changed appreciably? Has our customer mix changed?

4. **Has there been any erosion of our price premium or cost advantage?** The quality advantage Nissan once enjoyed over American carmakers is mostly gone, and its dowdy styling makes Toyotas and Hondas look positively fetching. Nissan turned to Peugeot for a bailout. Getting rescued by a *French* car company—now *that's* embarrassing.

5. **Has it been getting more difficult to attract world-class talent?** If you don't believe the best people work for the most vital companies, go ask anyone at Cisco. One senior vice president estimated the average IQ at Cisco to be a full 10 points ahead of the competition. A bit of hyperbole, perhaps, but an enormous advantage even if it's only partly true. Of course smart people can do stupid things, but in an economy where people are capital, your capacity to attract the best is a good indicator of their faith in your future.

Over
the last decade,
massive efficiency pro-
grams, share buybacks, and
a superheated acquisition market pushed share prices ever higher.
Beyond this, companies worked ever
harder to squeeze more revenue out of their
existing customers. And they employed legions
of consultants to teach them about "best practices."
These initiatives cannot be faulted, but too often they
were no more than life support for brain–dead strategies. Looking at the bedside share price monitor, top
management could convince itself that its strategy was still
alive. It will become harder and harder to maintain that fic-
tion in the years ahead. Average P/E ratios, which doubled over
the last decade thanks to a wave of investment from aging baby
boomers, the burgeoning ranks of momentum–driven day traders,
and the buoying effect of sky–high Internet stock valuations, will not
double again over the next decade. At the dawn of the new century,
American stocks were worth 172 percent of U.S. economic output,
more than double the level before the 1987 plunge. It may be a new
economy, but trees still don't grow to the sky. Neither can the pace of
M&A activity witnessed in the past few years continue indefinitely. And
with many companies already as skinny as Calista Flockhart, there are
few remaining opportunities for dramatic cost cutting.

HONESTY FIRST

If you want to escape the cul–de–sac of diminishing returns, the first
step is to admit that your current strategy, your dearly beloved business
model, may be running out of steam. Sooner or later, every business
model reaches the point of diminishing returns. And these days, it's more
often sooner than later.

Working ever harder to improve the efficiency of a worn–out strategy
is ultimately futile. Think of all those CEOs leading all those depressingly
mediocre companies. How many of them are willing to stand in front of
their shareholders, or their employees, and own up to the obvious—"Our
business model is busted"?

Dakota tribal wisdom says that when you discover you're on a dead horse, the best strategy is to dismount. Of course, there are other strategies. You can change riders. You can get a committee to study the dead horse. You can benchmark how other companies ride dead horses. You can declare that it's cheaper to feed a dead horse. You can harness several dead horses together. But after you've tried all these things, you're still going to have to dismount.

The temptation to stay on a dead horse can be overwhelming. Take one example. In a recent six-month period, the percentage of teenagers who named Nike as a "cool" brand shrank from 52 percent to 40 percent.[5] By the time teenagers are sporting T-shirts that read, "Just Don't Do It," it's a bit late to start work on revitalizing your brand. The time to begin searching for new wealth-creating strategies is long before the horse stumbles. Today's stock market darlings would do well to remember Toys "R" Us, Compaq Computer, Novell, and dozens of other highfliers that fell to earth when they couldn't escape the gravitational pull of dying strategies. If you believe the existing business model will generate profits in perpetuity, or if you don't have the guts to admit it won't, you will have little incentive to search for new wealth-creating opportunities, much less embrace the new innovation agenda.

Sun Microsystems' chief technology officer has estimated that 20 percent of his company's in-house technical knowledge becomes obsolete each year.[6] No wonder Sun sees itself as being on a never-ending hunt for new strategies. America's major television networks, dusty relics in an era of 500-channel satellite television, have been somewhat less than attentive to the risks of strategy decay. It's been nontraditional channels like MTV and Comedy Central that have pioneered edgy new shows (though it's hard to argue that *South Park* advances the art of television programming). Twenty years ago television networks were a bit like *Time* magazine—broad and shallow, with something for everyone. Now television is like a 30-foot-long magazine rack filled with specialty rags: The Classic Movie Channel, The Golf Channel, Animal Planet, MTV, and dozens more. Television has been parsed into hundreds of tiny markets. Just over the horizon looms full video Webcasting, which will turn television into a whatever-you-want, when-you-want medium. In the 1993–1994 season, the three major networks had an audience share of 61 percent. By the 1998–1999 season that had tumbled to 43 percent.[7] Says Robert A. Iger, the former head of ABC and now president of Disney, "We used to think the possibility existed that the erosion was going to stop. We were silly. It's never going to stop. As you give customers greater and greater choices, they are going to make more choices."[8] Denial is tragic. Delay is deadly.

There is solid evidence that world–beating strategies seldom last even a decade. Skeptical? Ask yourself this question: How many of the companies in the S&P 500 managed to deliver top–quartile shareholder returns for more than 5 years out of the last 10? Answer: 11. And not one company in the S&P 500 achieved top–quartile returns in more than 7 of the last 10 years. If we divide the last 15 years into three 5–year periods, we find that 24 companies got pushed off the list of America's 100 most valuable companies in the first period, 26 got replaced in the second period, and fully 41 were displaced in the last 5–year period. Success has never been more transient. Don't let anyone tell you otherwise.

Why do so few companies beat the odds? Because they can't bring themselves to abandon a seriously out–of–date business model. To create *new* wealth, a company must be willing to abandon its current strategy, at least in part, before it goes toes up. Gap went from selling Levi jeans and a motley assortment of teen clothing in an undistinguished mall format to owning a portfolio of couldn't–be–cooler brands sold in some of the freshest retail digs around. Cisco went from selling stand–alone routers to being an end–to–end supplier of digital communication solutions. Harley–Davidson went from supplying motorcycles to antisocial marauders to selling lifestyle makeovers to balding bad boy wannabes caught in the throes of midlife crisis. The companies that are creating new wealth are not just getting better; they're getting different—profoundly different.

In the age of revolution, the future is not an echo of the past. While every executive understands this intellectually, it is quite another thing to stand in front of your organization, and investors, and boldly confront the demon of decay. But investors and employees are smart enough to know that sooner or later every company has to do a strategy "un–install."

Without an explicit recognition of the onset of decay, there is little incentive for a strategy reboot. It is imperative, therefore, that you and everyone else in your organization be alert to the signs that your company's business model is approaching its "sell by" date—unless, of course, you particularly relish the chance to manage a turnaround.

So start with the truth. Executives must be willing to be brutally honest about the rate at which their current strategy is decaying. In 1999, when stock indexes soared ever higher, the majority of the stocks in the S&P 500 index actually fell. If you're one of the 256 CEOs whose stock price went *down*, you need to face up to the truth: no amount of incrementalism is going to solve your company's problem. Yet history suggests that top management has an enormous capacity for denial. Most senior executives grew up in a world where industry boundaries seemed inviolable, where business models aged gracefully, and where incumbency was often an over–

Never forget that good companies gone bad are simply companies that for too long denied the reality of strategy decay.

whelming advantage. That world is gone. Get over it. Anyone who fails to recognize this fact puts his or her company's future success in grave jeopardy. Executives and employees in every company have a set of little lies they tell themselves to avoid having to deal with the reality of a faltering strategy. Like an alcoholic who claims to drink only socially, managers often claim a dead business model is only sleeping. Here are some of the most used lies:

"It's only an execution issue."
"It's an alignment problem."
"We just have to get more focused."
"It's the fault of the regulators."
"Our competitors are behaving irrationally."
"We're in a transition period."
"Everyone's losing money."
"Asia/Europe/Latin America went bad."
"We're investing for the long term."
"Investors don't understand our strategy."

Sometimes people in a company will walk around a dead strategy for years before admitting that it has expired and gone to strategy heaven.

So what are the little lies that get told in your company? Recently I came across the corporate magazine for one of America's largest insurance companies. In this magazine the CEO was quoted as saying, "Insurance is very complex, I think people will always need agents." That's at least a medium-sized lie. InsWeb.com, Quotesmith.com, and a bunch of new insurance infomediaries can easily imagine a world without agents, as can anyone who bought insurance in this way. Oh yeah, we may still need claims agents for a while longer, but sales agents? Don't be too sure. Every business model is decaying as we speak.

If you want to lead the revolution you have to search for signs of diminishing returns in your efficiency programs, for evidence of unsustainable revenue growth or creeping convergence. Be honest: has "corporate strategy" been more about financial restructuring and mega–deals than about business concept innovation? Are you counting on some e–business whitewash to cover the cracks of a crumbling business model? You have to have the courage to speak candidly about the fragility of success in a discontinuous world. Never forget that good companies gone bad are simply companies that for too long denied the reality of strategy decay.

The nub of the matter is this: What will it take to get *your* company to reinvent itself? Will it take a competitor's success—a benchmark so clear and unequivocal that you will be forced to move? That's what it took to prompt Merrill Lynch to embrace online trading. But if you wait until a competitor hands you a paint-by-numbers kit, you're going to end up producing something highly unoriginal. Will it take a direct and immediate crisis—a threat so close you can smell failure on its breath? That's what it took in the U.S. airline business. Legislators in Washington were more attentive to the plaintive cries of American air passengers than were some airlines. You know you have a problem when Washington is paying more attention to your customers than you are. But should it take the threat of legislation to compel air carriers to tell their passengers the truth about delayed and cancelled flights? If the threat is already breathing in your ear, you're unlikely to escape without a mauling. Or does it take only a sense of the enormous possibility that exists in the age of revolution to get you and your company totally jazzed about the opportunity for radical innovation?

In the age of revolution, every company must become an opportunity-seeking missile—where the guidance system homes in on what is possible, not on what has already been accomplished. A brutal honesty about strategy decay and a commitment to creating *new* wealth are the foundations for strategy innovation. But you can't be an industry revolutionary unless you've learned to see the unconventional. You won't have the courage to abandon, even partially, what is familiar unless you *feel* in your viscera the promise of the unconventional. And you can't create radical new business concepts, or reinvigorate old ones, unless you first understand what a business concept actually is. So that is where we will turn our attention next.

WHAT WILL IT TAKE TO GET YOUR COMPANY TO REINVENT ITSELF?

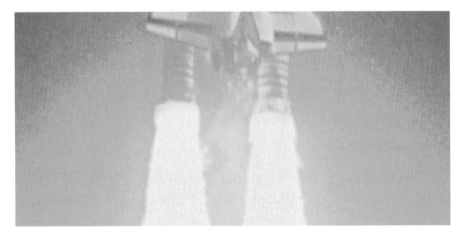

3

BUSINESS
CONCEPT
INNOVATION

CAN YOU THINK BEYOND NEW PRODUCTS
and new services to entirely new business *concepts*—
ones that meet deep customer needs in unconventional ways? Can you think of unconventional ways
of recharging an existing business concept? Can you
go nonlinear?

In most organizations there are few individuals who
can think holistically and concretely about new
business concepts, or envision radical adjustments to
existing business models. This is why so many great
ideas are stillborn—someone has a fragment of an idea
but doesn't know how to build a fully fledged business
model around it. It is also why so many companies get
squeezed by strategy convergence—they are locked into
a one-dimensional view of innovation and can't
imagine entirely new possibilities for differentiating
existing business models.

Can you imagine a world in which every time you
pick up the phone or connect to the Internet a little
infobot conducts a real-time auction to determine
which bandwidth provider will transport your bits

for the lowest possible price? Instead of switching telecom providers once every couple of years in search of a better deal, you might switch a dozen times a day. And your new infomediary will present you with a single, consolidated bill. Will it happen? Who knows? But unless you and your company become adept at this type of business concept innovation, more imaginative minds will capture tomorrow's wealth.

There are no more than a handful of companies that have even begun to build innovation systems that focus on creating a steady stream of new business concepts or new rules within current business concepts. In the chapters that follow, you will meet some of the individuals and companies

Unless you and your company become innovation, more imaginative minds

that have become masters at business concept innovation. But first, let's get some practice in thinking holistically about business concepts. Let's speculate about what *could* be. As a start, let's imagine a radically new business concept—a *cyber business school.*

CYBER B-SCHOOL

Maybe you're midcareer and would like to go to business school but don't relish the prospect of uprooting your family and putting your career on hold for two years while you attend a top–flight B–school. Or maybe you simply can't afford the exorbitant fees charged by those ivy–clad institutions. Could the way you buy business education change as dramatically over the next 10 years as the way you buy books (Amazon.com), trade shares (E*TRADE), or get your news (Yahoo!)? You bet. Let's try a little thought experiment, one that will illustrate the kind of wrenching innovation that will destroy old business models in the age of revolution.

Start with the salient characteristics of a typical top–10 B–school:

- *Geographically defined:* Faculty and students live within 20 miles of campus.
- *Tough to get in:* Admission requirements include an honor–student GPA and a ninetieth percentile score on the Graduate Management Admissions Test—for starters. On average, fewer than one out of five applicants gets accepted.
- *Classroom-based:* The typical format is one professor, 80 students, and a badly photocopied case.
- *Few "stars":* Twenty percent of the faculty have world–class reputations as "gurus," the rest don't. Stars earn as much as 90 percent of their

income from outside teaching and consulting.

- *Egalitarian pay structure:* The salary differential between the "stars" and newly hired assistant professors is typically no greater than three to one.

- *Publish or perish:* To get promoted, young faculty must publish within a narrowly defined "discipline." Peers within that discipline review their research. Faculty are generally unwilling to participate in multidisciplinary research and teaching.

- *Young customers:* For the core M.B.A. program, customers are college graduates, roughly 25 to 30 years of age, with three or four years of work experience.

adept at business concept will capture tomorrow's wealth.

- *Student numbers:* Top business schools admit anywhere between a couple hundred and around one thousand M.B.A. students per year.

- *High tuition:* Fees can amount to as much as $20,000 per year and even more.

- *Inflexible program of study:* The M.B.A. program comprises two years of intensive residential study with 20 classroom hours per week and classes offered at set times.

- *Academic research:* For faculty, the unstated goal is to publish "the maximum number of pages in journals read by the minimum number of people." Most research never gets applied. Even the best faculty find it difficult to pry research money out of the dean.

The top 10 business schools in America turn out fewer than 7,500 M.B.A. graduates a year. In a world of 6 billion people, what is the size of the unfilled demand for high-quality business education? The vast majority of would-be business students is relegated to a second-class education or none whatsoever. As market economies take root in Eastern Europe, Asia, Latin America, and the Indian subcontinent, the demand for management education will soar. Failure to meet this demand could slow the speed of economic development in some parts of the world. Is there room for a new business model in business education? Yeah, acres of room.

Imagine that Paul Allen, co-founder of Microsoft, or George Soros, the global financier, decides to establish a cyber management school—let's call it the Global Leadership Academy. The first step is to skim two or three star professors from each of the 10 best business schools and 10 or so of the most cerebral partners in the leading consulting companies—the ones who've written groundbreaking books. Faculty are attracted to GLA by the

chance to make a global difference in the quality of management—something that's difficult to do when your distribution channel is limited to a
few hundred 27-year-olds each year. Faculty members are given equity in
the new venture and a guaranteed income of $1 million per year. The new
venture can afford these salaries because it is built on a very different
economic model than a physical B-school. Instead of putting one professor in front of 80 students, GLA puts one professor in front of 100,000 students—through live satellite broadcasts and Webcasts. GLA also builds a
network of local tutors around the world, affiliated with second-tier uni-

New business models are more than replacements for what already is. Instead, they open up entirely new possibilities.

versities. These tutors meet occasionally with students and can facilitate
online discussions of cases and lectures. Students can share insights in
custom-designed chat rooms.

GLA's admission requirements are unlike those of traditional B-schools.
To enroll, an applicant must simply submit three letters of recommen-
dation from individuals outside his or her family. The first letter must
describe some sort of "against the odds" accomplishment—perhaps over-
coming drug addiction or helping to raise younger siblings after the death
of a parent. The second letter must describe the applicant in a leadership
role, however humble, and the third must outline a contribution the applicant has made to the community.

GLA's costs are largely unrelated to the number of students it serves.
Indeed, it wants as many "customers" as possible in order to better amor-
tize its fixed investment in online courseware and faculty salaries. Though
the entrance requirements may appear to be "soft," there is a demanding
exit exam. Those who pass it get a degree from GLA. Those who don't get a
certificate outlining their specific educational accomplishments. GLA
charges students a flat fee of $2,000 per year, irrespective of how quickly
they progress through the program. Dedicated students can finish the
program in three years.

In some traditional business schools, students are given a limited number of "points" with which they can bid for admission to the classes of the
most popular teachers. There are no oversubscribed courses at GLA. Every
student learns from the best. The elite faculty supervises the development
of Internet-based curricula and delivers key lectures.

GLA abandons the traditional discipline-based M.B.A. program and
opts for an issue-based curriculum instead. Courses include "Profiting
from Strategic Alliances," "Unleashing Innovation," "Building Digital

Strategies," "Accessing Global Capital Markets," "Inspiring a Gen–X Work-force," and other cross–discipline issues.

With a 50 percent gross margin, GLA is able to build a first–rate research team around each faculty member. Freed from the burden of repetitive teaching, and with a cadre of first–rate researchers, faculty members dramatically raise their research output.

While GLA doesn't have a hundred–year history as a noble university, the chance to study with the world's best business minds attracts a flood of students. The collective "brand" of the faculty soon outshines the brand of any offline university.

GLA's early success astonishes traditional business schools. Unlike first-generation distance learning programs pioneered by Duke University and other schools, GLA offers its students the very best faculty in the world, rather than those willing to live near some particular university. Business education begins to resemble investment banking and basketball, where the stars get paid star salaries. Traditional business schools that seek to emulate GLA find themselves caught in a thicket of intractable issues:

> How do we sign up faculty from "competing" business schools?

> How do we manage the tensions when one faculty member gets paid 10 or 20 times what another faculty member gets paid?

> How do we pay star rates, given a brick–and–mortar overhead structure?

> How do we blow up the functional chimneys that prevent us from building an issue–based curriculum?

> How do we justify high tuition fees when students can get the best faculty in the world for 90 percent less?

After three years of dithering and debate, Harvard, Wharton, Michigan, Northwestern, and the London Business School join forces and launch their own virtual B-school. But internal squabbling and the challenge of managing a five–way alliance hamper their efforts. Oxford, Cambridge, and other universities still struggling to build old–economy business schools simply give up.

An all–star B–school in cyberspace. Will this new business model material-ize? Without a doubt. New business models are more than disruptive *technolo-gies*, they are completely novel business concepts. They are more than *replacements* for what already is. Instead, they open up entirely new possibilities.

BUSINESS CONCEPT INNOVATION

In the new economy, the unit of analysis for innovation is not a product or a technology—it's a business concept. The building blocks of a business concept and a business model are the same—a business model is simply a business concept that has been put into practice. *Business concept innovation* is the capacity to imagine dramatically different business concepts or dramatically new ways of differentiating existing business concepts. Business concept innovation is thus the key to creating new wealth. Competition within a broad domain—be it financial services, communications, entertainment, publishing, education, energy, or any other field—takes place not between products or companies but between business models.

New business models sometimes render old business models obsolete. For example, it's easy to imagine Internet-based phone calls, based on packet switching, largely supplanting phone calls made on dedicated voice circuits. More often, new business models don't destroy old models, they just siphon off customer demand, slowly deflating the profit potential of the old business model. Sears still has a hardware department, and Craftsman is a great brand, but The Home Depot has captured a huge portion of the burgeoning demand in the do-it-yourself market. Digital photography is not going to kill the film business in one fell swoop, but it may maim it by capturing a significant part of the "imaging" demand.

> **When was the last time you caught your breath as you walked past the cosmetics counter?**

The goal of business concept innovation is to introduce more strategic variety into an industry or competitive domain. When this happens, and when customers value that variety, the distribution of wealth-creating potential often shifts dramatically in favor of the innovator. It's not value that "migrates" within and across industries, but the locus of innovation. Companies in one part of an industry will sometimes sit idly by while their strategies converge, while elsewhere some radical upstart creates a new business model and a gusher of new wealth. For example, Wal-Mart's bargaining power has allowed it to suck a lot of wealth out of its suppliers, but it would be only half right to say that value has "migrated" toward Wal-Mart. What actually happened was that Wal-Mart succeeded in doing something that few of its suppliers or competitors had done: inventing an entirely new and oh-so-attractive business concept—the super efficient hypermarket with "everyday low prices."

Business concept innovation is *meta*-innovation, in that it changes the very basis for competition within an industry or domain. The *American Heritage College Dictionary* defines "meta-" as "beyond" or "more comprehensive." Because it is nonlinear, business concept innovation goes *beyond* incremental innovation. Because it takes the entire business concept as the starting point, it is more comprehensive than innovation that focuses solely on products or technology.

Let's take cosmetics as an example. When was the last time you caught your breath as you walked past the cosmetics counter in some big department store? When was the last time you stopped, looked around, and thought, "This is *so* cool"? Never? Well, that's no surprise. The way cosmetics are merchandised and sold has hardly changed over the past couple of decades. If you parachuted into the cosmetics section of a major department store, could you immediately tell whether you were in Macy's, Saks Fifth Avenue, Bloomingdale's, or one of their competitors? If the product names

were disguised, could you immediately distinguish the Estée Lauder counter from the Lancôme counter? Probably not. No wonder the cosmetics industry has been in a funk.

Think for a minute about the cosmetics business concept. High-end beauty products are sold almost exclusively in upscale department stores and account for as much as 20 percent of store profits. Manufacturers jealously control the display of their products, with counters and staff dedicated to each brand. Salesclerks, who are often paid by the manufacturers, are on commission and trained to be pushy—to *sell* you something rather than just let you *buy* something. If you want a lipstick of a particular shade, you'll have to wander from counter to counter, trying to remember if that Chanel lip gloss over there is an eensy-weensy bit less pink than the Lancôme lipstick you're holding in your hand. Many times you have to ask a clerk to see a particular product—most are displayed under glass-topped counters. Merchandising often relies on a "gift-with-purchase," a freebie that shoppers increasingly take for granted.

Sephora, a French-born cosmetics chain, recently acquired by the luxury giant LVMH, is on a global growth tear. Why? Because it's been ripping up the cosmetics rule book. Walk into a Sephora store, and you'll be blown away. In front of you is a wall of video screens. The staff are robed in black, each wearing one black glove, the better to show off delicate perfume bottles. They work for a flat salary. The store layout is black and white and oh-so-sleek. You'll find beauty-related books, magazines, and videos; poetry inscribed on gleaming columns; and more than 600 different brands. But the biggest wow factor comes from the way Sephora displays the merchandise. Virtually every perfume in the world is arranged alphabetically along a wall. There's a lipstick counter with more than 365 hues, arranged by color. Face and body products are organized by category, rather than by manufacturer. You'll find everything from the hip (Urban Decay) to the *très chic* (Lancôme). Premium and mass-market brands often end up side by side. There's a fragrance organ—a multitiered rack of essences—where staff can tell you just what's in your favorite perfume and direct you to other similar fragrances. All the products are on open

WHEN IT'S MOST EFFECTIVE, BUSINESS CONCEPT INNOVATION LEAVES COMPETITORS IN A GUT-WRENCHING QUANDARY.

display. Pick them up, test them—even the lipsticks. There are no gifts. This is a temple of beauty, with the consumer as goddess.

Don't take my word for it, listen to Marianne Wilson of *Chain Store Age*:

> By the combined force of its ambience, design and merchandise mix, Sephora blows away all other competitors in its category. And it does so without the gift-with-purchase clutter, hard sell and often haughty sales people that define much of department store beauty retailing. In fact, what I most liked about Sephora was the egalitarian way it treats both shoppers and merchandise.[1]

By the spring of 1999, Sephora had captured 20 percent of the French retail cosmetics market. Within 18 months of opening its first U.S. outlet in Manhattan, Sephora had opened an additional 49 stores across the United States, and had plans to open as many as 200 more. Myron E. Ullman III, architect of Sephora's international expansion, has his own view on what Sephora is all about:

> Retailing is about change. I can't think of a single retail concept that hasn't changed that is now doing very well. That's why we have a group in Paris who sit around and do nothing else but think of different ways to do things. Chief among their tasks is to keep [our] flagships so stunning that people are compelled to walk in. When our customers stroll down Fifth Avenue, we want them to say to themselves, "Should I go to the Museum of Modern Art or should I go to Sephora?"

Sephora has trashed the typical cosmetics business model:

	Traditional Model	Sephora Model
Sales staff on commission	Yes	No
Gift with purchase	Yes	No
One brand per counter	Yes	No
Manufacturer controls display	Yes	No
Easy to sample	No	Yes
Shop unmolested	No	Yes
Easy to compare products	No	Yes
Customer in control	No	Yes

Without a doubt, this is business concept innovation.

With Sephora, the cosmetics makers lose their control of the sales force, product display, and merchandising—the very things they relied on for competitive differentiation at point of sale. Major ouch! Some cosmetics manufacturers, afraid of angering department stores, have refused to let Sephora handle certain product lines. You won't find Estée Lauder's MAC, Bobbi Brown, and Aveda lines at Sephora. Nor will you find Chanel's makeup lines—not, at least, for now.

Business concept innovation starts from a premise that the only way to escape the squeeze of hyper-competition, even temporarily, is to build a business model so unlike what has come before that traditional competitors are left scrambling. When it's most effective, business concept innovation leaves competitors in a gut-wrenching quandary: if they abandon their tried-and-tested business model, they risk sacrificing their core business for a second-place finish in a game they didn't invent, with rules they don't understand; yet if they don't embrace the new model, they forgo the future. Damned if they do and damned if they don't—that's business concept innovation at its best.

Business concept innovation isn't strictly about *competitive* strategy. It is not a way of positioning *against* competitors, but of going *around* them. It's based on *avoidance*, not *attack*. Here's the key thought: *what is not different is not strategic*. To the extent that strategy is the quest for above-average profits, it is *entirely* about variety—not just in one or two areas, but in all components of the business model. Business concept innovation often falls short of this lofty goal, but that's the objective.

Consequently, a capacity to first identify, then deconstruct and reconstruct business models lies at the heart of a high-performance innovation system. If your company is not experimenting with radically different business models, it's already living on borrowed time.

Business concept innovation is a religion in Silicon Valley. In the Valley, precocious 25–year–olds know what a business concept is. They relish the chance to deconstruct old ones and build new ones. Undergrad engineering students at Stanford University get *taught* how to do this—no kidding! Yet in most companies outside the Valley, I can't find one person in a hundred who can tell me what a business concept is, much less how to invent a new one or reinvent an old one. Moreover, I doubt you can find a dozen individuals in your company who share a common definition of your company's *existing* business concept. How could they if they can't even identify the elements of a business concept? Though consultants talk incessantly about "business models," I've never met one who has a coherent definition of what a business model actually *is*. It's hard to invent a new business concept if you can't agree on its components. So let's take a few minutes and learn how to decompose a business concept. This is an indispensable part of your training as an industry revolutionary.

UNPACKING THE BUSINESS MODEL

To be an industry revolutionary, you must develop an instinctive capacity to think about business models in their entirety. There are many ways of describing the components of a business model. I have created a framework that is complete, yet simple.

A business concept comprises four major components:

• Core Strategy

• Strategic Resources

• Customer Interface

• Value Network

Each of these components has several subcomponents, which will be described later in this section. For each element I have also suggested a few questions that should help you think more deeply and deftly about opportunities for business concept innovation. The fact is that most companies have *business concept blind spots* that prevent them from seeing opportunities for innovation in many parts of the business concept. In this chapter we'll remove those blind spots.

The four major components are linked together by three "bridge" components:

- Core Strategy ← *Configuration* of Activities → Resource Base
- Core Strategy ← Customer *Benefits* → Customer Interface
- Resource Base ← Company *Boundaries* → Value Network

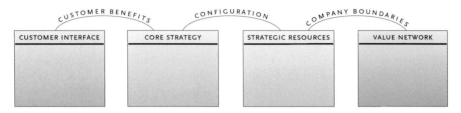

Underpinning the business model are four factors that determine its profit potential:

- Efficiency
- Uniqueness
- Fit
- Profit Boosters

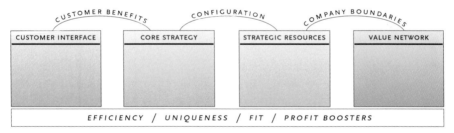

Core Strategy

The first component of the business concept is the *core strategy*. It is the essence of how the firm chooses to compete. Elements of the core strategy include the business mission, product/market scope, and basis for differentiation.

1. The Business Mission: This captures the overall *objective* of the strategy—what the business model is designed to accomplish or deliver. The business mission encompasses things such as the "value proposition," "strategic intent," "big, hairy, audacious goals," "purpose," and overall performance objectives. It implies a sense of direction and a set of criteria against which to measure progress. It is often unstated and often constrains a company's view of potential business concepts. A change in a company's business mission doesn't necessarily result in business concept innovation. But when a company brings a new or very different business mission into an industry dominated by companies with roughly similar business goals, the result may be business concept innovation. This was the case when Virgin exported its lifestyle–oriented, entertainment–focused business mission to the airline business. Traditional air carriers had business missions focused on maximizing the operational efficiency of their airlines. Virgin's business mission was focused on fun, value–for–money, customer feel–good factors. Anyone who has flown on Virgin will have noticed the difference this makes.

Example: Although it has long styled itself as "The Document Company," Xerox's implicit business mission has focused on copiers and copying. This definition created a *business concept blind spot* that  allowed Hewlett–Packard to build a commanding lead in the printer business. With most of their documents stored electronically, individuals use their printers, rather than copiers, to reproduce documents. You can argue that HP is also a "document company," but its business mission focused on printing rather than copying. After falling far behind, Xerox amended its business concept to include printing. 'Tis a pity for Xerox that this business concept innovation didn't occur a decade earlier.

Ask yourself: What is our business mission? What are we becoming as a company—can we describe a "from" and a "to"? What is our dream? What kind of difference do we want to make in the world? Is our business mission sufficiently broad to allow for business concept innovation? Is our business mission as *relevant* to customers as it might have been in years past? Most important, do we have a business mission that is sufficiently distinguished from the missions of other companies in our industry?

Thought: A business school that sees its business mission as granting degrees to residential students, rather than addressing the world's "management deficit," will have little incentive for business concept innovation.

2. **Product/Market Scope:** This captures the essence of *where* the firm competes—which customers, which geographies, and what product segments—and where, by implication, it doesn't compete. A company's definition of product/market scope can be a source of business concept innovation when it is quite different from that of traditional competitors.

Are there types of customers that have been generally ignored by companies in our industry?

Example: Amazon.com may have started as an online bookseller, but it is rapidly becoming the Wal-Mart of the Internet—offering products as diverse as videos, personal electronics, lawn and garden supplies, tools, toys, and much more. Leveraging its easy-to-use customer interface, Amazon seems intent on increasing its share of customers—to the detriment of single-segment Web retailers.

Ask yourself: Could we offer customers something closer to a "total solution" to their needs by expanding our definition of product scope? Could we increase our "share of wallet" as well as our share of market by expanding our scope? Would a different definition of scope allow us to capture more of the life cycle profits associated with our product or service? Are there types of customers that have been generally ignored by companies in our industry?

Thought: What if banks expanded the scope of their debit card offerings to include children? Wouldn't it be great if your daughter had her own debit card and her allowance was automatically transferred to her bank account each month? She could spend the available funds with her debit card. No more worrying about lost allowances, and no more arguments about whether you remembered to pay her or not. This isn't as far-fetched as you might think. Web sites such as iCanBuy.com, DoughNET.com, and RocketCash.com let kids shop online using mom's or dad's credit card. Don't panic. Parents set a spending limit and get a report on what the kids have bought.[2] You have to wonder why Visa or MasterCard didn't think of this.

3. **Basis for Differentiation:** This captures the essence of *how* the firm competes and, in particular, how it competes *differently* than its competitors.

Example: You don't know Jonathan Ives, but you know his work. At 30 years of age, the quirky Londoner was appointed head of Apple Computer's industrial design division. It is Ives, after all, who was responsible for the iMac, the curvy, translucent machine that has redefined what a computer should look like. For years, the PC was the ugliest thing in your house. It looked like a disemboweled robot with cords and cables spilling everywhere. And it came in only one color—deadly, boring beige. Why? Because most of the companies making PCs had an industrial products heritage—they were filled with engineers not artists. The iMac sold 400,000 units in the first month after its introduction, and introduced an

You can take $250 out of a cash machine with a piece of plastic. But if you want to check in to a $250-per-night hotel room, be prepared to give your life history at check-in.

entirely new dimension of differentiation—aesthetics—into the computer industry.

Ask yourself: How have competitors tried to differentiate themselves in our industry? Are there other dimensions of differentiation we could explore? In what aspects of the product or service has there been the *least* differentiation? How could we increase the differentiation in some of these dimensions? Have we searched diligently for differentiation opportunities in *every* dimension of the business model?

Thought: You can take $250 out of a cash machine with a piece of plastic. But if you want to check in to a $250-per-night hotel room, be prepared to give your life history at check-in. This is absurd. You take money out of the ATM, but you take nothing from the hotel but the soap. By the time you arrive, you've already guaranteed your room with a credit card, and they have your name on file, so why do you have to go through the whole check-in rigmarole? Why not use your credit card as a room key? Will it happen? Yep. Holiday Inn is planning a new hotel near the Atlanta airport where consumers will be able to use their credit cards as room keys.[3] Hey guys, ATMs have been around for years—what took you so long?

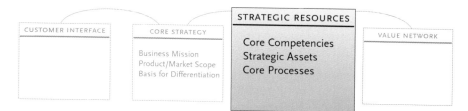

Strategic Resources

Every competitive advantage worthy of the name rests on unique firm-specific resources. Dramatically changing the resource base for competition can be a source of business concept innovation. Strategic resources include core competencies, strategic assets, and core processes.

1. **Core Competencies:** This is what the firm *knows*. It encompasses skills and unique capabilities.

   Example: Enron, a company that had its start in the gas pipeline industry and became the world's leading energy trader, is using its core competencies to shake up the telecoms model. Enron is extending its understanding of how to de-verticalize an industry and create highly efficient markets for commodity products into the bandwidth business. If Enron succeeds, industrial and individual customers will be able to grab more bandwidth anytime they need it. Want to suck some real-time video down the fiber-optic pipe? No problem. The Enron Intelligent Network is being designed to allow users to buy just the bandwidth they need, when they need it. Enron's competencies, honed in the energy business, are distinctly different from those possessed by traditional network operators like AT&T.

   Ask yourself: What are our core competencies? What do we know that is (a) unique, (b) valuable to customers, and (c) transferable to new opportunities? What are the deep benefits that our core competencies allow us to deliver to customers? How could we deploy those benefits in new ways or in new settings? What difference could our core competencies make if we introduced them into industries where competitors possess very different skills? Are there skills we don't currently possess that could undermine the role our traditional competencies play in some overall customer solution? What new competencies should we be adding to our business concept?

Thought: The skills eBay applies to the problem of creating an online, consumer-to-consumer marketplace are very different than the competencies a newspaper relies on in running its classified ads section. A newspaper would face a daunting challenge if it wanted to run real-time, coast-to-coast auctions. When business concept innovation changes the competence base of an industry, it puts traditional players at a profound disadvantage, which is, of course, the goal of business concept innovation.

2. **Strategic Assets:** Strategic assets are what the firm owns. They are things, rather than know-how. Strategic assets can include brands, patents, infrastructure, proprietary standards, customer data, and anything else that is both rare and valuable. Using one's strategic assets in a novel way can lead to business concept innovation.

Example: I think it's unlikely that Barnes & Noble will ever match Amazon.com's success as an online retailer. But Barnes & Noble has one strategic asset that Amazon.com can't match—its prime retail locations. Barnes & Noble has used this asset to deliver new forms of value to customers. First it sprinkled comfy sofas and overstuffed chairs amid the acres of books. Next it built coffee bars in its bookstores. Then it started scheduling poetry readings and music recitals. All this has transformed Barnes & Noble into a leisure destination—something more akin to a community center or the old town square than a bookstore.

Ask yourself: What are our strategic assets? Could we exploit them in new ways to bring new value to consumers? Could our strategic assets be valuable in other industry settings? Can we build new business models that exploit our existing strategic assets—that is, can we imagine alternate uses for our strategic assets?

Thought: If you're a boring old utility, how do you cash in on the bandwidth gold rush? Companies like Williams and Qwest are exploiting a valuable strategic asset—their "rights-of-way"—to build new communication networks. Like Enron, Williams started in the pipeline business. Williams is stringing thousands of miles of fiber-optic cable through decommissioned pipelines. Qwest's founder, Philip Anschutz, bought Southern Pacific Railroad 10 years ago. Now his high-speed communications company is building fiber-optic networks along the railroad's rights-of-way. Those who labored to clear these rights-of-way more than a hundred years ago would never have imagined that they would one day carry voices, images, and data at the speed of light. What old strategic asset could your company repurpose?

3. **Core Processes:** This is what people in the firm actually *do*. Core processes are methodologies and routines used in transforming inputs into outputs. Core processes are *activities*, rather than "assets" or "skills." They are used in translating competencies, assets, and other inputs into value for customers. A fundamental reinvention of a core process can be the basis for business concept innovation.

Examples: Dell's build–to–order system is one of its core processes and a powerful example of business concept innovation. Drug discovery is a core process for every pharmaceutical company. It is also a process that has been radically reinvented in recent years through bioinformatics, which makes it possible to rapidly screen thousands and thousands of compounds. Toyota's lean manufacturing was a process innovation that turned the car industry on its ear.

> **Thought: If you're a boring old utility, how do you cash in on the bandwidth gold rush?**

Ask yourself: What are our most critical processes—that is, what processes create the most value for customers and are most competitively unique? What is the rate at which we are improving these processes? Is that rate of improvement accelerating or decelerating? Can we imagine a radically different process that would deliver the same benefit? Are there opportunities for step function improvements in the efficiency or effectiveness of our processes? Could we borrow nonlinear process ideas from other industries? Conversely, could we use our process expertise to transform some other industry?

Thought: Have you ever had a house built? How long did it take? A year? Two years? A few years ago the San Diego–based Building Industry Association sponsored a seemingly ridiculous contest. Two teams were pitted against each other—each would try to build a house in less than four hours, using traditional materials. The teams planned every second of the building process with military precision. They struggled to invent new technologies, such as cement that would dry in a matter of minutes. They broke the work down into subtasks that could be carried out in parallel. While one group was laying the foundation, another would frame the walls, and another would build the roof. The frame would get bolted to the foundation in large sections, and the roof would be lifted onto the framing with the help of a crane. Each team brought hundreds of construction workers to the site, and every tradesman was given an intricately choreographed role to play. Improbably, one team

ONLY BY PUSHING THE PEDAL TO THE METAL IS IT POSSIBLE TO ESCAPE THE LIMITS OF CURRENT PROCESSES.

managed to build its three-bedroom bungalow, complete with land-scaping, in less than *three* hours. Of course the contest had a logic—only by pushing the pedal to the metal, by reaching for the seemingly impossible, is it possible to escape the limits of current processes and discover new possibilities. But don't you dare call *this* process reengineering—it's far more radical. So what kind of process innovation would allow you to transform *your* industry?

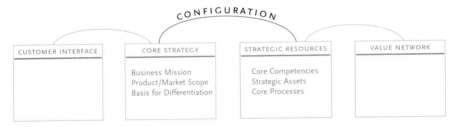

Configuration

Intermediating between a company's *core strategy* and its *strategic resources* is a bridge component I'll call *configuration*. Configuration refers to the unique way in which competencies, assets, and processes are *combined* and *interrelated* in support of a particular strategy. It refers to the *linkages* between competencies, assets, and processes and how those linkages are managed. The notion of configuration recognizes that great strategies (and great business models) rest on a unique blending of competencies, assets, and processes.

> *Example:* Chrysler has gained a substantial amount of advantage from the way it uses "platform teams" to orchestrate the functional disciplines involved in producing and marketing a vehicle. Most car companies are organized by function—design, engineering, manufac-turing, marketing, and sales. Employees sit in functional "silos" and are often more loyal to their function than to any particular car pro-gram. The result is a lot of friction, suboptimal trade-offs, and devel-opment delays. Chrysler used a new building to unite functional specialists around vehicle platforms, employing a team structure it first used in the development of the built-to-thrill Viper sports car. Each platform team has representatives from every function. They sit together in a stadium-sized room, where each employee has a line of

sight to every other employee. In the new configuration, it's clear that an employee's first loyalty is to the success of the program he or she is working on, not to some distant functional head. Chrysler's American competitors possess roughly similar technical knowledge, strategic assets, and processes, but Chrysler was the first American car company to configure all of these into boundary–busting platform teams. This is one reason Chrysler came to be regarded in the 1990s as one of the most innovative car companies in the world.

Ask yourself: How do we manage the interfaces between different assets, knowledge, and processes? Have we configured our assets, skills, and processes in unique ways? Has anyone in our industry or domain configured their strategic resources in an unconventional way? Do they gain any advantage from this configuration? Can we imagine very different configurations than what we have at present?

Thought: If your bank is like most, it sends you one statement for your credit card, another for your mortgage, another for your checking account, another for your savings or investment account, and still another for your car loan or any other borrowing you may have. The blizzard of statements you receive each month reflects the internal configuration of most banks—each product area is a separate profit center. It also reflects banks' eagerness to borrow money from you at one rate (what they pay you on a certificate of deposit, for example) and lend it back to you at a higher rate (the interest you pay on your credit card debt, for example). Virgin Direct, the innovative financial services arm of Sir Richard Branson's far–flung empire, offers customers a radically different approach based on a completely different configuration of banking resources. The Virgin One account works like this. Imagine you have a $200,000 balance on your mortgage, with an 8 percent interest rate. Imagine further that your monthly paycheck amounts to $8,000. When your paycheck is electronically deposited into your Virgin One account, your mortgage balance is immediately reduced by $8,000. Then, as you write checks during the month from the same account, your mortgage balance creeps back up. In this way, you're earning the equivalent of 8 percent on the money from your paycheck that sits in your One account. Compare that with what most banks give you on your checking account. Now let's say you splurge on a Tahitian holiday and end up with $10,000 of credit card debt. Instead of paying this down over a period of months and being subject to the typically exorbitant interest rates charged by credit card companies, you pay the credit card bill out of your One account. Your debt goes up by $10,000, but you're being charged interest at only 8 percent. And when, a few months later, you pay in that $20,000 inheritance from grandma, it reduces your debt by a similar account, and therefore earns an effective 8 percent interest rate—far better than what you could get on a deposit account. The radical premise behind the Virgin One account is this: you are one person with a single overall level of indebtedness. Your bank shouldn't treat you like you're suffering from a case of multiple personalities, nor should it gain financially from the fact that it is configured in a way that makes it impossible to consolidate your borrowing and savings into a single account.

CUSTOMER INTERFACE	CONFIGURATION		
	CORE STRATEGY	STRATEGIC RESOURCES	VALUE NETWORK
Fulfillment & Support Information & Insight Relationship Dynamics Pricing Structure	Business Mission Product/Market Scope Basis for Differentiation	Core Competencies Strategic Assets Core Processes	

Customer Interface

The third component of the business concept, *customer interface*, has four elements: fulfillment and support, information and insight, relationship dynamics, and pricing structure. The Internet has caused a radical shift in how producers reach consumers.

1. ***Fulfillment and Support:*** This refers to the way the firm "goes to market," how it actually "reaches" customers–which channels it uses, what kind of customer support it offers, and what level of service it provides.

   Examples: Webvan.com is the latest company hoping to create a revolution in the way Americans buy groceries. Webvan aims to build a nationwide network of distribution centers that will allow it to entirely bypass traditional supermarkets. Groceries are ordered online, and Webvan delivers them at a time convenient to the customer. Webvan has enrolled Bechtel, the world's leading construction company, to manage the design and construction of its distribution centers. The company claims its unique fulfillment process results in 50 percent less grocery handling than the industry average. Webvan's first distribution center, a 330,000–square-foot warehouse in Oakland, California, is more than double the size of a typical grocery store warehouse and boasts more than four miles of conveyor belts. Webvan claims its high level of automation trims 10 percent off the costs of an offline grocery store. There's no guarantee Webvan will prevail over other online grocery retailers, but whoever wins, the way groceries reach customers is changing in ways that will make life a lot easier for harried, two-career families.

Today, most consumers buy software in shrink-wrapped boxes, paying a one-time license fee for the product. But a new generation of "application service providers" aims to change all this. One pioneer is ThinkFree.com, an ASP that allows users to store important files on the Web and work on their Microsoft Office documents from any computer. Hotmail.com was one of the first ASPs—its free e-mail serv-

The way groceries reach customers is changing in ways that will make life a lot easier.

ice could be accessed from any computer, anywhere, and you didn't need to download any software to make it work. Software as a service versus software as a product is a dramatically different fulfill-ment strategy.

Ask yourself: How do we reach customers? What does a customer have to "go through" to buy our products and services? To what extent have we built our fulfillment and support system for our benefit rather than our customers' benefit? Could we make the process of fulfillment and support substantially easier or more enjoyable for customers? What would it look like if we designed our support and fulfillment processes from the customer backward? Could we dramatically reduce search costs? Could we provide customers with truly honest data for comparison shopping? Have we removed every element of customer aggravation in the support and fulfillment process?

Thought: Today Americans give to charity a smaller percentage of their income than ever before. We are so wrapped up in our lives, so constantly busy, that we have hardly a moment to think about doing good for anyone but ourselves. Could business concept innovation change this? Is there another way of linking donors to worthwhile causes—another "fulfillment" mechanism? Of course. One thing that blunts the impulse to give is the bureaucracy that intervenes between the giver and the beneficiary. You give to United Way or some religious organization that pools your money with other gifts and directs those funds to projects around the world. You have only a vague sense of where your money goes and no direct feedback on the difference it makes. Most of us wouldn't consider putting our financial investments in a "blind trust," but this is essentially what happens when we give to charity. What if you had the chance to pick the exact projects to which you'd like to contribute? What if you got a monthly report on the good that was being done? What if you were able to pick projects that were sized to the amount you could afford—projects where you could feel your contribution made a critical difference, whether it was $100, $1,000, or $100,000? What if you could easily build a portfolio of specific charity projects that reflected your own personal interests—be it abolishing hunger, ending child labor, reducing deforestation, or saving souls? Instead of United Way, it would be Your Way.

So let's establish a Web site called givemore.org. A small team of people will vet charity projects submitted from around the world. They will be assisted by local review teams. One project might be to build an orphanage in Rwanda, another to help a struggling church in Byelorussia, and another to help teens at risk. Each project will be posted to the Web. While today you can get a long list of charities on the Web, you can't easily make donations to specific projects. At givemore.org, project listings will include the amount of funding needed, the expected benefits, and the supervising organization. The review team will rate each project on some cost/benefit criteria. You will know what portion of your contribution is going to be absorbed by overhead and administrative fees. Projects will be posted by government agencies, churches, long-standing charities, and responsible individuals. Potential donors will go online and select a project from a menu of worthy causes organized by need and geography. They will get regular e-mail updates on the progress of their projects. Every year givemore.org will arrange a trip for large donors so they can review the impact of their giving on-site. With givers no longer divorced from the heartwarming gratitude of recipients, giving just might soar. Is this all a fantasy? Yeah, but it'll happen. Do you have a fantasy about how your company can reinvent its connection to customers?

2. **Information and Insight:** This refers to all the knowledge that is collected from and utilized on behalf of customers—the information content of the customer interface. It also refers to the ability of a company to extract insights from this information—insights that can help it do cool new things for customers. It also covers the information that is made available to customers pre- and post–purchase.

Example: Remember what it was like to shop for insurance in the bad old days? Many insurance agents represented a single insurer. You spent hours calling around to try and find the best rate. Comparing policies was torture. You'd come away convinced that the core competencies of the insurance industry were complexity and obfuscation. Now go to Quickeninsurance.com or Quotesmith.com. You can instantly compare insurance policies from dozens of vendors across a common set of criteria. Prices are clearly posted. No mystery here. And with just one click you can start your application. These and other online brokers are empowering consumers with information in ways that will dramatically change the insurance industry.

Do you have a fantasy about how your company can reinvent its connection to customers?

One big danger for traditional insurance companies: no more stupid customers. Soon every buyer will be armed with truly neutral information on which products represent the best combination of coverage and price.

Ask yourself: What do we actually know about customers? Are we using every opportunity to deepen our knowledge of our customers' needs and desires? Are we capturing all the data we could? How do we use this knowledge to serve them in new ways? Have we given our customers the information they need to make empowered and intelligent purchasing decisions? What additional information would customers like to have?

Thought: A senior executive of a large supermarket chain once told me of some research that suggested a top-quartile customer in an average store would spend 50 times more in a year than a bottom-quartile customer. The top-quartile customer lived locally, shopped a couple times a week, had a family, and was reasonably well off. The bottom-quartile customer was just passing through or didn't have a family, and wasn't so well heeled. I started thinking about this data. What if it were true? Every supermarket has an express lane for customers with "10 items or less." But who uses that lane? Bottom-quartile customers. Top-quartile customers are waiting in line with an overstuffed cart—they've come to buy more than beer and cigarettes. Why, I began to wonder, wasn't there a line for customers who spend $5,000 or more in a year? Why didn't these shoppers

It's one thing for people to buy your products. It's another for them to tattoo your name on their bodies.

have someone to help them load their groceries into their BMWs and Volvos? While many supermarkets give loyalty cards to their customers, few seem to have used the information gathered to provide truly differentiated service to their best customers.

3. Relationship Dynamics: This element of the business model refers to the nature of the *interaction* between the producer and the customer. Is the interaction face to face or indirect? Is it continuous or sporadic? How easy is it for the customer to interact with the producer? What feelings do these interactions invoke on the part of the customer? Is there any sense of "loyalty" created by the pattern of interactions? The notion of relationship dynamics acknowledges the fact that there are emotional, as well as transactional, elements in the interaction of producers and consumers, and that these can be the basis for a highly differentiated business concept.

Example: There's probably no company in the world that works harder to build genuine relationships with its customers than Harley–Davidson. The Harley Owners Group boasts 450,000 members. Every year Harley–Davidson sponsors an annual rally where the tattoo contest is one of the most keenly anticipated events. As the company says, "It's one thing for people to buy your products. It's another for them to tattoo your name on their bodies." BMW makes awesome motorcycles, but when was the last time you saw a bicep that read "Bayerische Motoren Werke"?

Ask yourself: How do we make our customers *feel*? What is the range of emotions that a customer experiences in his or her interactions with us? Have we invested in our customers? Could we reinvent the customer experience in ways that would strengthen the sense of affiliation the customer has with us? Where can we exceed customer expectations and raise the hurdle for competitors? What are the dozen greatest customer experiences in the world? Is there anything about those experiences we could replicate in our relationship with customers?

Thought: Perhaps nowhere is the alignment between customer expectations and the actual service experience more out of whack than in health care. A senior health-care executive recently described the current state of the U.S. health-care experience as follows: "Prison inmates and hospital patients have a lot in common. Both are subjected to excessive questioning, stripped of their usual clothing and possessions, placed in a subservient, dependent relationship, and allowed visitors only during certain hours." Adventist Health System, one of the largest church-affiliated hospital groups in America, is seeking to change this sorry state of affairs. It has examined each stage of the patient experience and has identified opportunities to revolutionize service delivery. A couple of examples: Instead of answering the same questions over and over again, patients will be given a Web-based "portable health record" that travels with them from clinical experience to clinical experience. Another innovation is the elimination of visiting hours. Family members will have visiting privileges 24 hours a day, even in the emergency room. While creating some inconvenience for the staff, this idea has greatly reduced litigation expense in the hospitals where it has been instituted. When a health event goes wrong, the family is less likely to point fingers at anonymous health-care providers if they were there and know the doctors and staff did all they could do for the patient. Adventist Health System is changing the relationship dynamics between the health-care consumer and the health-care provider.

4. **Pricing Structure:** You have several choices in what you charge for. You can charge customers for a product or for service. You can charge customers directly or indirectly through a third party. You can bundle components or price them separately. You can charge a flat rate or charge for time or distance. You can have set prices or market-based prices. Each of these choices offers the chance for business concept innovation, depending on the traditions of your industry.

Examples: Lawyers typically charge by the hour. While some lawyers are exceptionally well paid, charging hundreds of dollars per hour, the time-based pricing model puts an upper limit on revenue generation. Wilson Sonsini Goodrich & Rosati, based in the heart of Silicon Valley, often trades fees for equity in the start-up companies they serve. On New Year's Eve, 1999, the partnership was holding stock in 34 newly public clients worth $230 million. That's more money than the total 1999 revenues of 62 of America's top 100 law firms. If the $230 million windfall was divided among Wilson Sonsini's 120 partners, they would each take home $1.9 million.[4]

In pre–Web times, when you purchased a CD you were compelled to buy whatever tunes the producer chose to include. Yet today, you can buy songs one at a time from a host of online music sites. Fans who visit the Beastie Boys Web site can buy any 40 Beastie songs for $19.99. The chosen selections are burned onto two CDs and mailed to the devoted pop aficionado.[5]

Increasingly, General Electric, Rolls–Royce, and Pratt & Whitney— the world's leading makers of jet engines—don't sell a product. They sell "power by the hour." When airlines buy one of Boeing's ultra-long–range 777s, scheduled for launch in 2003, they'll get a pair of GE 90 engines that come with a fixed–price maintenance agreement pegged at so many dollars per flight hour. After all, airlines don't really want to own jet engines; they want guaranteed up time. Many Internet service providers used to charge by the hour for connect time. No more. Most now have a single monthly charge no matter how long you're online.

Ask yourself: What are you actually charging for? What is the dominant pricing paradigm in your industry? Can you break it? Do you really know what customers think they're paying for? Can you more closely align what you charge for with what customers actually value? Does the existing pricing structure implicitly penalize some customers and subsidize others? Can you change this?

Thought: What you charge for and what your customers think they're paying for are often quite distinct. Your pricing structure and a customer's value structure are not the same things. When I buy a magazine I pay for information or entertainment. When I buy a razor I pay for a cleanly shaven face. A company that understands a customer's value structure—the value that is placed on each of the benefits received—is in a great position to be a pricing innovator. If I visit the *New York Times* or the *San Jose Mercury News* online, I get the reporters or columnists that write for those particular papers. But why can't I go to a site that lists the top–100 columnists and news reporters, along with the titles of their latest stories or editorials? That way, I'd pay for and get to read the writers I most enjoy.

Customer Benefits

Intermediating between the *core strategy* and the *customer interface* is another bridge component—the particular bundle of *benefits* that is actually being

CUSTOMER BENEFITS · CONFIGURATION

CUSTOMER INTERFACE	CORE STRATEGY	STRATEGIC RESOURCES	VALUE NETWORK
Fulfillment & Support Information & Insight Relationship Dynamics Pricing Structure	Business Mission Product/Market Scope Basis for Differentiation	Core Competencies Strategic Assets Core Processes	

offered to the customer. Benefits refer to a customer–derived definition of the basic needs and wants that are being satisfied. Benefits are what link the core strategy to the needs of the customer. An important component of any business concept is the decision as to which benefits are or aren't going to be included.

> *Example:* It used to be that when you bought a car, you bought sheet metal and rubber. Now, if you buy a luxury sedan, you get a car bursting with ancillary benefits: 24/7 roadside service, expense reimbursement when your trip is interrupted by car trouble, a loaner when your car is in for major service, and a free car wash with every service. GM's OnStar system provides a 24–hour concierge who can secure a restaurant reservation or direct you to the nearest zoo. If your airbags deploy, OnStar automatically contacts emergency services and gives them your location. Having trouble locating your car in an airport parking lot? Call OnStar from your cell phone, and they'll flash your car's lights and sound its horn. They'll even unlock the doors remotely if you've been a particularly silly prat and locked your keys inside. OnStar may fall short of industry revolution, but it's certainly raising the ante for luxury carmakers and it's just the beginning of what carmakers hope will ultimately be a cornucopia of services that will generate a continuing stream of revenues long after the vehicle has been purchased.

> *Ask yourself:* What benefits are we actually delivering to customers? Are there ancillary benefits that the customer might value? What's the core need we're trying to address? Have we defined that need broadly enough? Conversely, are we delivering benefits that customers don't really care about? Can we change the benefit bundle in ways that will surprise customers and frustrate competitors? What's the context in which the product or service is used? Does that context suggest the possibility of enlarging the benefit bundle?

> *Thought:* Imagine you want to build a patio behind your house and you go online to check out a DIY superstore. You provide some information on the size of patio you want to build, the style of your house, and your budget. A virtual architect then presents a couple of

dozen plans from which you can choose. The program automatically resizes each plan to fit your available space. Once you've made your selection, a virtual contractor generates a list of all the tools and materials you're going to need and a construction blueprint. You can remove from the list any item that you already have. In a few hours a truck delivers everything you're going to need on one pallet. You print out a detailed construction guide from the Web site. When you make your purchase you get a telephone number to call for help if you should run into any problems. Now that's a uniquely tailored bundle of benefits, and it could it be the basis for some real business concept innovation for The Home Depot, Orchard Supply, or some other big home-improvement retailer.

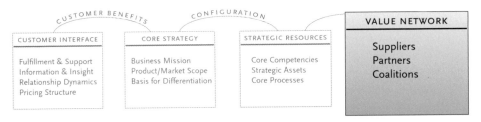

CUSTOMER INTERFACE	CORE STRATEGY	STRATEGIC RESOURCES	VALUE NETWORK
Fulfillment & Support Information & Insight Relationship Dynamics Pricing Structure	Business Mission Product/Market Scope Basis for Differentiation	Core Competencies Strategic Assets Core Processes	Suppliers Partners Coalitions

Value Network

The fourth component of a business model is the *value network* that surrounds the firm, and which complements and amplifies the firm's own resources. Today many of the resources that are critical to a firm's success lie outside its direct control. Elements of the value network include suppliers, partners, and coalitions. The design and management of the value network can be important sources of business concept innovation.

1. **Suppliers:** Suppliers typically reside "up the value chain" from the producer. Privileged access to or a deep relationship with suppliers can be a central element of a novel business model.

   Example: Part of what has made Cisco the most nimble competitor in the communications equipment business has been its use of outside suppliers. Says Cisco's Howard Charney, senior vice president, "Today, more than 50 percent of our product does not touch a Cisco factory or employee. It just gets magically assembled and shipped, and the customer doesn't even know we never touched it." Increasingly, companies like Cisco and Nokia are using their supplier networks to dramatically reduce working capital and increase flexibility.

   Ask yourself: How effectively are we using suppliers as a source of innovation? Do we regard them as integral to our business model?

An imaginative use of partners can be the key to industry revolution.

Do we gain competitive advantage from the way we manage the linkage with our suppliers (lightning speed, dramatically reduced inventory costs, etc.)? How closely are our business goals aligned with those of our suppliers?

Thought: Now more than ever, it is possible for companies to off-load noncore activities onto suppliers. Technology has steadily reduced the costs of communication and coordination. Industry standards, such as GSM in the cell phone business, have simplified the interface between different components of a system. Enormous economies of scale in the manufacture of high–volume "core products" such as semiconductors have made it necessary for downstream assemblers to rely on just a few suppliers. Add to this ever shorter product life cycles and a premium on flexibility, and it is easy to see why companies are becoming less vertical. Yet every company must guard against "outsourcing" things that might become critical sources of competitive differentiation. Once you've outsourced something to some big IT company, you can write it off as a source of competitive advantage.

2. **Partners:** Partners typically supply critical "complements" to a final product or "solution." Their relationship with producers is more horizontal and less vertical than that of suppliers. An imaginative use of partners can be the key to industry revolution.

Example: The success of Microsoft's Windows platform is in large part due to the support Microsoft has lavished on its software development partners. Making it easy for independent software vendors (ISVs) to write for Windows increases the number of applications running on Windows and further strengthens its market position. Microsoft's support includes offering development tools to ISVs that make it easier to write software for the Windows O/S, helping young companies get access to capital and offering them co-marketing opportunities, hosting dozens of developer events around the world,

COALITION MEMBERS ARE MORE THAN PARTNERS, THEY SHARE DIRECTLY IN THE RISK AND REWARDS OF INDUSTRY REVOLUTION.

and running a dedicated Web site that provides developers with extensive online support. In 1999, the Microsoft Developer Network included over 10,000 ISVs.

Ask yourself: Can we look at the world as a global reservoir of competencies? What opportunities might be available to us if we could "borrow" the assets and competencies of other companies and marry them with our own? How could we use partners to "punch more than our weight"? How can we use partners to achieve greater flexibility, focus more tightly on our own core competencies, build a first-mover advantage, or offer a more complete "solution" to customers?

Thought: A lot of "suppliers" would like to become "partners"—that is, they want to be more than order takers competing on price. Here's what this implies. First, you have to take responsibility for something more than a minor component in the overall solution. You need to take responsibility for an entire system or product. Second, you may have to be willing to share some of the commercial risk. To win an exclusive contract from Boeing to supply jet engines for a super-long-range derivative of the 777, GE had to behave like a partner. It agreed to put up as much as half of the $1 billion needed to launch the 777 derivative, thus reducing Boeing's development risk. Third, you have to work hard to make sure that your contribution is truly differentiated in a way that makes a difference to end consumers. This means you can't rely on your immediate downstream customer for your understanding of end-consumer needs. You must build your own point of view about what those end customers really want. If you're Dell or HP, the Taiwanese company that makes your computer monitors is a supplier. Intel is a partner. Every supplier would like to become "Intel Inside." But this won't happen unless you stop thinking of yourself as a supplier.

3. Coalitions: Business concept innovation often requires a company to join together with other, like-minded competitors in a coalition. This is particularly likely to be the case where investment or technology hurdles are high or where there is a high risk of ending up on the losing side of a winner-take-all standards battle. Coalition members are more than partners, they share directly in the risk and rewards of industry revolution.

Example: Airbus Industrie, a consortium of France's Aerospatiale Matra, Germany's DaimlerChrysler Aerospace Airbus, British Aerospace, and Spain's CASA, is one of the world's most successful coalitions. In 1999 Airbus rang up 476 orders to Boeing's 391. With Lockheed gone, and McDonnell Douglas now part of Boeing, Airbus is all that stands between the world's airlines and a Boeing monopoly.

Ask yourself: Can we look beyond our own resources and markets and imagine new resource combinations that could create new markets and services? Can we co-opt other firms into a "common cause"? Can we use their resources to alter the competitive dynamics of an industry? Can we use a coalition to bring a highly risky project into the realm of feasibility? Can we use a coalition to attack the entrenched position of an industry incumbent?

Thought: Business-to-business "hubs" and "exchanges" are simply one type of coalition. In April 2000, 11 of the world's largest retailers, including Target, Kmart, Safeway, Marks & Spencer, and Tesco, announced the formation of a global buying consortium. Their goal is to build a Worldwide Retail Exchange that would be open to all retailers. Interestingly, the original 11 members have a combined buying power of $300 billion per year, nearly twice that of Wal-Mart. Sears, Carrefour, Metro AG, J Sainsbury plc, and Kroger are combining much of their $200 billion purchasing power in their own GlobalNetXchange.[6] Whatever the ultimate fate of these new business-to-business coalitions, it is a sure bet that they will radically change the distribution of bargaining power within many industries. Pity the poor suppliers.

Beyond pooling buying power or sharing risk coalitions can also be used to partition the boundaries between collaboration and competition. For example, a number of wireless phone makers worked together to develop an operating system for cell phones that would allow them to access the Internet. Since standards battles are often winner-take-all, Nokia, Ericsson, Motorola, and others have decided to collaborate on the development of an operating system even though they compete vigorously in the market for handsets.

Members of the coalition would rather compete on dimensions other than who has the best operating system.

CUSTOMER INTERFACE	CORE STRATEGY	STRATEGIC RESOURCES	VALUE NETWORK
Fulfillment & Support Information & Insight Relationship Dynamics Pricing Structure	Business Mission Product/Market Scope Basis for Differentiation	Core Competencies Strategic Assets Core Processes	Suppliers Partners Coalitions

Company Boundaries

Intermediating between a company's *strategic resources* and its *value network* are the firm's *boundaries*. This bridge component refers to *the decisions that have been made about what the firm does and what it contracts out to the value network*. Again, an important aspect of any business model is the choice of what the firm will do for itself and what it will outsource to suppliers, partners, or coalition members. Changing these boundaries is often an important contributor to business concept innovation.

> *Example*: The PC industry's spectacular growth was driven by innovative boundary decisions by IBM, Microsoft, and Intel. Twenty years ago the computer industry was dominated by vertically integrated companies such as IBM, Data General, and Digital Equipment Corp. These companies made their own silicon chips, created their own proprietary operating systems, manufactured their own computers, and often wrote application software. The PC, with its open standards, changed all that. Microsoft did the operating system. Intel did the chips. Hundreds of suppliers from California to Taiwan to Ireland made specialized components such as SCSI cards, sound chips, monitors, and disk drives. Thousands of independent software vendors wrote applications, and assemblers, such as Dell, shipped the finished products to customers and handled technical support. Horizontal specialization allowed component manufacturers to reap enormous economies of scale as they were no longer limited to selling through their own channels, under a single brand. It gave the assemblers complete freedom to incorporate the very latest technology and the most cost-competitive components in the finished product. Indeed, it is difficult to believe that a vertically integrated company could have sustained the pace of innovation witnessed over the past couple of decades in the PC business.

> *Ask yourself*: Have you looked critically at where you draw the boundary between what you do and what you don't do as a

company? Is there a chance to change industry rules by "de–verticalizing" your industry, as Microsoft did in the computer business or Enron and others have done in the energy business? How explicitly do you consider boundary choices in thinking about new business concepts?

Thought: In the age of progress, companies were organized like hierarchies, where internal transactions were governed by some central authority and every business unit was 100 percent owned by the parent company. While this structure allowed, in theory, for a lot of internal coordination, as, for example, when General Motors sources engines for several model lines from a single factory, the sheer size of these hierarchies, and top management's distance from the market, often made them slow and unresponsive. The new economy is witnessing the development of a new corporate form that sits halfway between the traditional hierarchy, with its central control, and markets where there is no central control. *Red Herring* calls these companies economic networks, or "EcoNets."[7] CMGI and ICG are the archetypes, but dozens more are being formed all the time.

Originally designed as incubators for Internet start–ups, these companies are quickly evolving into twenty–first century *keiretsu*, where member companies rely on each other and on the parent for critical skills, market learning, legal help, financing, executive recruitment, and strategy development. The parent company acts as midwife, birthing young companies and pushing them toward their IPOs. But even after they go public, the parent company retains a significant degree of equity—enough to ensure a large measure of management control, and to keep the offspring firmly connected to the rest of the family. The advantage of an IPO is that gives each business an independent valuation and a pool of valuable equity that can be used to attract talent, to reward executives for their business-building prowess, and as currency in acquisitions. These advantages are not available to individual business units in a traditional, hierarchical company.

Like traditional conglomerates, corporate management in the EcoNets is not emotionally tied to any single business. This is a distinct advantage given the so–far rather short life cycles of many Internet start–ups. If one business dies, so what; there are a dozen more to take its place. Unlike conglomerates, EcoNet senior execs work hard to create value across and between individual companies. In short, EcoNets are struggling to resolve two fundamental paradoxes that have long beset old–line companies: how to nurture young companies without smothering them, and how to reap syner-gies without succumbing to bureaucratic bloat and pointless head-office meddling. So far the EcoNets seem to be succeeding: for example, only Dell Computer rewarded its shareholders more hand-somely than CMGI in the 1990s. If traditional companies want to create this kind of value, they are going to have to become as adept as the EcoNets at growing and supporting new companies.

WEALTH POTENTIAL

To be an industry revolutionary, you need a point of view on how you're going to inject innovation into each component of the business model. You also need a compelling story about how your business con-cept is going to *make money!* If you can't describe how your business concept will produce above-average profits, you're a comedian without a punch line.

There are four factors to consider in determining the *wealth potential* of any business concept:

- the extent to which the business concept is an *efficient* way of delivering customer benefits;
- the extent to which the business concept is *unique*;
- the degree of *fit* among the elements of the business concept; and
- the extent to which the business concept exploits *profit boosters* that have the potential to generate above-average returns.

Let's take each of these in turn.

EFFICIENT

To create wealth, a business model must be efficient in the sense that the value customers place on the benefits delivered exceeds the cost of pro-ducing those benefits. Many new business concepts founder on this very point—there's just no margin! Many Web-based business models have negative operating margins. Sites such as Buy.com are reputed to lose money on everything they sell, but to make it up on advertising. There are

Having an efficient business model does not mean having the lowest costs.

many who doubt whether such a model can be sustained in the long term.

Examples: Southwest Airlines has a business model that delivers air travel to budget-minded fliers more efficiently than any of its major competitors. With its point-to-point route structure, all-737 fleet, and flexible work practices, Southwest has the lowest seat-per-mile cost of any major airline. Despite Southwest's low fares, it has one of the healthiest margins in the airline business.

However, having an efficient business model does *not* mean having the lowest costs. Midwest Express Airlines doesn't match Southwest's fares, and Southwest would never claim to deliver the "best care in the air," as Midwest does. Filet mignon with lobster, a roll with butter, spinach, mandarin salad, and chocolate banana-split cake—when was the last time you ate like this in coach? That's a typical meal on Midwest Express. The company spends an average of $10 per passenger on meals, compared with Southwest's 20¢. (You can get peanuts really cheap when you buy in bulk.) Midwest offers its coach passengers two-by-two seating, with five more inches of knee room and four more inches of hip room than usual coach seats. Midwest earns healthy profits because it tightly controls costs in other areas—it flies an older fleet of mostly DC-9s, and it operates out of a low-cost hub, Milwaukee. The same coach fare that would buy a distinctly mediocre service experience on American or United buys a near-first-class experience on Midwest. No wonder the airline has been rated by *Travel & Leisure* magazine as the best domestic airline, and no wonder its stock has outperformed the Dow Jones Industrial Average. While Southwest offers less service for a much lower price than traditional airlines, Midwest offers more service for about the same price. Both companies have highly efficient business models.

Ask yourself: Have we tested our assumptions about the value customers will actually derive from our products or services? Do we understand in detail the costs we will incur in providing that value?

UNIQUE

As we saw in our discussion of strategy convergence in chapter 2, there are often a number of companies in an industry with business models that are essentially identical. The greater the convergence among business models, the less the chance for above-average profits. The goal is to create a business model that is unique in its conception and execution. Of course, the goal is not uniqueness for its own sake. To produce profits, a business model must be unique in ways that are valued by customers.

Example: Broadcast.com represents a fundamentally new approach to delivering radio and television programming. It can deliver content to your desktop (I recently watched ITN's news, live from London, on my laptop), and it does so without the need for a dedicated broadcast network. You can pick your favorite radio or television personalities, download past shows, and listen to stations from around the world. This is nothing like local radio and TV. By itself, uniqueness doesn't guarantee profitability, but it's a start. Broadcast.com was sold to Yahoo! in July 1999 in a deal that valued Broadcast.com at something north of $4 billion—that's the value of uniqueness.

Ask yourself: To what extent does your business concept depart from the average within your industry or domain? How many points of difference can be identified across the major components of the business concept? Will these points of difference bring new benefits to customers?

FIT

Consanguinity is a 10-dollar word that means "fit." A business concept generates profits when all its elements are mutually reinforcing. A business concept has to be internally consistent—all its parts must work together for the same end goal. Almost by definition, a company with mediocre performance is a company where elements of its business model work at cross-purposes.

Example: Four Seasons Hotels and Resorts, Inc., based in Toronto, runs the largest chain of luxury hotels in the world and defines "pampered" in nearly 20 countries. The company's success comes from the fact that every aspect of its business model—property location, staff selection and training, architecture, quality of decor, service levels, and catering—is focused on making you feel like a head of state. Few companies achieve the kind of consistency so much in evidence at Four Seasons. For example, on a recent first-class flight from San Francisco to London, there was an elegant caviar service at the beginning of the flight, and a breakfast at the other end that featured a plastic tub of Wheaties with a pull-off paper lid. Talk about a jarring inconsistency! This is how cereal is sold at McDonald's, and not quite what is expected for a $10,000 roundtrip airfare.

Ask yourself: Do all of the elements of the business model positively reinforce each other? Are there some elements of the business model that are at odds with other elements? What's the degree of internal consistency in our business model? Is there anything that looks anomalous to customers?

PROFIT BOOSTERS

Of course what you actually want to know is not whether your business model is going to be profitable, but whether it's going to be *really* profitable. There are a dozen *profit boosters* that can push profits into orbit. The trick is to figure out a way of bolting one or two these profit boosters onto your business concept.

These profit boosters can be grouped under four categories:

- Increasing Returns
- Competitor Lock–Out
- Strategic Economies
- Strategic Flexibility

You need to get acquainted with each of these profit boosters. They are what distinguish so–so profits from returns that make investors swoon.

The first two, *increasing returns* and *competitor lock-out*, are synonyms for monopoly. Business concept innovation is, after all, the search for temporary monopolies. While revolutionary business concepts tend to undermine entrenched monopolies, a business concept with strong monopolistic tendencies can often withstand a prolonged assault from would–be rivals before crumbling. In general, the stronger the monopoly, the greater the innovation necessary to unseat the incumbent. In this sense, business concept innovation is the quest for strategies that are, insofar as possible, impervious to further bouts of business concept innovation. Got that? To be clear, I am not using the word "monopoly" in a legal sense—I am merely referring to strategies that tend to be self-reinforcing. You don't have to engage in predatory tactics or set out to be a robber baron to create a business concept that ends up yielding monopolylike profits.

Economists start with an assumption of perfect, atomistic competition. They look at any firm earning above-average profits as an anomaly. Industry revolutionaries start with an assumption that the entire goal of strategy is to create *im*perfect competition. To them, strategy is all about building quasi monopolies. To an economist, above-average profit represents "market failure." To a strategist, it represents a killer business concept. The problem for economists is that there are a lot of anomalies these days. Microsoft's Windows operating system, Delta's control of gates in Atlanta and Salt Lake City, Intel's x86 architecture, and the patents behind the DVD are all examples of quasi monopolies. Recently, economists such as W. Brian Arthur and Paul Romer have discovered what savvy innovators have known all along: some business models, by their very nature, have built-in monopolies.

Oxford and Cambridge universities are two of the oldest examples of "increasing returns."

Increasing Returns

Founded more than 800 years ago, Oxford and Cambridge universities are two of the oldest examples of "increasing returns." Their continued dominance in British higher education is attested to by the fact that they are often known simply as "Oxbridge," a class of two that eclipses all other British universities. Imagine you're a brilliant young physicist who one day hopes to win a Nobel Prize. Where do you want to go to do your postdoctoral research? That's simple—to a university that already has a clutch of Nobel Prize winners. You also want access to the best Ph.D. students, who are, of course, attracted to the best faculty. The best attract the best—this virtuous circle has allowed Oxford and Cambridge to dominate British academia for the better part of a millennium. It wasn't Microsoft and W. Brian Arthur that invented increasing returns.

The term *increasing returns* simply refers to a competitive situation where the rich tend to get richer, and the poor, poorer. It denotes a flywheel effect that tends to perpetuate early success. Those who are ahead will get further ahead, and those who are behind will fall further behind. Perpetual motion is almost as rare in business as it is in physics, and every business model ultimately encounters some sort of friction, but a business concept characterized by increasing returns can produce fat profits for an immodestly long time. The notion of increasing returns is subtly different from the notion of scale. In an industry such as chemicals, which is characterized by significant economies of scale, you have to be big to win. In industries with increasing returns, if you win early, you're likely to *get* big. Economies of scale are largely static; increasing returns are dynamic.

To benefit from increasing returns, a business model must harness one of three underlying forces: network effects, positive feedback effects, or learning effects.

1. ***Network Effects:*** Some business models benefit from a strange kind of value multiplier known as the "network effect." In some cases, the value of a network increases as the *square* of the growth of the number of "nodes," or members in the network. If you model the growth of a business concept that exploits the network effect, you get a diagram that looks like the power curve for nuclear fission or the infection curve for a virulent virus.

   Examples: eBay is a classic example of network economies. You wouldn't go to an auction site that had only a dozen items for sale. But as the number of participants (nodes) increases, the chance you'll find what you want, or find a buyer for what you don't want, goes up geometrically. If you have something to buy or sell online, why *wouldn't* you go to eBay? With nearly two–and–a–half million items for sale, in more than 1,600 categories, eBay has exploited the dynamics of the network effect to the hilt. Where the value of the network is a function of the *number of members in the network,* there will be increasing returns for those who start earliest, work hardest, and build the biggest network. As their network gets bigger and bigger, it gets harder and harder for latecomers to build equivalent networks, and there is less and less incentive for customers to switch networks. While Cisco's business model doesn't benefit directly from the network effect, it benefits indirectly since Cisco is building much of the digital plumbing for the Internet. The growth of the Internet is the epitome of a network effect: the more people go online, the more interesting the Internet becomes to advertisers, merchants, and content providers. The more content and commercial options online, the greater the incentive for individuals to go online. Cisco has hitched its business model to this comet.

Network effects also account for the triumph of Visa, MasterCard, and American Express as truly global credit cards. The more merchants who accept these cards, the more likely you are to carry them. The more likely you are to carry them, the more merchants are apt to accept them. Another virtuous circle.

Ask yourself: Do we have a business concept that taps into the network effect? Can we find opportunities to create network economies where none currently exist? If not, can we somehow hitch our business concept to the network multiplier?

If you model the growth of a business concept that exploits the network effect, you get a diagram that looks like the power curve for nuclear fission.

2. **Positive Feedback Effects:** *Positive feedback effects* and *increasing returns* are sometimes used interchangeably to denote a situation where success breeds success. But I'd like to use *positive feedback effects* in a more limited way—to refer specifically to the way one uses market feedback to turn an initial lead into an unbridgeable chasm for

competitors. A firm with a large base of users, and a way of rapidly extracting feedback from those users, may be able to improve its products and services faster than its competitors. As a result, its products become better yet, and it captures even more customers. Another virtuous circle ensues.

Example: AOL has systematically exploited insights derived from its customer base to provide the easiest online service, and has steadily pulled ahead of other branded Internet portals. The better the content and online experience, the more users AOL attracts. The more users AOL attracts, the more advertising revenue it gets. The more advertising dollars it gets, the more it can afford to invest in upgrading and expanding its services, thus attracting more users. This positive feedback effect also works with advertisers. The more users, the higher the ad rates AOL can charge. The higher the ad rates, the more AOL can spend on differentiating its site and offering. The more it spends on making its site and content even better, the more users it attracts. Positive feedback effects are the hub in the virtuous circle of customer learning and improvement.

Ask yourself: Where's the flywheel that will perpetuate our early success? Where are we creating a virtuous circle of increasing returns? Where could we create positive feedback effects within our business model? Can we set up a very short learning cycle that will allow us to improve our products and services faster than anyone else? Should we be heavily discounting our products or services, or giving them away for free as a means to generate positive feedback effects that would allow us to outpace competitors?

3. **Learning Effects:** More and more industries are knowledge–intensive. A company that gets an early start in accumulating knowledge, and then continues to learn faster than its rivals, can build an almost insurmountable lead. Knowledge accumulation is often highly correlated with experience. (Remember Boston Consulting Group's experience curve?) The notion is simple: the application of knowledge begets new knowledge. This is particularly true in cases where the critical knowledge is both complex and tacit—complex in the sense that it represents the fusion of several different types of knowledge, and tacit in that it is not easily codified.

Example: In an industry—be it manufacturing semiconductors or strategy consulting—characterized by strong learning effects, it is difficult for latecomers to intercept the knowledge–building progress of the leaders unless they change the knowledge base of the industry.

Learning effects gave Sharp and Toshiba dominant positions in the manufacture of flat screen displays. In the early years, flat screen manufacturing yields were disastrously low. But perseverance paid off. For a long while, Sharp and Toshiba enjoyed virtual monopolies in the single most valuable component of a laptop computer. Hundreds of millions went to the bottom line. Of course, over time all knowledge tends to get commoditized—it gets acquired from supplies, equipment manufacturers, ex-employees, or through reverse engineering. As this has happened, new competitors have entered the flat screen display business.

Ask yourself: What parts of our business model might be subject to learning curve effects? Where does accumulated volume count, and

REALLY SLICK BUSINESS MODELS LOCK PREEMPTION, CHOKE POINTS, AND

how much does it count as a percentage of total costs? Are we taking full advantage of every opportunity to learn? Are we building that learning into our products and services on a real-time basis?

COMPETITOR LOCK-OUT

When you find a window of opportunity, the goal is to crawl through it and lock it behind you. You want *all* the loot, and you don't want to have to fight for it. Ghastly business, fighting. Always a chance that some of *your* blood may get spilled. That's why really slick business models lock competitors out through preemption, choke points, and customer lock-in.

1. **Preemption:** Where there is great potential for increasing returns, merely being first may be enough to put competitors out of contention. It's terrific when the first punch is a knockout blow. In industries that are R&D–intensive or that have high fixed costs, there's often no second place—you're either first or you're nowhere.

   Examples: Imagine that Early Bird, Inc., has just sunk $200 million into developing a new software product. In its first year of operation it finds 5 million customers for its WormFinder software, which sells for $250 a pop. That's $1.25 billion in revenue. With a variable cost of $50 per copy (to cover manufacturing, distribution, advertising, and admin), Early Bird's direct costs amount to $250 million. That leaves $1 billion—a 500 percent return on its R&D investment. If it's smart,

Early Bird will sink a couple of hundred million dollars back into R&D to bolster its lead. Slow As Snails, Inc., enters the market 10 months late with a competing product and manages to sell only 1 million copies. At $250 a pop, Snails' gross is $250 million. With variable costs of $50 per copy, Snails' gross profit is $200 million. That barely covers its own development costs. Going forward, there's no way it will be able to match Early Bird's escalating R&D investment. Now Early Bird has the chance to play vulture. It drops its price to $150 and the market expands to 11 million customers, of which Early Bird has 8.5 million. Its revenues inch ahead to $1.275 billion, but it is still making a very healthy gross profit of $850 million. Meanwhile, Slow As Snails matches Early Bird's price and rakes in only $225 mil-

COMPETITORS OUT THROUGH CUSTOMER LOCK-IN.

lion on 1.5 million customers. After deducting direct costs of $75 million, Slow As Snails can afford only $150 million for ongoing R&D. It may take another couple of rounds for the fight to be over, but Slow As Snails is going down. A business concept with this kind of fixed–cost leverage offers the fleet of foot the chance to create an almost unassailable position.

First–mover advantages are never absolute, but they are often pivotal in industries with a rapid pace of technological development and relatively short product life cycles. If you get in late, you're going to be fighting the U.S. Marines with slingshots and bottle rockets. Preemption requires a great product, a capacity to learn fast, and a willingness to double up your bets. Being first means nothing if you're trying to sell something nobody wants or if it takes you forever to respond to customer input. Apple may have been first with handheld computers, but the Newton was so woefully underdeveloped that it left the door wide open for the PalmPilot.

Johnson & Johnson pulled a Newton with its groundbreaking coronary "stent," a tiny metal frame that props open cholesterol-clogged arteries. Three years after the product's launch in 1994, it was closing in on $1 billion in revenues, and had a 90 percent market share and gross margins judged to be as high as 80 percent. But J&J left the stent window wide open. The company's overambitious pricing ($1,595), sluggish pace of product refinement, and offhand

Do you risk becoming a perpetual follower?

treatment of cardiologists opened the door for followers like Guidant Corp. and Boston Scientific Corp. Forty-five days after it launched its competing product, Guidant claimed a market share of 70 percent. J&J ultimately abandoned the market. Preemption without follow-through ain't worth squat.

Ask yourself: Do you risk becoming a perpetual follower—of being 3Com to someone else's Cisco? Are there any first-mover advantages implicit in your business concept? Where do you plan to preempt, and how do you plan to follow up on that? How are you going to turn being first once into being first again and again?

2. Choke Points: The famed military strategist Karl von Clausewitz called it the "command of heights." My colleague Peter Skarzynski calls it "choke point control," but the idea is the same. Whether it's 1452 and you're Sultan Mehmet II building a fortress to control the Bosphorus or it's the new millennium and you're trying to gain control of the cable television infrastructure that will allow broadband Webcasting, the logic is the same. Whoever owns the choke point collects the toll. If you're unwilling to pay up, you're locked out.

Examples: For years, AT&T's control of your telephone line constituted a choke point. Hard as it is to believe, there was a time when you couldn't connect anything to the phone network without AT&T's permission. Recently AT&T, Microsoft, and AOL all seem to have discovered the importance of owning one of the last true choke points in America—the cable TV connection into the home. For the foreseeable future, the coaxial cable that brings you Conan O'Brien and other sophisticates is one of only three broadband connections into the home (the others being satellite TV and DSL—digital subscriber lines). Like a compass seeking true north, AT&T's monopoly meter zeroed in on the late twentieth-century equivalent to the early twentieth-century phone line. AOL has been more than a little worried that AT&T might use its newly discovered choke point to put a brake on AOL's success. In a doomsday scenario, AT&T makes AOL pay an access fee (much as a grocery chain charges a food company a "slotting fee" to put new products on the shelves). Or worse, AT&T refuses to carry AOL in favor of an AT&T-sponsored portal. Statements such as the following, made by AT&T's CEO, Michael Armstrong, are hardly designed to assuage AOL's anxiety: "If you don't control the asset, I don't know how you control the destiny."[8] Sultan Mehmet II couldn't have said it better. No wonder AOL was attracted to Time Warner, another big cable TV operator. Ironically, one of AT&T's motives for getting into the TV business was to find a way around another choke point—the Baby Bells' control of "the last mile" of the phone network. Now AT&T has its own "last mile."

Microsoft's Windows may be history's most effective choke point. It is virtually impossible to build a PC, write a software application, or create a document without, in some way, sending a check to Microsoft. All of us who've passed through the Microsoft toll gate should be thankful for one thing: Internet Protocol (the standard that governs how packets of data are sent across the Internet) and HTML (the standard that governs how information is displayed on the Internet) are not only open, they're in the public domain. That must drive Bill Gates nuts, yet he should be grateful, for if anyone owned IP and HTML, Bill would probably be the second-richest person on the planet.

Choke points come in many shapes and sizes: a technical standard, control of some costly infrastructure, preferential access to a government buyer, a patent, or a prime location. Other choke point examples include the "anchor" store in a mall, Gatorade's prime position on the sidelines of every NFL football game, De Beers' historic control over the distribution of diamonds, or a critical patent. A truly strategic business concept lets you command the heights.

Ask yourself: Is there some standard, some protocol, an interface, or a bit of infrastructure that you could uniquely own? Are you creating any assets that will be critical to the success of other companies—so critical that you can effectively charge a "toll"? Are there some scarce assets or skills that you'd like to deny your competitors? Can you lock up these assets or skills in some way?

3. Customer Lock-In: Competitor lock–*out* often means customer lock–*in*. But even when you can't lock out *all* your competitors, you can lock in *some* of your customers—through long–term supply contracts, proprietary product designs that keep them coming back for upgrades and add–ons, or control over a local monopoly. There are many ways you can tie up your customers, but you have to be careful. A customer that *feels* locked in is a particularly angry beast. You gotta use velvet ropes.

Examples: U.S. airlines have earned graduate degrees in customer lock–in. First there's the matter of gates. Competition–phobic air carriers moved swiftly after deregulation to consolidate their control over so–called fortress hubs. During the 1980s, the Justice Department approved every airline merger that was presented to it. The result? A fellow traveler can tell where you live simply by looking at the frequent–flyer luggage tag that adorns your carry-on—yeah, that gold–colored emblem of your slavery. You got a US Airways tag? You probably live in Pittsburgh or Charlotte. Continen-tal? Houston or Newark. America West? Phoenix. TWA (poor sod)? St. Louis. Northwest? Detroit or Minneapolis, maybe Memphis.

Fortress hubs have been wildly successful, as lock–in strategies go, provoking some in the U.S. Congress to label airlines "unregulated monopolies." Few fliers are dumb enough to believe that the new spate of proposed semi–mergers and co–marketing agreements (Amer-ican and US Airways, United and Delta, Northwest and Continental) is really about "seamless travel." They're about better lock–in.

Frequent–flyer cards are an even more intricate set of manacles. Fail to fly enough with your airworthy monopolist, and you'll get stuffed into steerage on *every* flight. You'll never tally up enough miles for that second honeymoon either. You're not Platinum? Not 1K? Then don't even bother to ask an airline employee for a favor unless you're fully prostrate or more than halfway through a myocardial infarction.

Customer lock–in is just a fancy way of saying "switching costs." Once you've bought Microsoft *Word* and learned to navigate its Byzantine "features," you'll be well and truly on the hook. To Microsoft you're more than a customer, you're an annuity. Unless someone comes along with a truly radical new software business concept, you're going to be buying upgrades from Microsoft for a looooong time. Indeed, in a recent year, around half of Microsoft's software revenues came from upgrades. Talk about customer lock–in! You could escape the clutches of Philip Morris and a two–pack–a–day nicotine habit easier than you could wriggle free of Redmond Bill.

Only Intel has anything close to Microsoft's lock on customers. A few years ago Intel's co-founder and chairman, Gordon Moore, was asked whether he had been worried that his company's x86 chip architecture would be supplanted by new technologies such as RISC (reduced instruction set computing). His answer was telling: "No . . . we had this tremendous advantage: all of the software that people had bought that ran on our instruction set."[9] Intel may be paranoid about many things, but a new chip architecture that would knock it out of the PCs is probably not one of them. Customer lock-in? Handcuffs, straitjacket, and leg irons. Indeed, after years of trying, AMD has only recently taken a significant chunk of the microprocessor market in low-end PCs. And customers are glad for the alternative.

GE's jet engine deal with Boeing is a rather more palatable form of customer lock-in. GE's financial support for Boeing's development of the long-range 777 came with a price—Boeing would agree to sell the new 777 with GE engines *exclusively*. Lock-in is okay when the customer asks to be tied up.

All in all, be careful of customer lock-in. Lock-in is great while it lasts, but the moment those cuffs are off, your customers may well go for your throat.

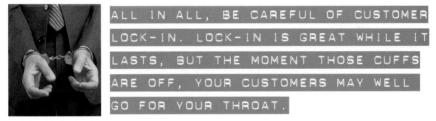

ALL IN ALL, BE CAREFUL OF CUSTOMER LOCK-IN. LOCK-IN IS GREAT WHILE IT LASTS, BUT THE MOMENT THOSE CUFFS ARE OFF, YOUR CUSTOMERS MAY WELL GO FOR YOUR THROAT.

Ask yourself: Could this business concept reduce our customers' ability or desire to buy from other suppliers? Is there anything in this business concept that would induce customers to limit their freedom of choice? How could we bind our fate with the fate of our customers even more tightly?

Strategic Economies

Unlike operational efficiencies, strategic economies don't derive from operational excellence, but from the business concept itself. Strategic economies come in three varieties: scale, focus, and scope.

1. ***Scale:*** Scale can drive efficiencies in many ways: better plant utilization, greater purchasing power, the muscle to enforce industrywide price discipline, and more besides. Industry revolutionaries often consolidate fragmented industries. Any

company that gets caught behind the consolidation curve and misses the chance to build scale advantages will be left at a notable disadvantage.

Examples: Wal-Mart consolidated Main Street retailing and reaped unimagined scale economies in logistics and purchasing. While scale economies tend to perpetuate the success of big incumbents, revolutionaries look for industries that are still fragmented or for scale advantages that haven't yet been tapped. Imagine starting a business one day and 16 months later having your 29 percent stake valued at $315 million. Another sickening Internet story? Not quite—it's a story about Brad Jacobs and heavy equipment rentals. Jacobs got his start in the garbage hauling business. Having watched that business consolidate, he thought there might be a chance to bring scale economies to the highly fragmented rental market for air compressors, cranes, forklifts, generators, and the like. United Rentals has consolidated more than 200 companies. After merging with a big competitor, United Rentals surpassed Hertz to become the largest equipment renter in the country, with over 600 locations.[10]

Ask yourself: Does our business model offer us the chance to build scale advantages? Where does size pay off in this business concept? Will the scale advantages outweigh any loss in flexibility?

2. **Focus:** A company with a high degree of focus and specialization may reap economies compared with competitors with a more diffused business mission and a less coherent mix of services or products. Focus is not about efficiency in a cost sense; it's about efficiency in a don't–get–distracted, get–all–the–wood–behind–one–arrow sense.

Examples: Focus is how little Granite Construction, Inc., of Watsonville, California, competes successfully with industry giants such as Morrison Knudsen and Bechtel. Granite Construction doesn't build chemical plants, and it doesn't do urban rail projects. It will, however, pave just about anything, be it an airport runway, a driveway, or a section of interstate highway. Sales amounted to $1.2 billion in 1998, double what they were five years before. The company has a portfolio of more than 30 gravel pits that supply paving materials. It also makes its own ready–mix concrete and asphalt.

Focus is what lets BMW take on the might of Ford and GM in the luxury car business and win. Large companies often impose competing and ambiguous demands on their various divisions. Certainly this seems to be the fate that befell Cadillac—how can one explain

Focus is not about efficiency in a cost sense; it's about efficiency in a don't-get-distracted, get-all-the-wood-behind-one-arrow sense.

products like the Cimmaron and the only slightly less insipid Catera? What BMW loses in scale, it makes up for in single–minded zeal. Is there anything else on this planet so tightly put together as a 325i? BMW is a pure, sweet note; Lincoln and Cadillac have often sounded like ill–disciplined orchestras still tuning up. If BMW is ultimately swept up in merger fever, its new owners would do well to leave the Bavarian car–meisters alone.

Ask yourself: Does our business concept have a laserlike focus? If not, do we run the risk of trying to "boil the ocean"? What advantages would we gain by being more narrowly focused? What economies of scope would we lose if we were more focused?

3. **Scope:** The idea here is almost the inverse of focus. A company that can leverage resources and management talents across a broad array of opportunities may have an efficiency advantage over firms that cannot. Scope economies come from sharing things across business units and countries: brands, facilities, best practice, scarce talent, IT infrastructure, and so on.

Example: Maybe you drink Moet & Chandon champagne, or perhaps your tastes run to Dom Perignon and Krug. Perhaps you carry a Louis Vuitton handbag or briefcase or wear a Tag Heuer watch. Your fragrance may have come from Christian Dior or Givenchy. And maybe that soft cotton shirt you're wearing came from Thomas Pink of Jermyn Street. Buy any of these brands and you're enriching the substantial coffers of LVMH, the world's premier luxury brands com–pany. The company's chairman, Bernard Arnault, a.k.a. The Pope of Fashion, built LVMH into a $7 billion–plus high–fashion juggernaut to capitalize on the substantial economies of scope that exist in man–ufacturing and marketing luxury goods. Scope economies come in a

Some business models are inherently easier to reconfigure than others—these are the ones that will endure in the age of revolution.

variety of flavors: channel power and access to distribution channels, economies in buying ad space and running high-tech distribution centers, and the chance to move experienced management teams into acquired businesses to help revitalize elite but stuffy brands. While Prada and Gucci have recently made significant acquisitions of their own, they lag far behind LVMH in the race to build a *de luxe* powerhouse. No one in the rarefied world of platinum-plated brands doubts that Bernard Arnault is an industry revolutionary.

Ask yourself: Where are the potential economies of scope within our business concept? Can we find any "dual use" assets—things we can exploit in more than one business? What skills could we leverage across businesses, countries, or activities?

Strategic Flexibility

In a fast-changing world, with unpredictable demand cycles, strategic flexibility can generate higher profits by helping a company stay perfectly tuned to the market and avoid getting trapped in dead-end business models. Strategic flexibility comes from portfolio breadth, operating agility, and a low breakeven point.

1. ***Portfolio Breadth:*** Focus is great, but if the world moves against you, you may lack other options. Linking the fortunes of your company to the fortunes of a single market can be a high-risk gamble. A company with a broad offering may be more resilient in the face of rapidly shifting customer priorities than a more narrowly focused competitor. A portfolio can consist of countries, products, businesses, competencies, or customer types. The essential point is that it helps to hedge a company's exposure to the vagaries of one particular market niche.

   Examples: Given the vagaries of drug development and approval, most pharmaceutical companies feel it necessary to support the development of a broad portfolio of drugs. A broad portfolio increases the chances that a company can sustain high levels of R&D year in and year out, rather than have its R&D budget whipsawed by the changing fortunes of one or two products. It also raises the odds of coming up with an out-and-out blockbuster. Cisco has one of the broadest product portfolios of any company in the data networking business. While other companies hitched themselves to a particular segment or technology, Cisco widened its horizons and spread its bets. It isn't dependent on the fortunes of any single technology or product line.

Ask yourself: What are the advantages of a wide portfolio of products or businesses? How can we hedge our bets in this business concept? Does this business concept force us to put all our eggs in a rather small basket? Is the reduction of earnings variability, for example, a positive strategic benefit?

2. ***Operating Agility:*** A company that is able to quickly refocus its efforts is better placed to respond to changes in demand and can thereby even out profit swings.

Example: Given the fact that Dell Computer owns few fixed assets, it is able to quickly reconfigure its selling approach and product line to suit changing market conditions. As one senior Dell executive put it, "We don't have to change bricks and mortar to change our strategy." Contrast that with Sears's 800–odd stores or GM's aging plants. Some business models are inherently easier to reconfigure than others— these are the ones that will endure in the age of revolution. Web- based businesses may offer the ultimate in flexibility. You can change a product description overnight, test a dozen different ad ideas and have the data back in 24 hours, and experiment with different price points—it's as if Web business concepts were made out of Play–Doh instead of steel and cement.

Ask yourself: How quickly does the demand function in our business change? Is there an advantage to investing in flexibility (i.e., in processes and facilities that would allow us to respond rapidly to shifts in demand)? Could we earn consistently higher profits if we were able to respond more quickly to changes in demand, or to changes in input needs (e.g., were able to quickly incorporate the latest components in our designs)?

3. ***Lower Breakeven:*** A business concept that carries a high breakpoint is inherently less flexible than one with a lower breakeven point. Capi- tal intensity, a big debt load, high fixed costs—these things tend to reduce the financial flexibility of a business model. In doing so, they also reduce strategic flexibility, in that they make it more difficult to pay off *one* thing so that you can go on and do *another* thing.

Example: For several decades Japanese car companies have been working to reduce the breakeven point of a car model. If you can break even on 50,000 units, instead of 250,000, you can trade that for a broader product range aimed at narrower consumer segments. More recently, the advantages of strategic flexibility have induced many companies to "de-capitalize" their business models.

THERE ARE 25-YEAR-OLD ENGINEERS IN SILICON VALLEY

Ask yourself: Does our business concept give us a **WHO DREAM** lower breakeven point than traditional business models? How could we tweak the business model to lower our breakeven point even further? What would be the benefits of a lower breakeven point? Could we use a lower breakeven to buy ourselves more flexibility or deliver more variety to customers?

Of course, none of these profit boosters can turn an awful product into a smash hit. On the other hand, a great business concept can sometimes compensate for a mediocre product—indeed, for years this is just what drove Apple aficionados nuts about Microsoft's success. For more than a decade, Microsoft's operating system was much less user-friendly than the Mac's, but Microsoft's profit boosters yielded an unprecedented financial windfall.

BECOMING A BUSINESS CONCEPT INNOVATOR

There are two reasons you must develop an instinctive ability to picture innovation in terms of novel business concepts, and competition as rivalry between business models. (Remember, the building blocks of a business concept and a business model are the same—a business model is simply a business concept that has been put into practice.) The first is so you can construct a well-developed business case around *your* billion-dollar insight. Half-baked ideas don't get funding. The second is so you can escape the hold the existing business model has on your imagination and your loyalties.

A successful business model creates its own intellectual hegemony. Success turns *a* business model into *the* business model. In *Dealers of Lightning,*[11] a cautionary tale for any preternaturally prosperous company, Michael Hiltzik pins down the reason Xerox failed so miserably to capitalize on the innovations that poured out of its Palo Alto Research Center. In the copier business Xerox got paid by the page; each page got counted by a clicker. In the electronic office of the future, there was no clicker—there was no annuity. How would one get paid? The hegemony of the pennies-per-page business model was so absolute that it blinded Xerox to an Aladdin's cave of other possibilities.

Many of the choices that define your company's business model were made years ago. Those choices were shaped by the logic of another age. In the fading glow of success, they may seem like inevitabilities. But they're not. It is your job to turn those inevitabilities back into choices. You do this by subjecting each element of the existing business model to fresh scrutiny: What are the alternatives? Does this choice still have merit? How would a company free of our prejudices tackle this? In decomposing the existing business model you create degrees of freedom where tradition reigns.

in Technicolor

business concepts.

you're a kid again

—with a very big Lego set.

So pretend

There are 25-year-old engineers in Silicon Valley who dream in Technicolor business concepts. But if you've been stuck for a decade in some functional chimney or you inherited a strategy from the village elders or you were taught to venerate "industry best practice," then thinking in terms of business models won't be a natural act for you.

So begin to practice. Pick the worst service experience you've had in the last year, and think about the business model that failed to meet your expectations. How would you change it—element by element? Find an industry where everyone seems to be stuck in the same cul–de–sac, and invent an exit strategy for one of the companies. Pick a company you care about—one you think deserves to be more successful than it is—and try to imagine a breakout business concept, your own equivalent of the cyber B–school. The great advantage of a business concept is that it is infinitely malleable. It is, at the outset, only an intellectual construct. So pretend you're a kid again—with a very big Lego set, one that allows you to re-make the very foundations of commerce. This isn't some meaningless exercise. This is mental training for industry revolutionaries.

BE
YOUR OWN
SEER

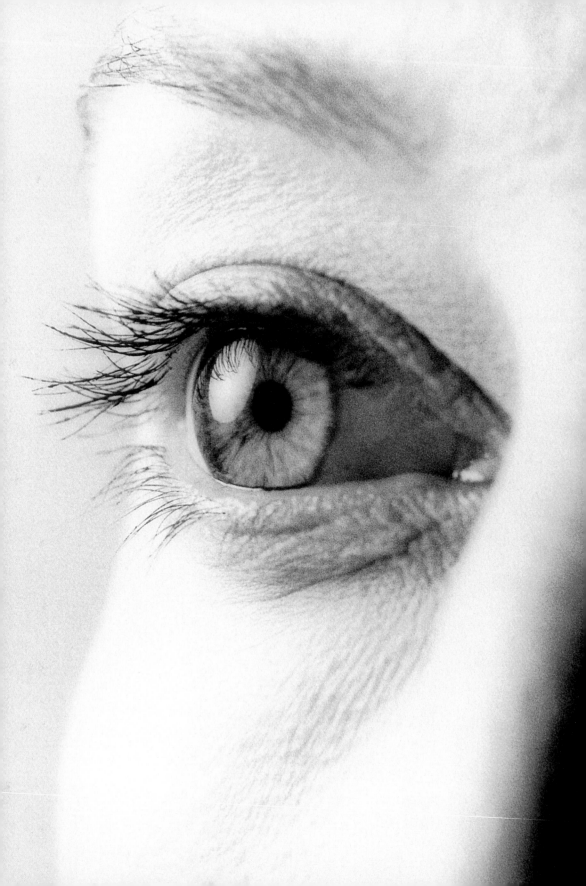

DO YOU HAVE THE PENETRATING
and unclouded eyes of a revolutionary? Do you just
know what's coming next? Is it real and inevitable and
three-dimensional for you? Can you see, *really* see, a
kick-ass opportunity for business concept innovation?
Is it so seductive that you can't even imagine turning
your back on it?

Are you the voice of opportunity in your company?
Are you the champion of the unconventional? Do you
know how to break through the hard, parched soil of
ignorance and dogma to find a gusher of an opportunity? Are you a source of strategic diversity? In the age
of revolution you have to be able to imagine
revolutionary alternatives to the status quo. If you
can't, you'll be relegated to the swollen ranks of
keyboard pounding automatons.

There are too many individuals who cannot yet
escape the dead hand of precedent. Too many who are
not fully vested in the future. Too many who cannot
distinguish between their heritage and their destiny. Is
this you? Wanna do something about it?

Look around you. Look at the individuals and companies that have been champions of business concept innovation. Do this, and you will see that rule–busting, wealth–creating innovation doesn't come out of corporate planning. It doesn't usually come from some corporate "incubator" division. It doesn't come out of product development. And it doesn't often come from blue–sky R&D. More and more, innovation comes not from the triumph of big science (important as it is in removing *physical* constraints to innovation), but from the triumph of contrarianism (which leaps over the *mental* constraints). It is the idiot savant, who asks a fresh question and then

answers it using parts that already exist, who is so often the author of the new. That's because industry revolution is *conceptual* innovation. It comes from the mind and soul of a malcontent, a dreamer, a smart–ass, and not from some bespectacled boffin or besuited planner.

FORGET THE FUTURE

From Nostradamus to Alvin Toffler, individuals and organizations have long been obsessed with trying to see the future. The goal is to somehow get advance warning of "what will be." Yet in my experience, industry revolutionaries spend little time gazing deeply into the future. While there are some aspects of the future that are highly probable—the cost of bandwidth will go down, our ability to manipulate genes will go up—most of what will constitute the future simply can't be known.

In 1984 the *Economist* magazine conducted a little study.[1] They asked 16 individuals to make predictions about 1994. Four Oxford economics students, 4 finance ministers, 4 corporate CEOs, and 4 London dustmen ("garbage collectors" to Americans) were asked to predict the pound/dollar exchange rate 10 years hence, the rate of inflation among OECD countries, the price of oil, and other macroeconomic unknowables. Not surprisingly, when 1994 rolled around, the forecasts turned out to be wrong. For example, the consensus forecast for OECD inflation was 8 percent. In actuality, it was barely 4 percent. Think about the difference that makes if you are trying to pick a discount rate to apply to a long–term capital investment. Interestingly, it was the finance ministers who made the least accurate forecasts. The best were made by the CEOs—who tied for first place with the dustmen. Yet even they produced forecasts so wrong as to be worthless.

Recently I heard the chairman of one of America's leading high-tech companies poke fun at a *Popular Science* article of some decades back that had predicted that the world's first computer, then just invented, would one day weigh 1 ton instead of 20. The corporate boss then made his own prediction: Within the next 20 years it would be possible to store the visual and aural data of an entire lifetime—the entire multimedia experience of a person's life—on a device no bigger than the proverbial credit card. I couldn't help but wonder whether someone writing 20 years from now would find this prediction equally amusing. When it comes to predicting the future, humility is a virtue.

Forecasting attempts to predict what *will* happen. This is largely futile. As Samuel Goldwyn once said, "Only a fool would make predictions—especially about the future." Recognizing this, companies have sought ways of coping with the future's inherent unpredictability. One response is to rehearse a range of futures via scenarios. Scenario planning speculates on what *might* happen. The goal is to develop a number of alternate scenarios as a way of sensitizing oneself to the possibility that the future may be quite unlike the present. By focusing in on a few big uncertainties—what might happen to the price of oil, how the Green movement might develop, what could happen to global security—scenario planning lets a company rehearse a range of possible futures.

THE GOAL IS NOT TO SPECULATE ON WHAT MIGHT HAPPEN, BUT TO IMAGINE WHAT YOU CAN ACTUALLY MAKE HAPPEN.

Scenario planning has many strengths, but it is not, by nature, proactive. Its implicit focus is on how the future may undermine the *existing* business model. In that sense it tends to be defensive—what might that big, bad future do to us—rather than offensive—how can we write our will on the future. There is little in scenario planning that suggests a firm can proactively shape its environment, that it can take advantage of changing circumstances *right now*. At least in practice, it is more often threat-focused than opportunity-focused. It is more about stewardship than entrepreneurship. Companies must do more than rehearse potential futures. After all, the goal is not to speculate on what *might* happen, but to imagine what you can *make* happen.

Another response to the future's inherent unpredictability is to become more "agile." Strategic flexibility is certainly a virtue in uncertain times. The ability to quickly reconfigure products, channels, and skills is essential to maintaining one's relevance in a world that is shaken, not stirred. But agility is no substitute for a vision of a radically new business model.

Agility is great, but if a company is no more than agile, it will be a perpetual follower—and in the age of revolution even fast followers find few spoils.

Companies fail to create the future not because they fail to predict it but because they fail to *imagine* it. It is curiosity and creativity they lack, not perspicuity. So it is vitally important that you understand the distinction

COMPANIES FAIL TO CREATE THE FUTURE NOT BECAUSE THEY FAIL TO PREDICT IT BUT BECAUSE THEY FAIL TO IMAGINE IT.

between "the future" and "the unimagined," between *knowing* what's next and *imagining* what's next.

To even talk about "the" future is a misnomer. There is no one future waiting to happen. While certain aspects of the future are highly probable (the earth will still be spinning tomorrow), there is little about the future that is inevitable. IKEA didn't have to be. eBay didn't have to be. Sephora didn't have to be. The future is the creation of millions of independent economic actors. Was cubism inevitable in art? Was deconstructionism inevitable in literature? Perhaps yes, in some cosmic sense. But their appearance at a particular point in history was far from a foregone conclusion.

SEE DIFFERENT, BE DIFFERENT

You can't be a revolutionary without a revolutionary point of view. And you can't buy your point of view from some boring consulting company. Nor can you borrow it from some rent-a-guru. You have to become your own seer, your own guru, and your own futurist.

Seeing over the horizon, finding the unconventional, imagining the unimagined—innovation comes from a new way of seeing and a new way of being. Learn to see different, learn to be different, and you will discover the different. Not only that, you will *believe* it, deeply. And maybe, just maybe, you will *build* it. How to see. How to be. Two more critical steps in your training as an industry revolutionary.

Listen to Bill Gross, founder of idealab!, a factory for new Internet businesses that spawned CarsDirect.com, NetZero, and GoTo.com among others.

It's almost better to look for where there's no market segment. Then companies that have that inertia, that have a cannibalization problem, stay off you for a while and give you a chance to get big enough to build a brand and get a network effect going. Then they'll have a hard time catching up.

Gross is not interested in bumping some other sumo wrestler out of the ring. He's interested in inventing games entirely outside the ring. This is the essence of industry revolution. Without a widespread capacity to imagine and design radical new business concepts, a company will be unable to escape decaying strategies. You know that tired old saw, "You have to be willing to cannibalize your own business"? Well, how likely is it that a company will cannibalize an existing business unless it has some incredibly compelling alternatives in view? I don't think the problem is that companies are unwilling to cannibalize themselves. I think the problem is that they don't have enough good *reasons* to cannibalize themselves. When was the last time you hung on to a good option when you had a much better option in view? It's simple. You have to have some fairly attractive birds in the bush to loosen your grip on the bird in the fist.

A FRESH WAY OF SEEING IS OFTEN MORE VALUABLE THAN SHEER BRAINPOWER.

But it's not always easy to spot the birds in the bush. That's why you must learn to see different and be different.

Alan Kay, who fathered the personal computer while at Xerox's Palo Alto Research Center and is now an "imagineer" at Disney, is a font of zippy aphorisms. One of my favorites: "Perspective is worth 80 IQ points." Alan knows that a fresh way of seeing is often more valuable than sheer brainpower. Impressionism. Cubism. Surrealism. Postmodernism. Each revolution in art was based on a reconception of reality. It wasn't the canvas, the pigments, or the brushes that changed, but how the artist perceived the world. In the same sense, it's not the tools that distinguish industry revolutionaries from humdrum incumbents—not the information technology they harness, not the processes they use, not their facilities. Instead, it is their ability to escape the stranglehold of the familiar.

The essence of strategy is variety. But there is no variety in strategy without variety in how individuals view the world. Do you see differently? Do you have a point of view that is at odds with industry norms? The point is simple: you're going to have to learn how to unlock your own imagination before you can unlock your company's imagination. You must become the merchant of new perspective within your organization.

So what are ways we can school ourselves in the art of seeing past the familiar to the truly novel? The rest of this chapter describes a variety of disciplines that will help you imagine what *could* be. They fall into two broad categories: be a novelty addict, and be a heretic.

BE A NOVELTY ADDICT

A whole lot of what's changing simply can't be seen from where you're sitting. You have an obstructed view. You have to get off your butt and search for new experiences, go to new places, learn new things, reach out to new people. In the age of revolution, the most dangerous words are "need to know." How the hell do you know what you need to know? You MUST find a way of continually surprising yourself. What you don't know but *could* know is much more important than what you don't know and *can't* know. You MUST become a novelty addict.

FIND THE DISCONTINUITIES

Would-be revolutionaries, intent on discovering uncontested competitive space, think about the future very differently than prognosticators and scenario planners. They know you can't see the future. Their goal is less to understand the future than to understand the revolutionary portent in what is *already* changing. More specifically, they are looking for things where the *rate of change* is changing—for inflection points that foreshadow significant discontinuities. Those who fail to notice these nascent discontinuities will be rudely awakened by those who were paying attention.

They are also looking for things that are changing at *different rates*. Sooner or later, the thing that is changing more quickly will impact the thing that is changing more slowly—in other words, rates of change between different phenomena ultimately converge. For years the cosmetics industry assumed that women were interested only in glamour, that their sense of self-worth was directly proportional to the sparkle in a man's eye. As Charlie Revson, the founder of Revlon, once put it, "We sell hope in a bottle." As women gained their economic independence, the image of women as "eye candy" lagged further and further behind the reality of their changing self-perception. This lag was exploited by The Body Shop with its message that glamour is fine, but sometimes you just want to pamper yourself a bit and take good care of your skin. *Change differentials* often point to revolutionary opportunities.

Here's a visual illustration. Imagine that you attach one end of a piece of elastic to a hardback book. You begin pulling the other end. Slowly the elastic stretches. The book doesn't move. But when you reach the limit of the elastic, the book starts moving with a jerk. The "slack" disappears when some revolutionary says, "Wait a minute. Why is this thing just sitting there when everything around it is moving?" For years the car selling paradigm in the United States has been stuck in neutral. While "category killers" consolidated distribution in other industries, car retailing remained a patchwork of mostly local dealerships. While you could get 24/7 technology support for your home computer, you could get your car serviced only between the hours of 8 A.M. and 5 P.M., and only Monday through Friday. While you could comparison shop a dozen different TV brands at Circuit City, no equivalent auto superstore carried the full range of leading brands. But recently a slew of outsiders, mostly Internet start-ups, has been working overtime to "snap" car retailing into the twenty-first century.

Think of how little auto styling has changed over the last decade. Can you tell a Taurus from a Camry from an Accord at 100 meters? Parking lots are seas of conformity. Now visit a dance club in Tokyo filled with Dankai Jr. kids—the rebellious offspring of Japan's baby boomers. You'll find multihued hair, clothes that are aggressively ugly, and fashion colors that are so loud they practically scream at you. In short, you won't find anything that reminds you of Japan's blue-suited, look-alike salarymen. So why hasn't this new style been reflected in auto design? That's exactly the question Yoshiki Honma, a boyish 33-year-old designer at Honda, asked himself. His answer? The Fuya-Jo, a slab-sided vehicle that is one part car and one part dance club. The car has seats that look like high-backed barstools, mammoth speakers in the doors, a gearshift that looks like a microphone, an instrument panel meant to resemble a deejay's mixing table, and storage space designed for skateboards and snowboards.[2] For now the Fuya-Jo is just a concept car, but it reflects a recognition at Honda that youth culture has changed a lot faster than automotive design over the past decade. This change differential creates an opportunity for a company with the courage to abandon conformist styling norms.

It's not enough to know what's changing. You also have to be aware of things that are changing at different rates, for it is the juxtaposition of the two that points to opportunities for industry revolution. Discontinuities and change differentials—that is where you look for inspiration.

Try to find the pattern in these three revolutions in sports equipment:

- A couple of decades back, Prince pioneered oversized tennis rackets, and it is still the number-one brand in the industry. The frying-pan size rackets have a giant sweet spot that helps to propel off-center shots across the net.

- Calloway invented the "Big Bertha" line of golf clubs, and Eli Calloway has become the patron saint of hackers everywhere. With an enlarged hitting area and perimeter weighting, the clubs dramatically increased the odds that high–handicap golfers could get the ball airborne and flying straight.

- Elan was the first to introduce super–sidecut, or "parabolic," skis, an innovation that has given the ski equipment industry a much–needed boost. With a broad tip and tail and a narrow waist, the new skis help even the most nonathletic skiers lay down curvaceous tracks.

What discontinuities were these three innovations exploiting? Beyond materials technology, they were exploiting the fact that baby boomers are the first generation in history that refuse to grow old. They may not have the eye–hand coordination they used to have, but they still love the sound

Individuals who get startled by the

of a tennis ball hitting the sweet spot. They don't have quite the rotation they used to, but they still want to hit the living daylights out of a golf ball. Their knees are a bit dodgy, but they still want to make turns like Hermann Maier. Come to think of it, Viagra's been exploiting the same discontinuity: seniors who refuse to grow old gracefully and want great sex right up to the end.

Here are some essential questions for every wannabe revolutionary:

- Where and in what ways is change creating the potential for new rules and new space?
- What is the potential for revolution inherent in the things that are changing *right now*, or have *already* changed?
- What are the discontinuities we could exploit?
- What aspect of what's changing can we come to understand better than anyone else in our industry?
- What's the deep dynamic that will make our new business concept oh–so–relevant right now?

If you don't have an answer to these questions, there is virtually no chance you or your company is going to be an industry revolutionary.

In 1984 John Naisbitt wrote in his book *Megatrends* that information would become a critical source of competitive advantage and that the "information float" would disappear as a way to make money. He argued that customers would demand a combination of "high tech" and "high touch." Instead of forcing technology on consumers, companies would learn how to use technology to improve service. He described a world in which hierarchies would give way to networks, and companies would become more virtual. He also hypothesized a shift from reliance on institutional help to more self-reliance in everything from health care to pensions. He foresaw a world in which consumers would use their wallets to enforce their values. Data mining, call centers, 24/7 customer support, outsourcing, supply chain integration, "green" energy, companies against animal testing—all these things are logical outgrowths of the forces Naisbitt described in 1984. How effective was your company in harnessing these discontinuities to create new business models and new sources of competitive advantage? If your company got caught behind the curve, it wasn't because these trends were invisible; it's because they were ignored.

If you're paying attention to discontinuities, there's little that will surprise you. It's pretty simple. Individuals who get startled by the future

future weren't paying attention.

weren't paying attention. One person's inevitability is another person's rude awakening. The question is, ARE YOU PAYING ATTENTION?

A novelty addict is always on the hunt for what's changing. Every discontinuity prompts a "where does this lead" question. Let's practice. We'll start with a particularly noisome discontinuity. A recent study suggested that the average middle manager gets 190 messages a day: 52 phone messages, 30 e-mail messages, 22 voice mails, 18 letters, 15 faxes, and so on. I don't have to tell you, this is a discontinuity. In the old days, when someone sent you a letter, they didn't expect to receive a response for at least a week. When they sent a fax, they expected a next-day response. Now, when they send an e-mail, they expect a reply within an hour or so. But it gets worse. With instant messaging, people *know* when you're online, and when they send you a message, they expect you to interrupt what you're doing and answer them *immediately*. It used to be that secretaries kept the world at bay—until downsizing turned middle managers into receptionists and filing clerks. It may be that we've taken accessibility to the point where meaningful work will simply grind to a halt. How ironic that in a world populated by "knowledge workers," there is virtually no time left to think. You may be able to manage the present in tiny splinters of time, but you certainly can't invent radical new business models if your attention has been smashed into minute-sized shards. This is a discontinuity. Can you see an opportunity in this? Let's take it a step further.

In a recent cartoon, a dad and his young daughter are walking along a beach. The dad is dressed in suit and tie and has a briefcase in one hand. His daughter is wearing her bathing suit. As she vainly tugs at her father's sleeve, he says, "Not now, dear, Daddy's working." Where *don't* you work these days? We are tethered to our jobs to an extent that is almost feudal. But there are opportunities lurking inside the insidious discontinuity of 24/7 accessibility. What about an electronic gatekeeper that could scan phone calls, e-mails, voice mails, and even faxes? Caller ID? Hah! I want automatic message screening. Every couple of hours a little menu would pop up on my computer screen telling me who was queuing for my at-tention. I could tell my digital gatekeeper who I was willing to communicate with in a given day or week and how important it was that I make contact with any given individual. I could also tell it when I was willing to be interrupted and when I was not. (Imagine never, ever having a telemarketer interrupt dinner again!) I could assign a different level of "interruptability" to different times of the day or week. People and issues that exceeded some urgency threshold would get to break through into my consciousness. People below the threshold wouldn't get through. I could also give a few people (family) an "attention override" privilege that would let them intrude anytime. Trust me, some revolutionary is going to help us regain control of our fragmented lives. There's a billion-dollar opportunity inside this discontinuity. You get the point? Keep asking yourself, What's changing? What's the opportunity this presents? Do this at least a dozen times a week. Get addicted to change.

> Most people in an industry are blind in the same way— they're all paying attention to the same things, and *not* paying attention to the same things.

Imagine the possibilities when an entire organization is alert to discon-tinuities. Recently, General Motors launched a number of initiatives aimed at getting everyone plugged into the future. In one, a diverse cross-section of individuals identified 19 broad change categories (e.g., global urban culture, entertainment in everything) that encompassed more than 100 discontinuities. Every discontinuity was illustrated by a visual image in order to help individuals connect with what's changing. The goal was to use this inventory as the backdrop for every serious strategy discussion.

After years of playing catch-up, GM is learning that you have to pay close attention to the discontinuities if you're going to get anywhere close to the bleeding edge of change.

Search Out Underappreciated Trends

There is no proprietary data about the future. Whatever *you* can know about what's changing in the world, so can everyone else. So you've got to look where others are not looking. The good news is that most people in  an industry are blind in the same way—they're all paying attention to the same things, and *not* paying attention to the same things. For example, if you work at Shell or Schlumberger, you know a lot about the three-dimensional representation of complex information. Complicated computer models portray seismographic data in a rich graphical format. This is how petroleum engineers "see" underground. Likewise, the folks at Pixar, the computer animation company, are experts at visualization. Now talk to a senior partner in a big accounting company. How much does this person know about complex graphical modeling? Not enough. If you want to understand the financial performance of a large global company, you have to comb through columns of black and white data, searching for variances and calculating financial ratios. Ugh! Why isn't this information presented in three dimensions, dynamically? Why can't you "fly" over the globe, and "drop into" your German subsidiary? See that red mountain over there? That's inventory, and it's growing. See that lake over there? That's one of those famous "profit pools," and it's shrinking by the hour. See all those people massed at the border? Those are your employees leaving for better opportunities. You get the idea. But you can't get the picture—yet. Odds are it won't be an accounting company that reinvents the display of accounting data—unless the senior partners start hanging around Silicon Graphics or Pixar. But there's little doubt that Excel will one day look as antiquated as green ledger paper.

Next time you go to an industry conference or pick up a trade magazine, ask yourself, What is *no one* talking about? Search for what's not there. There's a reason that outsiders typically reinvent industries. The outsiders

WHAT'S
THE BIG
STORY
THAT
CUTS
ACROSS
ALL
THESE
LITTLE
FACTS?

come from a different context—one that allows them to see new possibilities. William Gibson puts it beautifully: "The future has already happened, it's just unequally distributed." The future may not have happened yet in your industry, or your company, or your country, but it has happened somewhere. Revolutionaries are experts at *knowledge arbitrage*—moving insights between the hip and the un-hip, the knowing and the unknowing, the leading edge and the trailing edge. So get a bigger keyhole!

Find the Big Story

Next, search for transcendent themes. One of the reasons many people fail to fully appreciate what's changing is because they're down at ground level, lost in a thicket of confusing, conflicting data. You have to make time to step back and ask yourself, What's the big story that cuts across all these little facts? For example, consider five seemingly unrelated trends:

- In most developed countries, people are getting married later in life. No longer do people expect to find a mate while still at school.

- More people are telecommuting or working from home. Home-based businesses are one of the fastest-growing parts of the economy.

- The number of single-parent families has been steadily increasing. Single parents are run ragged trying to balance work and family— personal time is a rare luxury.

- New social standards governing the behavior of people at work make it ever more difficult to form romantic relationships with co-workers.

- E-mail and the Internet absorb more and more of people's time. All the hours in front of the PC are hours of aloneness—unless virtual communities fill *all* your social needs.

Can you see an overarching theme here? It's individual isolation. We're living in a world where it is more and more difficult for people to find time to connect. No wonder online dating sites like Matchmaker.com and eCRUSH are booming. But did *you* see it coming?

Recognizing patterns in complex data is a bit of an art. Some of it is just raw, conceptual ability. But if you've ever won a game of Scrabble or solved a challenging puzzle, you'll do fine. Keep a list of things that strike you as new or different. Every once in a while, scan that list and search for broad themes. If you can get above the trees, you'll have a view that few others can match.

Follow the Chain of Consequences

The world is a system. Something changes here, and it will affect something over there. Yet most people stop with first-order effects—they don't have the discipline to think through the knock–on effects. Jim Taylor, co-author of *The 500-Year Delta*, Iomega's executive vice president, and dedicated trend–watcher, predicted a 10,000 Dow Jones Industrial Average in 1992. Here's how he did it:

> *I saw a number that estimated how much people were going to save as they got older. About 15 million people a year would become 50 years old, and they would throw a lot of liquidity into the market. So I made a prediction that the Dow would pass through 10,000. When you see a trend, it's a matter of asking, "What would this mean?"*

Paul Saffo, director and Roy Amara Fellow at the Institute for the Future, makes the point this way:

> *I think about it as "orders of impact." First order, second order, etc. When an earthquake happens you have a whole series of waves that follow. The first order of the auto was the horseless carriage. The second order was the traffic jam. The third-order impact was the move toward the suburbs. This led in turn to the creation of huge metropolitan areas.*

No executive or manager should be surprised by the recent spate of books on corporate values and "loyalty." This concern around how to build organizational cohesion is the second–order effect of a first–order change: the steadily declining ratio of supervisors to operators or managers to staff in corporations. To cope, companies need a solid value system because more and more they must rely on people's judgment. Whenever you see something changing, begin to work through the chain of consequences. Get in the practice of asking a series of "and then what" questions. As you learn to do this, the future will become less and less of a surprise to you.

Dig Deeper

Sometimes creating proprietary foresight is just a matter of slogging through more data. You can't create economic value out of a superficial understanding of what's changing. For example, a short news item noting that some teenagers are spending more time online than in front of the TV is of almost no value. The real question is, Which kids are going online? Where are they going online? What, exactly, is it about the online experience that is more compelling to them than television? How much time do they spend online in a given day or week? What do they find cool or geeky online? And so on.

Faith Popcorn's BrainReserve interviews 4,500 consumers across 16 product categories every year. They also have a TalentBank of 6,000 experts globally who are subject area experts. No wonder Popcorn sometimes sees

You must be as perfectly attuned to the timeless as to the ever–changing.

the tectonic plates moving before others do—she's digging deeper. You probably can't spread your interests this broadly, but you can pick a few things to understand far more deeply than you do. Genetics, Generation Y, deregulation, ubiquitous computing, the market for online software services, the global revolution in how pensions are funded—every year pick a couple of the big things that are changing and resolve to dig deep.

Know What's *Not* Changing

The deep needs of human beings change almost not at all. Go back to Aristotle and the wants of man—little has changed. What changes is how we address our wants. Change gives us better tools. Opportunities come when we can imagine how to use our new tools to address our deepest desires. As Jim Taylor puts it, "The nature of human beings is the eye in the middle of the hurricane." We want to be loved, we want to be known, we want to communicate, we want to celebrate, we want to explore, we want to laugh, we want to know, we want to see new vistas, we want to leave some footprints in the sands of history. Any discontinuity that allows you to slake one of these thirsts more fully is an opportunity in the making.

If you think about human beings for a minute, you shouldn't be surprised that the Web was a chat room before it was a department store, or that Internet porn generates substantially more than 70 percent of all the revenue earned by online content providers (dwarfing games, sports, and music).[3] To be an industry revolutionary, you must be as perfectly attuned to the timeless as to the ever-changing. You must also let yourself be informed by the recurring themes of history. History has much to teach you about how discontinuities will play themselves out. For example, advances in genetics are slowly turning humans into creators. History suggests that the battle between the spiritual and the scientific over the proper use of genetic knowledge may be as heated as Galileo's clash with the Catholic church over humankind's place in the cosmos and Darwin's run-in with creationists.

The speed of the Internet's takeoff surprised most people, but that it happened should have been no surprise—because the interstate highway system provided an almost perfect historical analogy. The automobile had existed for around 50 years before the interstate highway system began to connect communities across America. Within a decade of the interstate's introduction suburbs were springing up, city centers were withering, corporations were building office towers in what had been cornfields, and commuters were commuting. It wasn't the car per se, but the ability to connect communities that changed the distribution of work and commerce. Likewise, computers had existed for about 50 years before the Internet took off. Before the Net, computers had been islands of computational power. Once connected, they began to transform society in ways even more dramatic than the interstate highway but also in ways that are entirely consistent with timeless aspects of human nature.

SEE IT, FEEL IT

You don't fall in love with a photograph or a resume, you fall in love with the experience of *being* with someone. In a similar way, you can't understand a discontinuity merely by reading about it, you can understand it only by living it. To be fully grounded in what is changing, you must move from the analytical to the experiential. Let me share a couple of examples. A few years back I was working with a large Nordic firm, perched on the edge of the Arctic Circle. This company was filled with brilliant engineers who designed technologically brilliant products that were boring to look at and sometimes difficult to use. I broke the bad

People don't embrace an opportunity because they see it, they embrace it because they feel it.

news—if they wanted their products to be highly desirable and highly relevant, they were going to have to learn something about global lifestyles. Off the engineers trooped—to Venice Beach in California, to Greenwich Village in New York, and down The Kings Road in London. They saw trendy style–setters wearing the latest fashion accessories. They came across people who had pierced every possible protuberance. They saw how designers in other fields were using colors and shapes in new ways. And they didn't see any of their competitors. How do you explain lifestyles with an overhead projector? Face to face with the edge, the engineers "got it." They went back and designed products in crazy hues with edgy designs and easy–to–use customer features.

People don't embrace an opportunity because they see it, they embrace it because they *feel* it. And to feel it, they have to experience it. If you want to teach someone in your organization about a discontinuity or give them a glimpse of a bold, new opportunity, you're going to have to design an experience.

To create a demo, or a prototype, or even tell a compelling story, you have to do some mental prototyping. You need more than a fragment of an idea. You have to build a story around it: why this is important, what difference it will make, who will care, how people will use this, what it will look like, taste like, and more. Radical alternatives are hard for people to imagine. You have to build a bridge between the world you're living in and the world everyone else is living in.

It's not always easy to make something new and ethereal, real and tangible. But think of this: Ask just about any kid to draw a picture of heaven, and you'll get back an imaginative illustration. If an eight–year–old can draw a picture of Paradise, *you* have no excuse.

GET A ROUTINE

Swim in the new. Sounds easy, but the ocean is a big place. How do you avoid drowning in data? You need some kind of routine. I can't tell you what your routine should be, but I can say what works for some folks.

John Naisbitt's routine for finding the edge is simple: he reads newspapers from around the world for several hours each day, hunting for patterns in things that get reported but don't yet generate a lot of ink. Marc Andreessen, the inventor of the Internet browser, has a different routine:

Pay attention to things that are taking off, even if they're only taking off at a small scale. One of the things that surprised me about the Internet is the number of things that I was aware of when they were small-scale things, not commercial, that are now picking up users and attention. Even if I was skeptical at the time, in most cases these are now billion-dollar companies. So you want to pay attention to small-scale successes because they're probably going to become large-scale successes.

 What are your routines? How often do you pick up a magazine you've never read before? How often do you go to an industry convention for an industry you know little about? How often do you hang out with people who are very different from you? Are you on the edge or in the hinterlands? Do you have any friends in venture capital who can tell you what's happening out on the fringe? Do you know what kind of start–ups are calling on the VP for business development in your company? Have you been tracking all the IPOs across your broad competitive domain? If not, get plugged in. Find the small things, play an imaginary game of "scale up," and then ask, If this thing became really big, what kind of a difference would it make? Who would be affected?

Each of us tends to discount what is new and small. As a discipline, start exaggerating what is new and small. You're not investing in these things, for goodness sake, you're simply opening your mind to new possibilities.

Faith Popcorn's BrainReserve is a lightning rod for cultural discontinuities. Says Popcorn:

> *We do something called "Brailleing the Culture"—monitoring the top 10 of everything.*
>
> *Anytime we see something that is weird, we key in on it. We look for things that are not part of the puzzle. How come* Touched by an Angel *was big on TV? How come the Dalai Lama is on posters? Don't dismiss the weird.*
>
> *We ask people, "What's sitting on your night table?" We're looking for culture hogs. They have to see everything, go everywhere. They're always on to the next thing.*
>
> *We look for cultural lingo. We review the soundtracks of sitcoms. We review the top 10 CDs, and what the artists are saying.*
>
> *I love to watch what new 12-step programs are emerging—recent ones are for people addicted to chat rooms or online pornography.*

Start exaggerating what is new and small.

Popcorn isn't looking for fads, for cultural ephemera, but for the tip of deep icebergs, for leaves carried along by powerful currents that are otherwise

THE REAL ISSUE IS NOT THE PRESENT VERSUS THE FUTURE BUT THE ORTHODOX VERSUS THE HETERODOX

almost imperceptible. The weird are the harbingers. If you dismiss the stuff that strikes you as weird, you have virtually no chance of finding the new. It's as important to be weird as wired. What's the hippest club in your city? Have you ever been there? What's the trippiest video game out there? Have you played it? Go ahead, do a little cool hunting.

Jim Taylor of Iomega takes yet another tack:

> *I watch the evolution of art, especially folk art. It's a wonderful precursor of what's changing in society. Look at the cubists in the 1930s. First it was art, then the structure of building, and finally the structure of most organizations. Right now we're seeing the "outsider" movement in art—it's creating a sense that everyone is an artist.*
>
> *I also pay attention to a set of deep underlying questions: What's the big idea in society and how will it play itself out? What's the latest technology that's about to be generalizable [about to go mass market]? What's the latest organ they can grow in a test tube?*

Artists have few constraints. Like magnifying glasses, they collect and concentrate the diffused light of cultural change. Taylor knows this. He also knows that if you develop a set of questions to ask yourself as you encounter the unfamiliar, you will increase the odds of actually taking away some meaningful insights.

John Seely Brown, for years the head of Xerox's famed Palo Alto Research Center, favors travel as a routine for discovering the new. Recently, he took a 7,500–mile motorcycle trip across America, entirely on back roads. Hundreds of conversations with people across America put Seely Brown in touch with what's changing away from the coasts. Says Seely Brown: "Everywhere one goes there's a chance to learn something. You keep asking, 'What's causing this?'…for example, a teenager doing something weird on the street. It's really active listening."

Insights come out of new conversations. All too often, strategy conversations in large companies have the same 10 people talking to the same 10 people for the fifth year in a row. They can finish each other's sentences. You're not going to learn anything new in this setting. Travel is still the fastest way to start a bunch of new conversations. It has the added benefit of turning the background into the foreground. When you travel to an exotic destination you're suddenly reminded of how much you take for granted and how there are alternatives to the familiar habits of your life. It was his experience with the casual warmth of Italian coffee bars that gave Howard Schultz the idea for Starbucks. Familiarity is the enemy. It slowly turns everything into wallpaper. Travel makes you a stranger. It puts you at odds. It robs you of your prejudices. If you can't travel, find a good bookstore and pick up the *Globe & Mail* (Toronto), *The Daily Telegraph* (London), *The South China Morning Post* (Hong Kong), *The New Straits Times* (Singapore), or some other foreign newspaper, or find them online. If your understanding of what's changing in the world comes from network television news, the *Wall Street Journal*, and *Time* magazine, you're going to miss the future.

BE A HERETIC

It is not enough to be a novelty addict. You must be a heretic as well. Heretics, not prophets, create revolutions. You can immerse yourself in what's changing, but you'll only see the opportunities to leverage change in novel ways if you can escape the shackles of tradition. There is much that individuals cannot imagine simply because 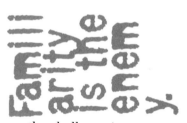 they are prisoners of their own dogma. In this sense, the challenge is not "long-term" thinking but "unconventional" thinking. The real issue is not the present versus the future but the orthodox versus the heterodox.

There is an enormous danger in viewing what's changing through the lens of what already is. People saw plastic, when it was first invented, as a substitute for existing materials—steel, wood, and leather. (Remember Corfam shoes?) Eventually, plastic got the chance to be plastic. Can you imagine a hula hoop, compact disc, or videotape made out of anything else? In the age of revolution the future is not just more of the past—it is profoundly different than the past. Whether or not *you* succeed in escaping the past is, in a way, quite irrelevant. The future's going to get invented, with you or without you. But if you want to build the new, you must first dismantle your existing belief system and burn for scrap anything that is not endlessly and universally true.

Ask yourself this question: What are the industry dogmas my company has knowingly chosen to violate? Can't think of any? Then don't expect to outperform industry averages. Industry revolutionaries create strategies that are subversive, not submissive. To do this, you must "deconstruct" the belief system that prevents individuals in your organization from imagining unorthodox strategies.

In most companies it is virtually impossible to redesign business models without first challenging the dominant mental models. Mental models spring out of and reinforce the current business model.

A business model is a "thing." The mental model is a set of beliefs about the "thing." The mental model reflects the "central tendency" of beliefs around the key business concept design variables:

- What is our business mission?
- What is our product/market scope?
- What is the basis for differentiation?
- What core competencies are important?
- What strategic assets do we need to own?
- What core processes are critical?
- How can we best configure our resources?
- How do we go to market?
- What kind of information do we need to serve customers?
- What is the kind of relationship we want with customers?
- How do we price our products and services?
- What is the particular benefit bundle we deliver?
- How do we integrate with suppliers and partners?
- What profit boosters can we exploit?

The more successful a company has been, the more deeply etched are its mental models. In even moderately successful companies, most people take 90 percent of the existing mental model as a given. Design choices made years earlier are seldom revisited. It's difficult to imagine revolutionary strategies when you start with nine-tenths of your brain tied behind your back. Design choices of long ago are seldom challenged in the absence of a crisis. Even then, it often takes a new management team to pull out the old beliefs by their roots. You and your colleagues must learn how to systematically deconstruct the existing set of beliefs around "what business we're in," "how we make money," "who our customers are," and so on.

The first step in your training as a heretic is to admit that you are living inside a mental model—a construct that may not even be of your own making. Alan Kay tells a wonderful little story about how he came to recognize this deep truth:

On the third day of a conference at a Buddhist center I asked people why they put their palms together several times a day. The Buddhists believe that the world is an illusion, but we have to go along with the illusion for efficiency reasons. When they put their hands together it is a semicolon, an acknowledgement that whatever they may think is going on right now is largely a fabrication of their own mind.

For much of life we simply go along with the illusion—yeah, this is the only way to sell a car, get a date, or sell perfume. But every once in a while you need to put your palms together, pause, step outside yourself, and examine what you believe and why. And in the age of revolution you have to do this more consistently and consciously than ever before.

Look for disconfirming evidence, for things that don't fit, for things that are ajar.

You have to know that things are not as they seem—and you must know this at such a deep level that you can challenge the very foundations of what others regard as axiomatic. We are all caught inside theories, inside constructs. Most of us spend our lives elaborating someone else's theory—about how to run an airline or publish a magazine or sell insurance. New facts are either absorbed into the construct or rejected. Seldom do the constructs themselves get altered. The challenge is to break the construct— or at least bend it a bit. To do so, you must first acknowledge that you are inside the construct. Jim Taylor puts it like this: "The more you pay attention to information that supports your worldview, the less you learn. There tends to be a convergence in what any group of people believe is important, despite what might really be important out there."

The problem with the future is not that it is unknowable. The problem with the future is that it is different. If you are unable to think differently, the future will always arrive as a surprise. You know that old bumper sticker, "Question Authority"? Well the authority you most need to question is the authority of your *own* long-held beliefs. This isn't about pricking someone else's conventions. We are all reassured when the world conforms to our prejudices. But confirmation of what you already believe is a complete waste of time. You must look for *disconfirming* evidence, for things that don't fit, for things that are ajar. This is hard, because it forces you to write off your depreciating intellectual capital—you must admit not only that you do "not know" many things but that you "wrongly know" many things.

SURFACE THE DOGMAS

So how do you cultivate contrarian tendencies and surface the dogmas in your company? One simple device is to ask yourself and your colleagues, What are 10 things you would never hear a customer say about our company or our industry? For example, no customer is ever going to say, "The airline treats its customers with dignity and respect." Few customers would ever say, "It's easy to shop for a better rate on electricity." Fewer still would say, "Banking is fun," or "Hotels always have great food." Once you've identified what customers wouldn't say, ask yourself why they wouldn't say those  things. What orthodoxies do they reveal? What opportunities do these orthodoxies create for some unorthodox newcomer? And finally, what would happen if we turned this orthodoxy on its head?

Another way in is to ask, What are the 10 things that all the major competitors in this industry believe in common? Then ask, What would happen if each of these assumptions were inverted? What new opportunities would present themselves? How would customers benefit? Clearly, not all industry beliefs are stupid. There's a difference between dogma (the earth is flat) and physics (things fall downward rather than upward). It is seldom a good idea to defy physics. Nevertheless, much of what people in an industry will tell you is God–given is merely human–made. It is your job to turn certainties back into choices.

> **What are 10 things you would never hear a customer say about our company or our industry?**

Time again for a little practice. Think for a moment about the orthodoxies in the American health–care industry. The sick are considered patients, not consumers. Health–care providers dispatch cases, they don't build relationships. The goal is to cure illnesses rather than promote wellness (you don't get reimbursed for wellness). Insurers are in the business of dodging risks rather than improving the health of a population. The entire industry has been organized from the payor backward rather than from the consumer forward. This has led to the greatest orthodoxy of all: Americans spend too much on health care. Says who? As compared to what? Do doctors perform unnecessary procedures? Yes. Do hospitals perform needless tests? Sure. Is there room for huge economies? Yup. So cut the waste. But before going any further down the health–care rationing road, someone needs to challenge the assumption that American citizens believe they are devoting too much of their resources to health care.

How can anyone say what percentage of their income aging baby boomers might be willing to pay for health care? The question's never been put to them. Today it is employers who decide how much is too much when it comes to health care. It is employers—who are purchasing agents, not consumers—that contract with health–care providers and insurance companies. Imagine if we let purchasing agents choose our toilet paper, or our cars, or the kind of food we eat. We'd all be using single–ply toilet tissue, driving puke–green Chevy Luminas, and eating the kind of food you buy in bulk at warehouse clubs. We wouldn't put up with that. Why do we put with employers telling us how much health care we can have? Managed care, which is more accurately described as managed reimbursement, isn't a revolution—it's just the health–care version of vigorous cost–cutting. There's nothing nonlinear about it. Whether we ever get a real revolution in health care will depend on whether anyone ever succeeds in taking a wrecking ball to the edifice of industry orthodoxy.

Never Stop Asking Why

Like children, heretics play an endless game of "why" and "what if." If you've been paying attention to what's changing, you can play a very intelligent game of "what if." For example, What if everything in the world were able to communicate with everything else? What would a vending machine want to talk about? "Hey, it's hot, and at this rate I'm going to be out of orange sodas in a couple of hours." What would a fuel pump say? "Oh, hi there, Jaguar XK8. I know you need premium fuel. That's what I'll pump." What would a refrigerator say? "My sensors tell me there's something rotten down in the crisper drawer."

Wayne Huizenga asked "why." Before AutoNation, no major car dealer had ever gone public. Says Huizenga:

> Every one of the dealers told me that Ford and General Motors and all the manufacturers would never let a publicly held company own a new-car dealership. And I'd always ask, "Why?" I never got a good answer. So we put some gentle pressure on the manufacturers and made it happen.

Revolutionaries simply ask "why" more than the rest of us.

Celebrate the Stupid

We've all been taught that good answers are more important than good questions. What was true in first grade is infinitely more true when you're in front of the board or your boss. But new questions are at the heart of business concept innovation—and if you're going to ask "why," you've got to be prepared to look foolish once in a while. Listen once more to Marc Andreessen:

In many companies the premium placed on being "right" is so high that there is virtually no room for

> *If your goal is to create something new and big, you're going to have to do something that everybody else will laugh at—so that becomes the test. If they're not laughing at it, and you don't get turned down a few times, it's probably not a great idea. In other words, if it's something that makes everybody nod their heads and say, "Yeah, that makes sense," there are probably already a dozen people doing it.*

Only stupid questions create new wealth. Of course, there are stupid stupid questions, and there are smart stupid questions. I remember asking a senior executive in one of America's leading hotel chains, "Why is it that someone who checks in at two in the morning has to check out at the same time as the guy who checks in at two in the afternoon?" When I got a blank stare I barged ahead. "Why can't you just have everyone check out 20 hours after they checked in? If I arrive at three in the afternoon, I'll have to check out at eleven the next morning. But if I arrive at ten in the evening, I can keep the room until six P.M. on the day of departure." The hotelier looked at me with a face full of condescension. "Gary," he said, "you don't understand the hotel industry." "*That*," I replied, "is my comparative advantage." You don't ask stupid questions when you're an industry expert. I suggested he go study Hertz. When you rent a car at Hertz, they don't ask you to bring it back at noon. You have it for 24 hours. And the hotel operator has an advantage Hertz doesn't have—the rooms never move. No one promises to leave the room in Chicago and ends up leaving it in Milwaukee instead!

In many companies the premium placed on being "right" is so high that there is virtually no room for speculation and imagination. If you insist on being incontrovertibly right, you will never be new. It's that simple. The fear of being wrong is so strong in many organizations that any idea not backed by a dumpster of data is automatically suspect. The training given M.B.A. students and managers reinforces this tendency. In course after course the message is driven home: the quality of your analysis counts for more than the quality of your imagination. John Naisbitt explains:

> *Academics are afraid to go beyond their data. Alfred North Whitehead said that a proposition doesn't have to be right, it just has to be interesting. Academics don't under-*

stand how liberating it is not to have to be right. When you have to be right you become a prisoner.

speculation and imagination.

So students get steroids for the left side of their brain, while the right side gets put on a starvation diet. How absurd. Analysis can help you avoid truly bad strategies, but it will never help you find truly great strategies.

Go to Extremes

Pick a performance parameter that's important in your business—time, cost, efficiency, quality, speed, whatever. Push this to extremes and ask, Why not? Pushing boundary conditions to the limit is one of John Seely Brown's favorite tricks for blowing up orthodoxies.

My heuristic is, "Take it to the limit and see what happens." Xerox wants to make copiers that make less noise. I told our people that this wasn't an interesting problem. If you ask us to make a machine that makes no noise, that gets interesting. They said, "That's impossible." I said, "Not if the copier has no moving parts." The question led to a radical shift in architectures in terms of how to think about copiers, printers, and mechanical systems. You'll see some radical products from Xerox that came from exploring impossible questions.

Think of every strategy conversation as your own personal version of the X Games. Get radical.

Find the "And"

Revolutionaries find a way to transcend trade-offs. They just hate it when someone says you can have A or you can have B. Screw it. I want 'em both! Toyota's "and" was a car that was economical to buy *and* of high quality. Where Mercedes–Benz and Chevrolet gave consumers an either/or, Toyota offered an *and*. Look around. Where have people accepted "ors" when they would have rather had "ands"? Take one example. There are many who believe we have an educational crisis in America. Our kids live in a culture literally saturated with entertainment. The number of alternatives to homework grows each year. Hmmm, *South Park* or algebra—that's a tough one. Unless teachers can find a way to make learning educational *and* fun, media moguls will be the real teachers in America. *Edutainment* was the original idea behind *Sesame Street*—no wonder it became one of the most popular kids shows in history—it offered an "and" instead of an "or."

This is how John Naisbitt puts it:

You just have to hang out with the paradoxes, hang out with the contradictions until you understand them. When there is a perceived contradiction, I like to look for something that helps to resolve the contradiction. A lot of people have an either/or mentality. We get the Internet and everyone says, "Well newspapers are going to go away." It's not either/or. There will be a change in the mix, that's all.

Bridle whenever you hear an "or." Search for novel solutions that make trade-offs unnecessary.

DISTINGUISH FORM FROM FUNCTION

Why did people think the Internet would kill newspapers? Because they saw newspapers as a *form* (ink smeared on dead trees) rather than as a *function* (sifting through all that happens in a day and selecting out what's really important). While the form of a newspaper may disappear, its function certainly won't. If a newspaper company sees itself in the business of running giant printing presses and distributing newsprint, it may one day be rendered irrelevant. If it sees itself as a current events editor, it will learn to live as happily online as off.

One way of distinguishing function from form is to substitute a verb for a noun. Richard Kovacevich, chief executive of Wells Fargo bank, provides an example: "Banking is essential, banks are not." Banks are things—bricks and mortar. Banking is a function. If I can divorce the function from the thing, I can think about how to deliver the function in radically different ways.

There are some IT executives and technologists who argue that computing is about to enter the "post-PC era." High-capacity networks, linked by powerful hub computers, will feed data to millions of information appliances. International Data Corporation has estimated that by 2005 more information appliances—including set-top boxes, screen phones, and handheld computers—will be sold than PCs. Couple this with online application service providers that remove the need for you to load up any software other than a browser, and you have a major threat to the existing PC business model. Yet many at Microsoft find this hard to swallow. Their loyalty is to the *form* of the PC, rather than the *function* of network computing. One senior vice president at Microsoft has termed the next wave of computing as the "PC-plus era." At best this is wishful thinking, at worst it is denial. There is little doubt that the form of computing will change dramatically over the next decade or so. Any company that can't distinguish between form and function will get caught inside an obsolete form factor.

START A NEW CONVERSATION

In most companies there is no distinction between a conversation about business concept innovation and a conversation about how to improve the operational performance of an existing business. Thus the same standards of analytical rigor are applied to both—whether the subject is the return on a new piece of production machinery or the chance to create an entirely new market. Strategy conversations at GE Capital are labeled "dreaming sessions." Questions about internal rate of return and EVA are disallowed. No one mistakes them for budget meetings. A conversation about business concept innovation is supposed to be fun, open-ended, and inquisitive. It ends with a set of hypotheses to be field-tested. An operational conversation is supposed to be businesslike, bounded, and filled with certainties. It ends with an implementation plan. In fact, there are a number of ways in which an operational conversation can be distinguished from a strategic conversation[4]:

Operational	Strategic
FOCUS	
Present focus	Future focus
Certainties	Possibilities
"Real"	"Play"
NATURE OF KNOWLEDGE	
Knowledge confirmation	Knowledge development
Static language	Dynamic language
Set within an industry	Focused on creating an industry
Implicit assumptions	Explicit assumptions
CONVERSATIONAL RULES	
Advocacy	Dialogue
Authoritative	Hypothetical
Reach for closure	Open new conversations
Need for expertise	Need for generalists
Get a decision	Keep learning

The next time you're thinking about how to turn the world upside down and someone asks you for an NPV, take a minute to educate them on the difference between a strategy conversation and an operational conversation. Then tell 'em to cut you some slack!

The disciplines I've described here are reliable ways to help you discover opportunities for business concept innovation. Yet there's no surefire, mechanical process for creating a bold new "aha." Instead, you must marry a thorough understanding of business concept innovation with the wide-eyed curiosity of a precocious five-year-old. Phrases such as "disciplined imagination," "routine creativity," and "informed intuition" capture the challenge. You already understand the part about being disciplined, well-informed, and following a routine, but what about imagination, creativity, and intuition? These qualities have been bred out of you—first by school, then by work. Yet you can, and must, regain your lost curiosity. You must learn to see again with eyes undimmed by precedent. What is familiar and drab must become wondrous and new. The goal of this chapter has been to help you regain your innocence.

Profound insights come out of a cocktail of unexpected problems, novel experiences, random conversations, and newly discovered facts. The goal is to mix this cocktail again and again. Indeed the goal is to *be* the mixer—to encompass within yourself and your team all the elements that combine to produce bursts of deeply creative insight. Not only is this an individual imperative, it is an organizational imperative. No single individual can encompass all that is changing in the world. Your cocktail shaker is just so big.

You can, and must, regain your lost curiosity.
Learn to see again with eyes undimmed by precedent.

5

CORPORATE
REBELS

YOU UNDERSTAND THE REVOLUTIONARY
imperative. You feel it in your bones. You're vibrating with excitement at the thought of doing something new, building something radical, and you can't shut up about it. But your industrial-era boss, with a black belt in corporate gamesmanship, is immune to your ramblings. Every time you start to pitch your idea you get "the look"—you know the one I mean—the look that says, "Who hired this idiot, anyway?"

So whaddya do? Beat your head against the walls of your cubicle? Throw yourself in front of the chairman's limo? Bide your time until the morons recognize your genius and promote you? Take early mental retirement? Enroll in a seminary? Steady on. There's another option—a path, too-seldom trod, that is rocky and steep but leads to opportunity. It is a path unfamiliar to corporate types, but well known to thousands of otherwise powerless individuals who've succeeded in knocking history out of its grooves.

A middle–aged woman who takes on the Marcos oligarchy in the Philippines. An African–American woman who refuses to sit in the back of the bus. A group of mothers who press lawmakers to stiffen drunk–driving penalties. A 12–year–old kid who founds an environmentalist group that ultimately attracts 25,000 members. A Czech poet who stands up to totalitarianism. These are the people who change the world. And you can't change your own company? Give me a break.

Of course no one is going to give you permission. You're not going to get a "mandate" from on high. But you've got to decide. Are you a courtier, kissing corporate butt? Or a rebel challenging your company to reinvent itself? Are you there to buff up top management's outsized ego, or are you there to help your company stay relevant in a revolutionary world? If it's the latter, you're going to have to learn to punch more than your weight and to cast a much bigger shadow across your organization than you do right now.

FROM SUBJECT TO CITIZEN

Let's start with the facts. Big, complicated social systems (such as the company where you work) don't get changed from the top—not unless they're already on the verge of collapse. To understand why, take a minute and imagine the traditional corporate pyramid, with senior management at the top and the minions—sorry, I mean the valued "associates"—at the bottom. Where in the pyramid are you going to find the least genetic diversity? Where are you going to find people who have most of their emotional equity invested in the past? Where will you find the folks who are most tempted to venerate history? The answer to all three questions is "at the top." Now ask yourself, Who holds the monopoly on setting strategy and mapping out corporate direction? The same small group. Is this stupid or what? No wonder there is so little business concept innovation in most companies. No wonder it's newcomers who create most of the new wealth.

The organizational pyramid is a hierarchy of experience. Senior executives got promoted for doing one thing very well. But sooner or later, the organization must learn how to do another thing. Today the competitive terrain is changing so fast as to make experience irrelevant or dangerous—you can't

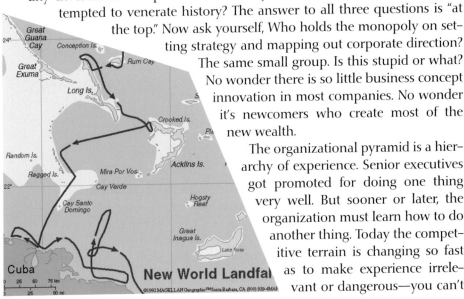

use an old map to find a new land. If you're a senior executive, ask yourself, After two or three decades of industry experience, am I more radical or more conservative? Am I more willing to challenge conventions or less willing? Am I more curious than I've ever been in my adult life, or less so? Am I a radical or a reactionary? Am I learning as fast as the world is changing? Senior executives have the same chance to be radicals as everyone else—but it is hard, because they have more to unlearn. Look at a company that is underperforming, and invariably you will find a management team that is the unwitting prisoner of its own out–of–date beliefs. When it comes to business concept innovation, the bottleneck is at the top of the bottle.

Rousseau once said, "Law is a very good thing for men with property and a very bad thing for men without property." The worshipful observance of precedent is a very good thing for those who sit at the top of organizations, because precedent protects their prerogatives. It rewards the skills they've perfected and the knowledge they've acquired in running the old thing. But precedent and a narrow distribution of strategy-making power is a very bad thing for anyone who wants to create a new future.

You can't use an old map to find a new land.

For business concept innovation to flourish, the responsibility for strategy making be must broadly distributed. Top management must give up its monopoly on strategy creation. In this sense, you can't have innovation in business models without innovation in political models.

Every company is comprised of four distinct models (see the figure "Creating Space for Business Concept Innovation"). On the bottom is the "operating model." This encompasses what people actually do on a day–to–day basis—how they're organized, what activities they perform, how they interact with customers, and what processes they run. Sitting atop the operating model is the "business model." This represents all the choices, conscious and unconscious, the company has made about the various components of its business concept. On top of the business model is the "mental model," which encompasses all the beliefs that individuals hold about what drives success in their industry. It is the prevailing set of dogmas or orthodoxies about what customers to serve, what those customers want, how to price, how to organize, which distribution channels to use, and so on. Finally, on top of everything else is the "political model."

CREATING SPACE FOR
BUSINESS CONCEPT INNOVATION

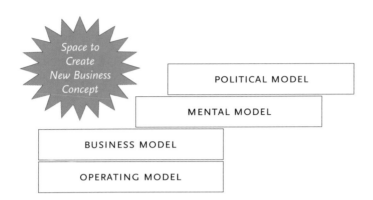

The political model refers to the way power is distributed throughout an organization and, in particular, the distribution of power to enforce mental models. So ask yourself, Who in your organization has the power to kill an idea and keep it dead? Who can make you feel like an imbecile just by saying, "We tried that five years ago and it didn't work"? Who can rule unconventional options "out of bounds"? Who has the last word on whether to try a new experiment? In most companies, political power is highly concentrated at the top of the organization, and precedent is a despot.

In a highly successful company the operating model, business model, mental model, and political model are all perfectly aligned—each one sits squarely atop the one below. Human resource professionals call this "alignment." And alignment is fine—if the world isn't changing. But perfect alignment destroys any chance of innovation, because it brooks no dissent and allows no alternatives. Alignment is the enemy of business concept innovation.

In a discontinuous world, business models don't last forever. And when they begin to decay, the temptation is to pour human energy and capital into improving the efficiency of the operating model. But better execution won't fix a broken business concept. Ultimately, you need to invent new business concepts or dramatically reinvent those you already have. Yet there is no way of innovating around the business concept unless you can first move your company's mental model off dead center. You have to upend deeply cherished beliefs. You have to create some misalignment between the mental model and the business model. This is why you must learn to be a heretic. But there's a hitch. You won't succeed in changing your company's mental model unless you first push the political model off-kilter and temporarily redistribute the power to make strategy. Put simply, if the power to create strategy and enforce mental models is narrowly distributed, you may find it difficult to get heard. When's the last time your CEO invited *you* to address the Executive Committee? When's the last time your boss's boss told the board that the company was counting on *you* to come up with the next great business concept?

ALIGNMENT IS FINE—IF THE WORLD ISN'T CHANGING, BUT PERFECT ALIGNMENT DESTROYS ANY CHANCE OF INNOVATION BECAUSE IT BROOKS NO DISSENT AND ALLOWS NO ALTERNATIVES.

So how do you overthrow top management's monopoly on strategy making? Well, you're not going to stage a palace coup. You're not going to shoot a senior vice president. Instead, you must become an activist. You must build a powerful grassroots constituency for business concept innovation. You must help to build a hierarchy of imagination, where an individual's share of voice in strategy making and innovation is a function of imagination and passion, rather than position and political power.

The good news is this: rule-busting change can start anywhere. Ever hear someone say, "Change must start at the top"? What utter rubbish. How often does the revolution start with the monarchy? Have you ever seen Queen Elizabeth II out in front of Buckingham palace, waving a placard that reads, "We want a republic"? Nelson Mandela, Václav Havel, Mohandas Gandhi, Susan B. Anthony, Martin Luther King—how often has profound change started at the top? Indeed, the fact that America has suffered but one civil war owes much to the principles of constitutional democracy enshrined in the Constitution. These principles create ample opportunity for change to emerge from below. It is not Congress that sets the social change agenda in America, it is activists.

Do the names Peter Benenson, Florence Kelly, Samuel Hopkins Adams, Irving Stowe, Sarah Brady, and Linda Carol Brown mean anything to you? Perhaps not, but you may well have enjoyed the fruits of their activism. Benenson was the founder of Amnesty International. Kelly was a consumer and labor activist who established the National Consumer's League and fought for the passage of minimum wage, child labor, and working hour laws. Adams was a muckraking journalist who was instrumental in getting the Pure Food and Drug Act passed in 1906. Stowe helped organize Greenpeace. Brady, whose husband James Brady was shot during the

attempted assassination of Ronald Reagan, is one of the most effective gun–control activists in America. Her lobbying helped bring about the Brady Bill, which requires a five–day waiting period on all gun purchases. Brown was the gutsy, young African–American student who tried to enroll in an all–white school in Topeka, Kansas, in 1950, prompting the landmark Supreme Court case *Brown vs. Board of Education of Topeka*, which declared the racial segregation of schools to be unconstitutional. These individuals and thousands of less celebrated activists badgered, harangued, organized, plotted, schemed, and ultimately prevailed. What they lacked in power they made up for in passion. They were citizen–activists.

The resilience of a democratic government rests not on one person, one vote, but on its capacity to give voice to the activists, provide a platform for the aggrieved, and harness the energies of those dissatisfied with the status quo. A democracy is a free market for causes—be it feminism, environmentalism, right–to–life, racial equality, or a hundred other movements. Those who lead these causes and shape society's agenda are truly citizens. The rest of us are subjects. It is unfortunate that the idea of democracy has become so enervated and the individual's sense of responsibility to the community so diminutive that they both can be summarized in the slogan, "One person, one vote." One person, one vote represents not the full ideal of democracy, but its most minimal precondition. If you exercise the rights of citizenship only once every four years, at the polling station, can you really claim to be a citizen? Likewise, if you willingly relinquish your responsibility to influence the destiny of the organization to which you devote the majority of your waking hours, can you really claim to be anything more than an employee?

Take a moment and reflect on the tragic price humankind so often pays when a society is unable to reshape itself through peaceful activism, when there is no escape valve for the disaffected and the disgruntled. Genocide, coups, and bloody uprisings become the only way to alter policy. Is it any different inside companies? Many companies suffer for years under mediocre leadership before the generals, sorry, the shareholders demand a change of the guard. Instead of being tied to a stake and shot, discredited CEOs take early retirement for "personal" reasons.

American constitutional democracy has survived two and a quarter centuries of unprecedented social and technological change. Democracy in America and elsewhere in the world provides more than an escape valve for the disgruntled; it provides the means for altering the very foundations of the political institutions themselves—in the case of the United States, through the legislative process and, ultimately, Constitutional amendments. In the same way, if companies are going to thrive in the age of revolution, they are going to have to become less like autocracies and more like democracies. And if you want to be a corporate citizen, rather than a subject, you're going to have to learn to be an activist.

Activists are not anarchists. They are, instead, the "loyal opposition." Their loyalty is not to any particular person or office, but to the continued

 *Activists are not anarchists. They are, instead, the "loyal opposition." Their goal is to create a movement within their company and a revolution outside it.*

success of their organization and to all those who labor on its behalf. They are patriots intent on protecting the enterprise from mediocrity, narrow self–interest, and veneration of the past. They seek to reform rather than to destroy. Their goal is to create a movement within their company and a revolution outside it. Here's how Webster's defines a movement: "a series of organized activities by people working concertedly toward some goal." By contrast, a revolution is the "overthrow of a government, form of govern-ment, or social system." A movement is what you create to raise conscious-ness and mobilize resources inside your company. A revolution is what you want to foist on your competitors.

Activists are "tempered radicals."[1] They are committed to their company, but they're also committed to a cause that is at odds with the pervading values or practices in their organization. They behave as responsible mem-bers of their organization, but they are also a source of alternative ideas and transformation. They challenge the status quo in two ways: first, by their refusal to "fit in" and, second, through their intentional acts to unbal-ance the status quo. They are idealists and nonconformists. But they're also street–smart pragmatists who know how to bend the political system to their own ends. They are cold–blooded hotheads.

You're probably asking yourself two questions: first, Why should I care? Why should I take a risk for a company that considers me expendable? Second, Is it really possible to change the direction of some-thing as big and unwieldy as a company, particularly when one doesn't hold the levers of power?

For a decade now, senior management has been telling employees that they have no entitlements. There's no job for life, no sinecure, no guarantee. Take responsibility for your career. Stay current. Justify your job. But the flip side of no entitlements is no dependency. For years companies mistook dependency for loyalty. But you're no longer dependent, you have choices. Nevertheless, there are three good reasons to put your head above the parapet.

Reason #1: You deserve something more than a paycheck and stock options. Do you remember that famous line often attributed to John Lennon: "Life is what happens while you're busy making other plans"? Yeah, maybe there's a hereafter, but that's no excuse to treat life as a dress rehearsal. Ask yourself, Have you done anything in the last three years that you will talk about for the rest of your life? Just what are you working for? Material well–being, granted, but is that it? Individuals become activists because they know that their self-worth is determined by the causes they serve. You need a noble cause.

Reason #2: The organization isn't "them," it's "you." Stop whining about "them." That's just an excuse you use to justify inaction. Start thinking of your company as the vehicle for your dreams, as you writ large. That's not an ego trip, that's the truth. Every organization is no more or less than the collective will of its members. And you can shape that will.

Reason #3: You owe it to your friends and colleagues. Your company has a face—you see it every time you peer into the next cubicle or share a table in the cafeteria. Like you, these people deserve the chance to make a very cool difference in the world. They may lack your courage, but they yearn to create, and they're ready to dream. You're not doing this to pump up the value of the CEO's stock options; you're doing it to give ordinary people the chance to accomplish extraordinary things.

That's why you bother. But can it be done? Yes. You're about to meet several corporate activists who succeeded in changing the direction of some of the world's largest companies.

JOHN PATRICK AND DAVID GROSSMAN: IBM's WAKE-UP CALL

Do you remember when IBM was a case study in complacency? Insulated from the real world by layer upon layer of dutiful managers and obsequious staff, IBM's executives were too busy fighting their endless turf battles to notice that the company's once unassailable leadership was crumbling around them. The company that took the top spot on *Fortune's* list of Most Admired Corporations for four years running in the mid–1980s was in dire need of saving by the early 1990s. Fujitsu, Digital Equipment Corp., and Compaq were hammering down hardware margins. EDS and

Andersen Consulting were stealing the hearts of CIOs who had long been loyal to IBM. Intel and Microsoft were running away with PC profits. Customers were bemoaning the company's arrogance. By the end of 1994, Lou Gerstner's first full year as CEO, the company had racked up $15 billion in cumulative losses over the previous three years and its market cap had plummeted from a high of $105 billion to $32 billion. Armchair consultants were near unanimous in their views: IBM should be broken up.

How did a company that had lagged behind every computer trend since the mainframe catch the Internet wave—a wave that even Bill Gates and Microsoft originally missed? Much of the credit goes to a small band of activists who built a bonfire under IBM's rather broad behind.

Despite Gerstner's early assertion that IBM didn't need a strategy (the last thing he wanted was to start another corporatewide talkfest), IBM was rudderless in gale force winds. Yet over the next seven years, IBM transformed itself from a company that primarily sold boxes into a company that sold services and delivered end-to-end IT solutions. IBM Global Services grew into a $30 billion business with more than 135,000 employees. Fine, you may say, but IBM was still playing catch up to Andersen, CSC, EDS, and a host of other IT service companies. Perhaps, but IBM's more recent transformation into the world's premier supplier of "e-business" solutions cannot be so easily gainsaid. By the end of 1998, IBM had completed 18,000 e-business consulting engagements, and about a quarter of its $82 billion in revenues was Net-related. In a few short years IBM had gone from being a metaphor for corporate sloth to being the first stop for any large company eager to become Net-enabled. Now how weird is that? How did a company that had lagged behind every computer trend since the mainframe catch the Internet wave—a wave that even Bill Gates and Microsoft originally missed? Much of the credit goes to a small band of activists who built a bonfire under IBM's rather broad behind. This is their story.

The first match was struck in the backwoods of IBM's empire, on a hilltop in Ithaca, New York, by a typically self-absorbed programmer. David Grossman was a midlevel IBMer stationed at Cornell University's Theory Center, a nondescript building hidden away in the southeast corner of the engineering quad. With access to a supercomputer connected to an early version of the Internet, Grossman was one of the first people in the world to download the Mosaic browser and experience the graphical world of the Web. Grossman's fecund imagination quickly conjured a wealth of interesting applications for the nascent technology. But it was an event in February 1994, as snow dusted the ground around the Theory Center, that hardened his determination to help get IBM out in front of what he knew would be at least "the next big thing," and might be "the ultimate big thing."

The Winter Olympics had just started in Lillehammer, Norway, and IBM was its official technology sponsor, responsible for providing all of the results data. Watching the games at home, Grossman saw the IBM logo on the bottom of his TV screen and sat through the feel–good ads touting IBM's contribution to the event. But when he sat in front of his Unix workstation and surfed the Web, he got a totally different picture. A rogue Olympics Website, run by Sun Microsystems, was taking IBM's raw data feed and presenting it under the Sun banner. "If I didn't know any better," says Grossman, "I would have thought that the data was being provided by Sun. And IBM didn't have a clue as to what was happening on the open Internet. It bothered me."

The fact that IBM's muckety–mucks were clueless about the Web wasn't exactly news to Grossman. He remembers when he had landed at IBM a few years earlier, and everyone was still using mainframe terminals: "I was shocked. I came from a progressive computing environment and was telling people at IBM that there was this thing called Unix, there was an Internet. No one knew what I was talking about."

This time, though, he felt embarrassed for IBM, and he was irked. After logging on to the corporate directory and looking up the name of the senior executive in charge of all IBM marketing, Abby Kohnstamm, Grossman sent her a message informing her that IBM's Olympic feed was being ripped off. A few days later, one of her minions working in Lillehammer called Grossman back. At the end of a frustrating conversation, Dave had the feeling that one of them was living on another planet. Ever persistent, Grossman tried to send the Olympic marketer some screen shots from Sun's Web site, but IBM's internal e–mail system couldn't cope with the Web software. That didn't stop IBM's diligent legal department from sending Sun a cease–and–desist letter, which succeeded in shutting down the site. Most frontline employees would have left it at that. But there was a bigger point that Grossman felt the rest of IBM was missing: Sun was about to eat their lunch. After

everyone had come back from  the Olympics, he drove down to IBM headquarters, four hours away, in Armonk, New York, to show Kohnstamm the Internet himself.

When he arrived, Grossman walked in unattended, a Unix workstation in his arms. Wearing a programmer's uniform of khakis and an open-necked shirt, he wound his way up to the third floor—the sanctum sanctorum of the largest computer company in the world. Borrowing a T1 line from someone who had been working on a video project, Grossman strung the line down the hall to a storage closet where he plugged it into the back of his workstation. He was now ready for his demo—a tour of some early Web sites, including one for the Rolling Stones. As sober-suited IBM executives scurried through their rounds, Mick Jagger could be heard wafting out of the closet.

Two people in addition to Kohnstamm were present at that first demo. One was Irving Wladawsky-Berger, head of the supercomputer division where Grossman worked. The other was John Patrick, who sat on a strategy task force with Wladawsky-Berger. Patrick, a career IBMer and lifelong gadget freak, had been head of marketing for the hugely successful ThinkPad laptop computer and was working in corporate strategy, scouting for his next big project. Within minutes, Grossman had his full attention. "When I saw the Web for the first time," says Patrick, "all the bells and whistles went off. Its ability to include colorful, interesting graphics, and to link to audio and video content blew my mind."

Not everyone saw what Patrick saw in that primitive first browser. Says Patrick:

> Two people can see the same thing, but have a very different understanding of the implications. When Java first came along and you saw a little clown dancing on the Web page, some people said, "So what?" and others said, "Wow, this is going to change everything." Part of it is, I'm always intrigued by anything new. A lot of people did say, "What's the big deal about the Web?" but I could see that people would do their banking here and get access to all kinds of information. I had been using online systems like CompuServe for a long time. So for people who weren't already using online systems, it was harder for them to see.

Their passions fueled by the Web's limitless possibilities, Patrick and Grossman would become IBM's Internet tag team, with Patrick doing the business translation for Grossman and Grossman doing the technology translation for Patrick. Patrick would act as a

sponsor and broker for resources. Grossman would develop intimate links with Netheads in IBM's far-flung development community. "The hardest part for people on the street like me," says Grossman, "was how to get senior-level attention within IBM." Patrick became his mentor and his go-between.

After seeing Grossman's demo, Patrick hired him, and they soon hooked up with another Internet activist within IBM, David Singer. Singer was a researcher in Alameda, California, who had written one of the first Gopher programs that fetched information off the Net. Grossman and Singer started building a primitive corporate intranet, and Patrick published a nine-page manifesto extolling the Web. Entitled "Get Connected," the manifesto outlined six ways IBM could leverage the Web.

1. Replace paper communications with e-mail.
2. Give every employee an e-mail address.
3. Make top executives available to customers and investors online.
4. Build a home page to better communicate with customers.
5. Print a Web address on everything, and put all marketing online.
6. Use the home page for e-commerce.

The "Get Connected" paper, distributed informally by e-mail, found a ready audience among IBM's unheralded Internet aficionados. The next step was to set up an online news group of the sort that allowed IBM's underground hackers to trade technical tidbits. "Very few people higher up even knew this stuff existed," says Grossman. Within months, more than 300 enthusiasts had joined the virtual Get Connected team. Like dissidents using a purloined duplicator in the old Soviet Union, Patrick and Grossman used the Web to build a community of Web fans that would ultimately transform IBM.

As Patrick's group began to blossom, some argued that he should "go corporate" and turn the nascent Web initiative into an officially sanctioned project. Patrick's boss, Jim Canavino, disagreed. "You know," Canavino remarked to Patrick, "we could set up some sort of department and give you a title, but I think that would be a bad idea. Try to keep this grassroots thing going as long as possible." Patrick needed to infiltrate IBM rather than manage some splendidly isolated project team. It would be easy for others at IBM to ignore a dinky department, but they couldn't stand in the way of a groundswell. Still, Canavino wasn't above using his role as head of strategy to give the fledgling initiative a push. To avoid the danger of IBM quickly going from having no Web site to dozens of uncoordinated ones, Canavino decreed that nobody could build a Web site without Patrick's approval. Though few in IBM had any inkling of what the Internet would become, Patrick had become IBM's semiofficial Internet czar. Pretty good for a staff guy.

Patrick's volunteer army was a widely dispersed group of Net addicts, many of whom had been unaware that there were others who shared their passions. "What John ended up providing," says Grossman, "was the ability to articulate and summarize what everyone was doing and to open a lot of doors." In turn, "the kids in black" introduced Patrick to the culture of the Internet, with its egalitarian ideals and trial–by–fire approach to developing new technologies. When the Get Connected conspirators gathered for their first physical meeting, remembers Grossman, "the question on everybody's lips was how do we wake this company up?"

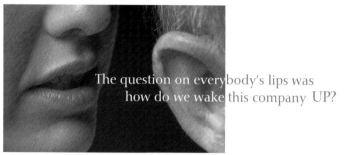

The question on everybody's lips was how do we wake this company UP?

Patrick gathered a small group of his Get Connected renegades, including Grossman, at his vacation house, set deep in the woods of western Pennsylvania. There they cobbled together a mock–up of an IBM home page. The next step was to get through to Gerstner's personal technology advisor, who agreed to make Lou available for a demo of the prospective IBM corporate Web site. When Gerstner saw the mock–up, his first question was, "Where's the buy button?" Gerstner wasn't a quick study, he was an instant study. But Dave and Patrick knew that an intrigued CEO wasn't enough. There were thousands of others who still needed to get the Internet religion.

Their first chance for a mass conversion came at a senior management meeting of IBM's top 300 officers on May 11, 1994. Having schemed to get himself on the agenda, Patrick drove his point home hard. He started by showing IBM's top brass some other Web sites that were already up and running, including ones for Hewlett–Packard, Sun Microsystems, the Red Sage restaurant in Washington, D.C., and a page for Grossman's six–year-old son Andrew. The point was clear: on the Web, everyone could have a virtual presence. Patrick ended the demo by saying, "Oh, by the way, IBM is going to have a home page too, and this is what it will look like." He showed the startled executives a mock–up of www.ibm.com, complete with a 36.2–second video clip of Gerstner saying, "My name is Lou Gerstner. Welcome to IBM."

Still, many IBM old-timers remained skeptical. Recalls Patrick: "A lot of people were saying, 'How do you make money at this?' I said, 'I have no idea. All I know is that this is the most powerful, important form of communications both inside and outside the company that has ever existed.'"

Shortly after the May meeting, Patrick and a few colleagues showed up at one of the first Internet World trade conventions. The star of the show, with the biggest booth, was rival Digital Equipment. Like Grossman before him, Patrick's competitive fires were stoked. The next day, when the convention's organizers auctioned off space for the next show, Patrick signed IBM up for the biggest display at a cost of tens of thousands of dollars. "It

was money I did not have," admits Patrick, "but I knew I could find it somehow. If you don't occasionally exceed your formal authority, you are not pushing the envelope." Now that IBM's name was on the line, Patrick had a rallying point around which he could gather all of the company's various Internet-related projects. Patrick was as concerned about the internal audience he wanted to reach as he was about the outside world. Here was his chance to seed his message across the entire company. He sent letters to the general managers of all the business units asking for anything they had that smelled like the Internet. They would only have to put in a little money, and he would coordinate everything. It turned out that IBM had a lot more Web technology brewing than even he had expected. But none of it was really ready to go to market. Still, by that December, Patrick was able to showcase IBM's Global Network as the world's largest Internet service provider and a Web browser that preceded both

Netscape's Navigator and Microsoft's Explorer. IBM stole the show and became a fixture at every Internet World thereafter.

Constantly fighting IBM's penchant for parochialism, Patrick took every opportunity to drive home the point that the Web was a companywide issue and not the preserve of a single division. At the next Internet World, in June 1995, he challenged his compatriots to leave their local biases at the door: "The night before the show, I got everybody together in an auditorium and said, 'We are here because we are the IBM Internet team for the next three days. You are not IBM Austin or IBM Germany.' That is part of the culture of the Internet: boundary-less, flat." The huge IBM booth generated a lot of curiosity among the show's other participants. When people asked Patrick to whom he reported, he said, "The Internet." When they asked him about his organization, he replied, "You're looking at it, and there are hundreds more."

Patrick was a relentless campaigner, spreading the good word about the Internet in countless speeches both inside and outside IBM. "Somebody would invite me to talk about the ThinkPad," he recalls, "and I would come talk about the Internet instead. I'd use the ThinkPad to bring up Web page presentations rather than PowerPoint slides." He also made himself very accessible to the media. People inside IBM would learn about what Patrick was doing by reading the newspaper. But even when talking to the media, Patrick's prime constituency was still the vast swath of unconverted IBMers. He just couldn't shut up about the Internet. Says Patrick: "If you believe it, you've got to be out there constantly talking about it, not sometimes, but all the time. If you know you're right, you just keep going."

While Patrick and his crew were throwing Internet hand grenades into every meeting they could wheedle their way into, Gerstner was fanning the flames from above. Gerstner's early belief in the importance of network computing dovetailed nicely with the logic of the Internet. Having bought into Patrick's pitch, Gerstner was ever ready to give IBM's Webheads a boost. He insisted that IBM put its annual and quarterly reports up on the Web well before most other companies were doing so. Gerstner also signed up to give a keynote address at Internet World, saying that the Internet was really for business. This was while Bill Gates and others were still dissing the Web as an insecure medium for consumer e-commerce.

Within IBM, Patrick became a trusted emissary between the company's buttoned-down corporate types and the T-shirted buccaneers who were plugged into Net culture and living on Internet time. Patrick had the ear of IBM's aristocracy, and his message was simple and unequivocal: "Miss this and you miss the future of computing." At the same time, Patrick con-

Grossman's on-the-fly development was the complete antithesis of IBM's traditional development process, which was to push developers to perfect products before letting them out the door. It was the difference between improv comedy and a carefully rehearsed Broadway play.

vinced Grossman and his ilk that not everyone at head office was a Neanderthal. Says Grossman:

I used to think that IBM at senior levels was clueless, that these guys had no idea how to run a company. But one of the many things that has impressed me is that the people who are running this company are really brilliant business people. Somehow we connected them to the street. Knowing how to shorten paths to those decision makers was key.

When IBM finally set up a small Internet group, with Patrick as chief technical officer, he insisted that the team stay separate from IBM's traditional software development organization. Patrick's logic: "I do believe there's a benefit in being separate, otherwise we'd have to start going to meetings. Pretty soon we'd be part of someone else's organization, and a budget cut would come along and we'd be gone."

Many of the folks in Patrick's fledgling organization weren't old enough to rent a car, and many were younger than his daughter.

Although IBM now had a formal Internet organization, Patrick and Grossman didn't disband their grassroots coalition. As the 1996 Summer Olympics approached, this group went through several watershed events. Patrick loaned Grossman out for 18 months to corporate marketing, which was in charge of the Olympics project. For the first time, the Olympics would have an official Web site, and IBM would build it. Grossman launched himself into building the Olympics Web site and was soon begging Patrick for extra bodies. "Patrick did the magic to get them hired," says Grossman, "and I morphed from doing the grunt technical work to being Tom Sawyer and getting other people to help whitewash the fence." Ultimately, more than 100 IBMers got involved.

To prepare for the Olympics, Grossman and his team had started developing Web sites for other sporting events such as the 1995 U.S. Open and Wimbledon. For the U.S. Open site, he gave a couple of college interns from MIT the task of writing a program to connect a scoring database to the Web site. "By the end of the summer," remembers Grossman, "we were sitting in a trailer, barely keeping together a Web site with a million people a day pounding away at it for scores. It was held together by Scotch tape, but we were learning about scalability." It was amazing, thought Grossman, that all of these people would come to a site merely for sports scores. IBM's second surprise came when it was caught off guard by the flood of global interest generated by a chess match between world chess champion Garry Kasparov and an IBM supercomputer named Deep

Blue in early 1996. Corporate marketing had asked Grossman earlier to build the Web site for the match, but he was booked with too many other assignments, so the site was outsourced to an advertising agency that did little more than put up a cheesy chessboard. The day of the first match, the site was overloaded with traffic and crashed.

"Nobody had any idea this was going to be such a big deal," says Patrick. IBM went into panic mode. Grossman and a hand-ful of IBM's best Web engineers jumped in to take over the site. They had about 36 hours to com-pletely revamp the site before the next match. They got Wladawsky–Berger to pull a $500,000 super-computer off the assembly line. The site didn't crash again, but the incident raised the anxiety level about the upcoming Olympics. If IBM was having difficulty running a Web site for a chess match, then what were the Olympics going to be like? The incident also succeeded in convincing a few more skeptics that the Internet was going to be beyond big.

DEEP BLUE

IBM had to build an Olympics Web site that could withstand anything. Patrick went tin–cupping again, asking all the general managers to loan him their best people and their best equipment. He got not one super-computer, but three. Grossman's team eventually grew to about 100 peo-ple. IBM was learning in the crucible of the world's most visible sporting event. By the time it was over, IBM had built the world's largest Web site (at the time), which withstood up to 17 million hits a day with few shut-downs. The content on the site was replicated in servers across four conti-nents. IBM even learned how to do a little e–commerce when a demo site for online ticket sales attracted a flood of credit–card numbers and $5 mil-lion in orders.

For Patrick and Grossman, the Olympics was just one more high–profile way to show IBM the possibilities of the Internet. It was also an easy way to get funding for development. Admits Grossman:

I used the Olympics as a front basically. What I was doing, without telling anyone, was getting computing resources. I also thought the fastest way to get IBM to change was to work from the outside in. If IBM saw itself written about in the papers, then it would change faster than if we got mired in an internal process.

Grossman's on–the–fly development, in public no less, was the complete antithesis of IBM's traditional way of doing things, which was to push de-velopers to perfect products before letting them out the door. It was the difference between improv comedy and a carefully rehearsed Broadway play. The old model didn't make much sense on the Web, where if something breaks, you can fix it universally without sending out millions of CD-ROMs with new software. You just fix the software on the server, and everyone who logs on automatically gets the new version. In the super-heated development climate of the Web, there is a big premium on getting stuff out fast, learning quick, and improving the breed as you go along. Grossman and Patrick quickly concluded that creating Web–enabled software called for a new set of software development principles, which they summarized and shared with the burgeoning Web community within IBM:

Start simple, grow fast

Trial by fire

Just don't inhale (the stale air of orthodoxy)

Just enough is good enough

Skip the krill

(go to the top of the food chain when trying to sell your idea)

Wherever you go, there you are (the Net has no bounds)

No blinders

Take risks, make mistakes quickly, fix them fast

Don't get pinned down (to any one way of thinking)

Much of the technology that Grossman and his crew first prototyped would later make its way into industrial–strength products. For instance, the Web server software developed for the Olympics evolved into a product called Websphere, and much of what his group learned formed the basis for a Web–hosting business that today supports tens of thousands of Web sites.

Following the Olympics, the Internet group turned its attention to pros-elytizing within IBM. Grossman, who had become the senior technical staff member on Patrick's team, set up an Internet lab to bring in executives from all over the company so they could experience the Web's possibilities. The group started a project called "Web Ahead" that worked to revolutionize internal IBM IT systems that had always had a low priority. For instance, the team took the old terminal–based corporate directory and wrote a Java application that gave it a great graphical interface and cool features. With a few clicks, employees could look up a colleague, see what computer skills he or she had, and then ask the directory to list every other employee at IBM with those same skills. These "Blue Pages" were an instant hit across IBM.

Patrick and Grossman never rested in their campaign to infiltrate the rest of IBM with their Internet thinking. The Internet group had only a few dozen people officially working for it, so Patrick was constantly pleading to borrow people (who were usually already part of his virtual team) from other departments. His most important ally was the team's ever-lengthening list of success stories. People could argue with position papers, but they couldn't argue with results. Repeatedly, Patrick put his whole organization on the line, and taking that risk and delivering results gave him credibility no fancy title or mega-budget could match. Patrick recounts how he co-opted line executives into sharing their resources:

> I have never been turned down on anything I have asked for, and I have asked for a lot. There was a lot of evangelizing and selling. I would go to a general manager and say, "I need you to pull some disk drives from the assembly line and I need your top engineer. What you will get out of it is unique. Your guy is going to come back to your group, and you are going to have a hell of a reference story to talk about. It will be great PR. We will make your stuff work on the Internet." I never did any name-dropping, but I didn't have to. Also, I was making a real commitment. I had 20 people working on these things.

Patrick was hard to refuse, partly because it was clear that he was fighting for the interests of all of IBM, rather than for the interests of his own little group. As he explains:

> I didn't have any allegiance to any one product group. Although I had a budget that came out of the software group, I didn't think of us as part of the software group. When somebody calls us and asks for help, we don't ask them for a budget code. We say, "Sure." We have never been a threat to any other part of the company. From the beginning our goal was to help IBM become the Internet Business Machines company.

Patrick was quick to assure would-be donors that the relationships he was forging worked both ways. He would borrow people from various business units, but at any given time about a quarter of his own people would be out on loan to other units. Further, Web Ahead alumni were regularly posted to permanent positions across IBM. When that happened, he would tell his remaining staff, "We did not lose Bill, we colonized the network hardware division. Now there is one of us living there." Patrick also helped start an internship program called "Extreme Blue" that paired some of the brightest engineering students with top IBM researchers. When IBM later hires these students, few come to work in Patrick's group, but all will be part of his virtual network.

Again and again, throughout their Internet campaign, Patrick and Grossman broke long-standing IBM rules and overstepped the boundaries of their own authority. But because their cause was so thoroughly righteous and their commitment to IBM's success so visibly selfless, they got away with things that had often sunk careers at IBM. Then and now, Patrick is unapologetic:

If you think of yourself as being in a box, with boundaries, you're not going to have any breakthroughs. I expect this of my people on my team, if they come to me and say, we failed because we didn't have the authority to do something, I'll say that's crazy.

Again and again Patrick and Grossman broke the long-standing IBM rules and overstepped the boundaries of their own authority.

Inside IBM and out, Patrick and Grossman are today recognized for their pivotal contribution to IBM's e-business metamorphosis. John and Dave's excellent activist adventure is full of lessons:

- They were relentless in getting their message across.
- They ignored hierarchy and directly lobbied Gerstner and his deputies for support.
- They borrowed resources from wherever they could find them.
- They enrolled true believers from the distant reaches of the IBM empire in a virtual network.
- From the Kasparov–Deep Blue chess match to the Summer Olympics to the Blue Pages, they put their butts and their reputations on the line to prove new technologies and build demos that would make the Internet's possibilities real to the uninitiated.
- Web Ahead developers produced the seeds of dozens of commercially viable products and services, which legitimized not only their own Web projects but everyone else's as well.

These two unlikely heroes—a software nerd and a corporate staffer—along with a pro-change CEO, helped give IBM the chance to do something it hadn't done for a couple of decades: lead from the front.

KEN KUTARAGI: SONY'S DIGITAL BANDIT

Throughout its history, Sony has had a knack for coming up with gee-whiz products, from one of the world's first transistor radios to tiny TVs to the Walkman, CD player (with Philips), and 8mm camcorder. Its archrival, Matsushita, may be bigger, but Sony's relentless innovation has made it synonymous with what's new and cool. Yet by the mid-1990s, Sony was in a deep funk. Its profits had sunk from a high of $1.3 billion in 1992 to a loss of $3.3 billion in 1995. Its foray into Hollywood had proved expensive and embarrassing, generating a $3 billion write-off in 1995. More worrying, Sony had mostly missed three of the biggest opportunities in consumer electronics: personal computers, cell phones, and video games. Compaq, Dell, HP, Toshiba, and a dozen other companies had trounced Sony in PCs. Motorola, Nokia, and Ericsson had run away with most of the cell phone business, and Nintendo and Sega had staked out the video game market.

All these new markets were either based on or quickly moving to digital technology. Yet Sony's historical strengths lay with analog technologies—of the sort found in televisions, VCRs, and tape players. With the exception of a handful of engineers scattered throughout the company, few at Sony were in tune with the digital revolution that was rendering analog technology obsolete and fueling entirely new businesses. One of the few cognoscenti, buried deep in a corporate R&D lab, was Ken Kutaragi. Lacking any formal mandate, Kutaragi launched a bandit project that eventually led to the establishment of the Sony Computer Entertainment division in 1993 and the introduction of the PlayStation video game console the following year. Less than five years later, the PlayStation business had grown to comprise 12 percent of Sony's $57 billion in total revenues, and an incredible 40 percent of its $3 billion in operating profits.[2] But more than simply being an astounding financial success, the PlayStation provided the springboard for Sony's leap into the digital age.

From his earliest days, Kutaragi had been infused with an engineer's curiosity. At the age of 10 he built a guitar amp for a friend. By the time he was a teenager he was putting together go-carts from old scooters. Unlike most of his peers, he grew up in an entrepreneurial household, working after school in the printing company his father had started following his return from World War II. After graduating from engineering school in 1975, Kutaragi applied for a job at Sony. The oil crisis had put a damper on hiring, and Kutaragi was one of only 46 male university graduates Sony took on that year.

Kutaragi's first job was to work on a liquid crystal display for calculators. The potential of LCDs captured his imagination. He explains:

I thought it would be nice not just for calculators, but also for future televisions. I cre-ated a very small LCD TV set. Unfortunately at that time Sony was making CRT [cathode ray tube] TV sets, so this was not a mainstream area. I was the only one pushing for flat screen displays, and I was just an insignificant engineer.

His mini–TVs, which prefigured the Sony Watchman by about a decade, got stuck in the lab. Still a tinkerer, he was fascinated by the brand–new microprocessors that companies such as Hitachi, Intel, and NEC were just beginning to produce. He bought samples of the first 4–bit and 8–bit chips and reverse–engineered their simple instruction sets. He also explored the intricacies of CP/M, an early personal computer operating system. With this knowledge, Kutaragi created a computer system in the tiny laboratory he occupied. "It was a nice toy for me," he recalls.

Kutaragi's digital hobby came in handy in the early 1980s when Sony began replacing some of the electromechanical components in its tape decks and video recorders with digital microcontrollers. His frustrations in designing a chip to measure sound levels convinced Kutaragi that the de-velopment tools provided by the chip companies were inadequate. In re-sponse, he created his own hardware and software tools for developing chips aimed at audio and video applications. Ultimately, these tools be-came standard issue for all Sony engineers. By the mid–1980s, Kutaragi had become fully convinced that the digital revolution was inevitable. With dozens of companies being formed around the world to exploit the new technologies, Kutaragi started to get an entrepreneurial itch. "I was in corporate R&D, but I wanted to enter the business area," he says. In R&D he was heading up part of a project to develop the first–ever digital cam-era for the consumer market, the "Mavica." Instead of using film, it stored its images on a two–inch disk.

It was during this time that Kutaragi purchased one of Nintendo's first–generation, 8–bit video games for his eight–year–old daughter. "She begged me to play every day," says Kutaragi, though he readily admits he needed little encouragement. But two things about the Nintendo system disturbed him: its sound was awful, and the games were stored on magnetic car-tridges. Ever the technical perfectionist, these shortcomings irritated Kutaragi. "Why," he asked himself, "did the game use such an unsophisti-cated magnetic storage system with such a sophisticated 8–bit processor?"

Convinced that he could make Nintendo's product better with the floppy storage system he had developed for the Mavica, Kutaragi tracked down the one salesman in Sony who had a relationship with Nintendo, and the two of them met with the game maker's head of technology. Kutaragi would have preferred to help Sony get into the video game business, but he couldn't find anyone internally who shared his enthusiasm for digital entertainment. Indeed, recalls Kutaragi, "When Nintendo introduced its first 8-bit system, no one in Sony mentioned it. They hated the product. It was a kind of snobbery. For people within Sony, the Nintendo product would have been very embarrassing to make because it was only a toy."

So began Kutaragi's collaboration with Nintendo and his bandit project. Ultimately, Nintendo decided not to use Kutaragi's floppy disk technology. Yet several of Nintendo's senior managers were intrigued by Kutaragi's unorthodox views and invited him to an offsite meeting in 1986 to further discuss the company's upcoming 16-bit system. Kutaragi suggested that Nintendo should let Sony make a special, digital, audio chip for its next game system. The new chip would greatly improve the machine's sound. Nintendo accepted.

Kutaragi's bold proposal left him with a problem. He was a researcher, not a businessman—he had no authority to strike a deal with Nintendo. To complicate matters, Sony had just embarked on an ill-fated foray into 8-bit computing with its line of MSX personal computers. Hoping to create an alternative to Microsoft's DOS operating system, a number of Japanese companies had converged around the MSX standard. The MSX project was something of a sacred cow within Sony as it was led by the son of Akio Morita, Sony's much-revered founder. Still, Kutaragi was unimpressed: "I hated the idea. We wanted to sell the MSX. But we saw the MSX as a subset of the PC. The MSX was no good at real-time graphics. Nintendo realized the importance of real-time entertainment. The architecture was totally different."

So Kutaragi kept his deal with Nintendo a secret. Only his boss, Masahiko Morizono, the head of R&D, was made aware of the budding relationship with Nintendo. Says Kutaragi, "I realized that if it was visible, it would be killed."

As the launch date for the new machine approached, Nintendo sprung a surprise on Kutaragi. The game maker wanted to release a joint statement touting Sony's new sound chip. Kutaragi's boss could no longer protect him. The project was out in the open. Kutaragi would have to come clean. Thus, he found himself in the unenviable position of standing in front of a group of furious senior executives trying to explain why Sony was helping a rival. Remembers Kutaragi: "They were upset. The executives hated to know that we were allied with Nintendo and were competing with an internal product [the MSX machine]. Many of them wanted to kill our project. But Ogha-san protected us."

Ogha-san was then president Norio Ogha, who later became Sony's CEO and chairman. Ogha was intrigued by the new market. In the end

"I realized that if it was visible, it would be killed."

Nintendo was given permission to use Sony's chip, and the product's success brought Kutaragi some credibility—at least outside of Sony. When Nintendo started to think about developing a 32-bit system in 1989, the company wanted Kutaragi to contribute to its design. In addition to a better sound chip, Kutaragi still wanted to replace the magnetic-based storage device—this time with a CD-ROM drive.

Within Sony, Kutaragi was viewed with suspicion. If he was going to continue his collaboration with Nintendo, he would need to find someone who could help him make his case to top management. Trolling for sponsors, Kutaragi approached Shigeo Maruyama, one of Ogha's disciples within Sony Music Japan. Maruyama expressed interest in the project because a CD-based system would be able to play not only games but music as well. Using Maruyama as a conduit, Kutaragi asked Ogha to create a dedicated group around the Nintendo project that would sit outside Sony's major businesses. Kutaragi feared that without this separation, his project, and his dream, wouldn't survive. Ogha, who had years earlier resorted to the same tactic in creating the music division, agreed to put Kutaragi's fledgling business in a separate unit.

This was a very lonely time for Kutaragi. He felt isolated from the rest of the company. "I was the outsider," he says. "No one would use my team's technology for internal projects." Here he was, developing key components for Nintendo's next game machine, which was likely to generate hundreds of millions of dollars, and his colleagues were ignoring him. Kutaragi recalls: "We were in a separate facility. No one accepted our project. This was a very difficult time for me. I moved my project out of the headquarters building, and located in a different area of Tokyo."

Then in 1991, just when he thought things couldn't get worse, Nintendo backed out of the deal. This change of heart came after Kutaragi had already devoted two long years of his life to the project. Nintendo was frightened that a CD-ROM drive might weaken Nintendo's hold over the production of game software. Magnetic cartridges required longer lead times to produce and were much more expensive than CD-ROMs, but it was a technology that Nintendo controlled. Nintendo was concerned that a CD-based machine might weaken the company's position in the game software business, which was where the real profits lay.

With his project in tatters, Kutaragi was more lonely than ever: "People inside Sony hated us. I was aligned with Nintendo, so when they cancelled the project I was homeless. I was arguing that computer entertainment would be a very important area for the future of Sony, but no one agreed."

Undeterred, he once again approached Ogha through Maruyama. Kutaragi recalls: "I wanted to convince Mr. Ogha that we needed to make

Sony a digital company, and the video game was the only project I could think of that would let us take a first step in this direction."

The MSX project, Japan's attempt to create its own PC operating system, had sputtered and died. Kutaragi saw game machines as Sony's best chance at becoming a digital company. But more than that, he wanted the company to make a commitment to computer entertainment. Sony sold millions of CD players, and by then there were digital components in most of its consumer electronics, but it still did not see itself as a digital company. The CD was seen as a replacement for vinyl records, rather than just one example of what would become an explosion of digital media. Kutaragi lobbied tirelessly to change this view. He explains:

> I convinced them that computer entertainment would be very important for the future of Sony. Sony's technology was analog-based. Analog would be finished by the end of the century in terms of being able to make a profit. The first age of Sony was analog, but it had to convert to a digital, information-based company in the future. No one realized that.

To underscore his commitment to the project, Kutaragi threatened to leave Sony if he wasn't allowed to proceed with his video game project. Not only that, he made an outrageous promise: if the company would fund his R&D efforts, he would create a platform for Sony's future growth. Ogha's go–ahead, when it came, reflected not only his reluctance to lose a creative engineer, but his annoyance that Nintendo had breached a contract with his own signature on it. Thus Nintendo's fears pushed the start button on Sony's PlayStation.

Kutaragi wanted to give the project a grand name, Sony Computer Entertainment, to match his grand vision for how chip technology would one day carry Sony far beyond games. At first, Ogha wasn't convinced. Recalls Kutaragi:

> I proposed the name to Mr. Ogha. I didn't want the project to be seen as games, I wanted a more sophisticated image. Mr. Ogha, said, "It's a very big name." Sony Music Entertainment, that's big business, but what is Sony Computer Entertainment? That is not a big business like Sony Music or Sony Pictures.

Despite the reservations, Kutaragi's project got the outsized name.

Already Kutaragi could envision an opportunity to vest bland business computers with fun, personality, and emotion. Two years of development came and went before Kutaragi and a handful of engineers completed the PlayStation. The 1–million–transistor chip underneath its plastic shell was one of the first to combine a 32–bit processor, a graphics chip, and a decompression engine on the same piece of silicon, otherwise known as a *system-on-a-chip*. Launched in Japan at Christmas 1994, the PlayStation was the first 32–bit game machine on the market. It would be a full year and a half before Nintendo released its next–generation system, the Nintendo 64. In a market where being first with the fastest is everything, Sony had pulled off a coup.

Sony's sterling brand name and the machine's engineering superiority gave the PlayStation a rapid liftoff. As sales shot skyward, Sony Computer Entertainment was awarded divisional status within the company, but Kutaragi was not immediately appointed as its president. Instead, he was asked to head up the division's engineering efforts.

Where Nintendo had been notorious for taking a tough line with game designers, Sony coddled independent game developers and made it easy for them to design games for the PlayStation. The PlayStation quickly became the world's top–selling game machine. Kutaragi, the onetime outcast, became CEO of the division in March 1999, when his boss moved on to become Sony's deputy CFO. By the end of its 1999 fiscal year, Sony had sold 55 million PlayStations worldwide and 430 million copies of video game software. Over 3,000 different game titles were available. All told, Sony Computer Entertainment racked up $6.5 billion in revenues, with a mouth–watering 17 percent operating margin, compared with 5 percent for the company as a whole (see the table "Sony Computer Entertainment Growth in Revenues and Operating Profits as Percentage of Corporate Profits").

SONY COMPUTER ENTERTAINMENT GROWTH IN REVENUES AND OPERATING PROFITS AS PERCENTAGE OF CORPORATE PROFITS, 1995–1999 (IN BILLIONS OF YEN)

	FY95	FY96	FY97	FY98	FY99
Sony Computer Entertainment Revenue	35	201	408	700	760
Sony Computer Entertainment Operating Income	n/a	(9)	57	117	137
Sony Corporate Operating Income	(167)	235	370	520	339

Kutaragi had proved himself. Former critics were now praising his courage and perseverance. He had made good on his promise. The returns on his bandit project had kept Sony afloat through the Asian financial crisis in 1997 and 1998, contributing nearly half of the company's profits. And Sony Computer Entertainment had become the company's second–largest business, surpassing Sony Music and Sony Pictures and second only to Sony Electronics. For a company that had staked billions on hardware-software synergy, Sony Computer Entertainment was proof that integration could pay off. Sony's software partners would sometimes spend as much as $40 million developing and marketing a single new game—that's the kind of budget more typically associated with Hollywood blockbusters. Video game software had come to generate more revenue than movie ticket sales. Nor was the PC safe from the onslaught. In 1998, software produced for dedicated game machines captured more than two-thirds of all the revenue derived from entertainment software. PC-based titles took the other third.

But Kutaragi's ambitions for Sony were far from sated. With sales of the PlayStation still climbing, Kutaragi began working on his next development masterpiece, informally known as the PlayStation II. Even though he was now CEO of Sony Computer Entertainment, he led the engineering team that set out to design the new machine. More than just a game machine, the PlayStation II would be built around a 128-bit processor called the "Emotion Engine," a chip Sony claimed to be three times faster than a Pentium chip of the same vintage. The new chip would be able to render images and movement more realistically than a Silicon Graphics workstation. Costing a cool $1 billion to develop, the chip would be powerful enough to recognize speech and render characters that could be controlled down to their facial expressions. The PlayStation II would play DVD movies, as well as all 3,000 CD-ROM games developed for the original PlayStation. Its graphics would be comparable to an animated movie, its sound quality superior to that of a music CD, and its computing power more than that of a high-end PC. Plus, it would connect to the Internet because, as Kutaragi says, "Communications is the biggest entertainment of all for humans. Even the telephone is a form of entertainment." Kutaragi's hope was that the PlayStation II would become a "home server" that would link households to all kinds of broadband services. A senior executive at Sony described the PlayStation II as an entirely new *dohyou*, using the Japanese word for sumo ring.

But even this groundbreaking product was just one step toward an even bolder goal. Explains Kutaragi:

> My intent is to create a new type of entertainment. Music has a 1,000-year history, movies have a 100-year history, but the computer is new. The microprocessor is a 30-year-old product, and IBM and Intel want to use it as an enhanced calculator. They are focused on productivity in the office, not entertainment. Spielberg saw our demonstration and he said, "Wow." Lucas thinks the PlayStation II can deliver his dream to the home. They did not expect that this type of technology would be available in this decade.

What Kutaragi is describing is nothing less than some future melding of TV, film, computers, music, and the Internet. Whether Sony will actually make this happen remains to be seen. But there is no doubt that the PlayStation II is more than just a game machine, and a few of the world's digerati wondered whether Sony might have Intel or Microsoft in its sights.

Yeah, Kutaragi could have left Sony and started his own video game company, but then he wouldn't have been able to leverage Sony's considerable marketing muscle, manufacturing capability, and money. Kutaragi muses:

If I had started this business as a venture outside a big company, it would have worked, but the moving speed would not have been fast enough. Sony had great human resources, capital, and manufacturing capability, but it did not have a vision at that time. But my team had the vision. We wanted to use Sony's infrastructure to enhance the time to market. If we were a Silicon Valley company, we would have created another Silicon Graphics. But our ambition is bigger than to be another Silicon Graphics.

In spring 1999, Sony announced a restructuring that placed Sony Computer Entertainment at the core of the company, and Kutaragi joined Sony's corporate management team. Kutaragi's odyssey from ignored engineer to corporate mogul provides a real–life seminar in what it takes to make a great company greater still:

- Start with a vision that is so bold and seductive that it is capable of sustaining you when others try to shut you down.
- Don't start with grand projects; start with something you can achieve right now, with your own resources (such as that first sound chip for Nintendo).
- Go underground if you have to, even if the price is isolation.
- Don't ask permission until you have achieved an early success and are ready to scale up.

become a highly visible champion of renewable energy.

safety of his anonymous staff job to

he was willing to abandon the

- Be willing to put your job on the line for what you believe.
- In a world where most people can't see beyond the next quarter, perseverance pays.

In his new role, Kutaragi is no less intent on changing the world than he was as a lonely engineer. From exile to divisional CEO, an activist indeed!

SHELL'S RENEWABLE RADICAL

When he joined Royal Dutch/Shell's planning group in 1993, peering into the future was Georges Dupont–Roc's job. But Dupont–Roc was more than a soulless planner playing scenario mind games. He was a dreamer and a doer. He could see a world of opportunities for Shell that lay beyond fossil fuels, a world so compelling and real that he was willing to abandon the safety of his anonymous staff job to become a highly visible champion of renewable energy. Before he was done, Dupont–Roc had convinced his century–old company to make renewable energy Shell's fifth core division, alongside exploration and production, chemicals, oil products, and natural gas.

As head of planning for the energy group, Dupont–Roc's job was to "look at the world energy scene and understand long–term issues that might have an impact on various sources of supply." In doing so, he became intrigued with the challenge of meeting the energy needs of a world

THE SCOPE OF DUPONT-ROC'S REPORT WAS AUDACIOUS—IT LOOKED OUT NOT 5 OR 10 YEARS, BUT MORE THAN 50!

with a rapidly increasing population in a way that would be environmentally sound and capable of sustaining economic development. Eager to deepen his thinking, Dupont–Roc sought out the world's energy experts at both universities and other corporations. He visited experts at MIT, Berkeley, Boeing, and Mercedes–Benz in his quest to develop a view on how the world energy system would evolve and what role renewable energy sources—such as sun, wind, and wood—would play. In 1994, he put his findings into a seven–page report, immodestly titled "The Evolution of the World's Energy Systems."

The report looked out not 5 or 10 years, but more than 50! Even for an oil company accustomed to making investments in exploration that don't pay off for 10 or 20 years, the scope of Dupont–Roc's report was audacious. But it was also grounded in a wealth of hard data about the progress of energy over the previous 100 years and what this might mean for the future. During the past century, world GDP had grown an average of 3 percent a year, supported by a supply of available energy that had grown at a 2 percent annual rate. During that time, the annual worldwide consumption of energy had increased from the equivalent of 4 barrels of oil per person to 13. Given these historical trends, Dupont–Roc came up with two potential story lines for the next century. The first one, which he labeled "sustained growth," assumed that energy consumption would continue to grow at its historical rate, in which case people would be burning the equivalent of 25 barrels of oil per capita by 2060. The second alternative, dubbed "dematerialization," assumed that energy growth would become somewhat disconnected from GDP growth as information technology, biotechnology, and lighter materials improved energy efficiency. In this case, people would be consuming the equivalent of only 15 barrels of oil a year by 2060.

In Dupont-Roc's view, the sustained growth scenario was the most probable. It assumed that energy efficiency would continue to increase at 1 percent a year, the same as it had for the past century. For the dematerialization scenario to occur, energy efficiency would have to increase at twice the historical rate, a phenomenon that had never occurred for more than a few years at a time. Even if dematerialization did take hold, it would begin in the fully developed nations and take several decades to spread to underdeveloped regions. However Dupont-Roc cut the data, he couldn't see any way to avoid an energy supply squeeze as the world's population grew and as the environmental perils of fossil fuels became ever more inescapable. Says Dupont-Roc: "I saw the potential for renewable energy sources to reduce their cost and take market share from traditional energy sources, going from a small niche to a serious competitor in the way that oil did at the beginning of the twentieth century."

To convince his skeptical colleagues, Dupont-Roc drew a powerful analogy. He pointed out that in the beginning, oil had been a niche product, used almost exclusively in lamps and stoves. In 1890, even after 20 years of 8 percent annual price declines because of improved refining and production techniques, the market share for oil was still only 2 percent compared with coal and wood. It wasn't until Winston Churchill switched the British Navy from coal to oil, in order to give ships more power and make their emissions less visible, that oil started to become the world's dominant source of energy. Dupont-Roc was simply reminding his colleagues of what they already knew: energy markets take a long time to develop. Every time energy consumption increased, the market diversified to meet those growing needs—from coal to oil and from oil to gas and nuclear. Wasn't it possible that renewable energy would come next—both from existing renewable sources like solar and wind and from other renewable sources yet to be exploited? Wasn't renewable energy one of history's freight trains? You could either jump on board before it gathered speed or get run over. Under the sustained growth scenario, Dupont-Roc figured that renewable energy would be fully competitive with oil, gas, and other traditional types of energy by 2020 (see graph "Energy Market Share, 1860–2060").

Dupont-Roc reminded his colleagues that, in the early stages, it was impossible to predict exactly which technologies would eventually triumph. In the early part of the century, for instance, the zeppelin looked like a surer bet than the airplane, and even electric cars looked more promising than those powered by combustion engines. An aluminum car powered by an electric battery broke the land speed record in 1899, clocking in at 105 kilometers per hour. On the last page of Dupont-Roc's report were excerpts from an article titled "What May Happen in the Next Hundred Years" from the *Ladies' Home Journal*, December 1900. One of the entries pre-

ENERGY MARKET SHARE, 1860–2060

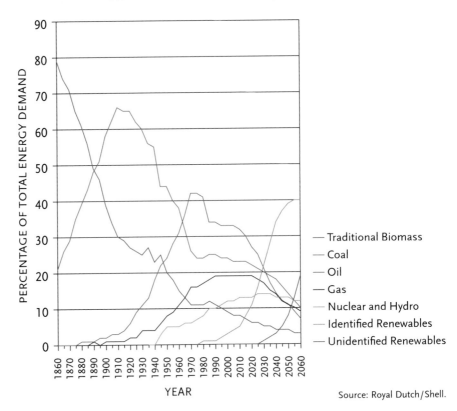

Source: Royal Dutch/Shell.

dicted, "There will be Air-Ships, but they will not successfully compete with surface land and water vessels for passenger traffic. They will be maintained as deadly war vessels by all military nations."

Obviously, there is no such thing today as British Blimpways. Dupont-Roc was saying that the future's big trends, such as how much energy 10 billion people will need, can be fairly guessed at, but the details, exactly which technologies will provide that energy, are more difficult to discern. For this reason, he advocated a technology–agnostic approach to renewable energy: experiment with everything from solar to wind to biomass (burning wood and other renewable resources) to geothermal. The goal would be to take options on a wide range of renewable energy sources.

Dupont-Roc wanted more than a nod to renewables from Shell's top brass. He was after more than a PR campaign to assuage the environmentalists. He wanted an ironclad corporate commitment. But first he would have to buttress the case for renewables. Dupont-Roc argued that the cost of making solar panels, growing trees, and converting wind into electricity would drop at a rate similar to the decline in the cost of producing oil during the late 1800s. His report showed that during the 1970s and 1980s the cost of making solar panels declined 15 percent a year and that during the 1980s and early 1990s the cost of electricity from wind turbines had drifted downward at the rate of 10 percent per year. Wind energy was already competitive in some markets. Solar panel costs would continue to decline through advances in silicon manufacturing, thin-film technology, and the scaling up of manufacturing. Through better cloning techniques and genetic manipulation, trees could be made to grow faster and burn hotter. In the meantime, production of hydrocarbon fuels would continue to rely on mature technology, and oil companies would be forced to go deeper offshore or look for smaller pockets of oil in older fields.

"Shell people were surprised that we were saying this sort of thing. It wasn't politically correct to talk about a world in which fossil fuels didn't dominate."

"I wasn't saying that oil was a dead business," recalls Dupont-Roc, "but that new energy segments would be able to improve their productivity faster and become competitive in the marketplace." Under his sustained growth model, the use of fossil fuels would continue to rise moderately until about 2020 or 2030, when renewables would come into their own and allow the total energy supply to keep growing at a time when energy from fossil fuels would be hitting a plateau.

Not everyone was immediately convinced by Dupont-Roc's thesis. In part, their skepticism was based on the disappointing results achieved in Shell's earlier experiments with renewable energy. In the 1970s, the company started a small solar energy project. But by the mid-1980s, after having spent about $100 million, it shut the business down. Photovoltaic energy was simply not cost-effective yet. In the 1980s, Shell also experimented with nuclear energy in a joint venture with Gulf, a dalliance that produced a $500 million write-off. By 1994, all that had survived of Shell's earlier experiments were a small photovoltaic research unit in Holland and a small forestry business with operations in Uruguay and Chile.

Undeterred, Dupont-Roc published his short strategy paper and began spreading the word about the new promise of renewables. He traveled from one Shell operating company to another, giving 80 speeches in 20 countries over the span of 18 months. Says Dupont-Roc, "Shell people were surprised that we were saying this sort of thing. It wasn't politically correct to talk about a world in which fossil fuels didn't dominate." Others suspected that it was all just a PR exercise. Yet every time he told his story, it got stronger:

*People would contribute to my stories by giving more examples and providing clarifi-
cation, which I would feed back into my model. It was a bit of a democratic debate.
The biggest thing I learned was not to be arrogant. Shell people have a reputation for
being arrogant, of trying to push a story instead of sharing it and trying to hear what
other people have to say.*

Finally, Dupont–Roc got his chance to give his presentation to Shell's
executive management committee. He received a cautious endorsement.
His case was helped by the steady trickle of positive feedback Shell's top
management had been getting from country managers who were pleased
to see Shell leading a dialogue about new energy sources. The fact that
Greenpeace had succeeded in mobilizing public opinion in opposition to

You have to remain focused

Shell's plans to sink an old oil platform in the North Sea also added urgency to the renewables cause. With Shell getting pummeled in European
newspapers, top management was especially receptive to any ideas that
would make their company more environmentally friendly.

The executive committee asked Dupont–Roc to prepare a business plan
outlining how Shell might poke its toe into the water of renewable energy.
They were perhaps looking for nothing more than a token, but this was
just the opening that Dupont–Roc needed to make his concept of a renewable energy business a reality.

Tree huggers notwithstanding, Dupont–Roc knew that he had to make
his proposal financially credible if it was ever to see the light of day. He
was certain that renewables would become economical over the next couple decades, but couldn't say exactly when or how. During the mid–1980s
Dupont–Roc had been leading a drilling project in the North Sea when the
collapse in oil prices forced everyone to find innovative ways to reduce
the project's costs (through three–dimensional seismic technologies, sub-
sea satellites, and unmanned platforms). He was sure a similar wave of innovation would one day push renewables into the energy mainstream.
But if Shell waited for that inflection point, it would be too late. Shell
would lack the experience to catch up to those who had started earlier.

In the fall of 1995, Dupont–Roc sidestepped all of Shell's numerous
barons during a one–hour meeting with the chairman in which he asked
for $25 million to test the commercial potential of some renewable energy
business concepts over a three–year period. Dupont–Roc wanted to concentrate on the two areas where Shell already had some competence: solar

energy and biomass (specifically, the growing of trees for power generation). In photovoltaics, he wanted to automate the way solar cells were
made and increase energy plant production from the equivalent of 2
megawatts of power a year per plant to 20 megawatts a year. His goal for
biomass was to demonstrate that Shell could grow trees sustainably, harvest them, and produce wood fuel for no more than the cost of natural
gas. "We had to convince the chairman that Shell could do something real
and credible," says Dupont-Roc. By the end of the meeting, the chairman
gave him his $25 million.

Dupont-Roc had the cash, but he still had to enlist the support of the
local line executives who control people and facilities
across Shell's global empire. Applauding his
speeches was one thing, but actually dedicating
or you will fail. resources to a nascent business project was another. With his little band of warriors, which in-
cluded three other people at Shell Central in
London, he embarked on a new campaign. "It was very
exhausting. We had to convince the chief executives of the operating companies to help us," he says. Dupont-Roc chose his targets carefully. If the
operating companies were too big, the project would get lost. If they were
too small, it might prove too distracting. So he focused on about two
dozen of Shell's medium-sized operating companies. Typical reactions
would be, "We are sorry, we're trying to rationalize our oil operations," or
"The local strategy cannot support renewables—although we support
you." Finally, his team narrowed the candidates down to about a dozen
medium-sized subsidiaries. These test beds had the advantage of repre-
senting different types of economies and climates. Some of the experiments failed, and some were unqualified successes. In Germany, for
instance, Dupont-Roc had to temper the local enthusiasm. He reflects:

> You have to keep a balance between retaining some type of central steering and letting
> the local initiative develop. In Germany, they went a little overboard. They started
> looking at solar heating, wave power, and wind power, which was good, but it was
> trying to do too much. We said, "We don't want to go that far right now." You have to
> remain focused or you will fail.

By the time the executive committee reviewed Dupont-Roc's progress
in December 1996, he was well ahead of plan. His group had planted 300
hectares (741 acres) of trees in Uruguay and had set up a 3-megawatt, photovoltaic demonstration plant in Holland. The committee was thrilled.
Even though the three-year trial period was not yet up, it asked him to
come back with a plan to substantially expand his renewable activities.

This time he developed a broad 15-year business plan for an entirely new division, which would not only expand the scope of Shell's biomass and solar power activities but also create a platform for entering two new areas: wind and geothermal. In preparing the plan, Dupont-Roc consulted about 20 senior executives throughout Shell who helped him fine-tune the commercial aspects of the plan. They would grill him: "What are you selling me? How will you produce it? In what countries? Who will find the customers?" When he finally presented the plan to the executive committee in June 1997, it was concrete. Its target was to create a portfolio of businesses by 2010 with assets in at least 20 different countries, $100 million in profits, and a 15 percent annual earnings growth rate. The businesses would be run locally, but a central team in London would assist in replicating successful ventures across the corporation.

Shell now faced a choice: it could either house the subsidiary within an existing division or create an entirely new one. It decided to pursue the latter option so that the business would be more visible and have a chance to grow. In the fall of 1997, the company established Shell International Renewables with a commitment to invest $500 million in the venture over the following five years. While Dupont-Roc was gratified that all his speeches and lobbying had finally paid off, he was profoundly disappointed that he wasn't asked to head up the new unit. Unfortunately, Shell was still an aristocracy, and he wasn't a blue blood. The job went instead to a more senior executive who had recently been reorganized out of his job in the chemicals division. Nevertheless, Dupont-Roc was heartened by the fact that his vision, aligned as it was with the tides of history, had helped to create the first major new division in Shell in decades. After staying to help the ex-chemicals executive set up the new renewables business and jump-start a geothermal energy project, Dupont-Roc quietly resigned to work for the French energy company TOTALFINA.

Despite his departure, Dupont-Roc left an indelible mark on Shell. By 1999 the first batch of trees, which had been planted in Uruguay under his watch in 1996, was ready to be harvested, and a new 20-megawatt solar panel factory was up and running in Germany. In South Africa, Shell International Renewables was marketing home solar systems to 50,000 people who lived too far away to get electricity from the power grid—the largest commercial rural electrification project ever to be based on solar power. It was also installing 10,000 solar home systems in Bolivia. In Germany and Holland, it opened a handful of solar-powered service stations where people driving electric cars could charge up in an environment-friendly way. And it was combining solar home systems with biomass-

They worked within the system, fomenting discontent, mobilizing kindred spirits, leading outlaw projects, and, ultimately, changing the destiny of some of the world's largest, most complicated companies.

fueled power plants in a "Sun Station" project that provided electricity for 80 homes, a mosque, a government building, and 11 street lamps in a village in Indonesia.

Back when the renewables business was still a $25 million project trying to prove itself, Dupont–Roc received a postcard from a politician in the French Alps, where he had grown up. The postcard showed two children playing in front of an extraordinary mountain scene, with a quote from the French novelist Antoine de Saint–Exupéry: "We do not inherit the land from our forefathers, we borrow it from our children." Shell's chairman

Mark Moody-Stuart would later repeat these words in a 1998 letter to shareholders.

Dupont-Roc's success is instructive:

- Invest relentlessly in your own learning. The endless meetings with experts and academics gave Dupont-Roc the weapons and armor he would need to win his arguments inside Shell.

- There's no substitute for impeccable data. While data alone is seldom enough to convince a company to do bold, new things, shoddy analysis will sink an activist's career before it even begins.

- A great cause (e.g., a cleaner planet and sustainable development) is as important as a great business case.

- If you're not willing to be an apostle, don't expect anyone else to be.

- Use analogies and experiences from your company's own history to buttress your credibility. Dupont-Roc's analysis of how oil, natural gas, and nuclear power had come to complement earlier energy sources was a powerful argument for renewables.

- Start small. Small successes are the platforms for big successes.

David Grossman, John Patrick, Ken Kutaragi, and Georges Dupont-Roc. They worked within the system, fomenting discontent, mobilizing kindred spirits, leading outlaw projects, and, ultimately, changing the destiny of some of the world's largest, most complicated companies. They were citizen-activists.

So where do you start? How are you going to organize a movement? Do you have what it takes? What can you actually learn from Ken and Dave and John and Georges? Read on.

GO AHEAD!
REVOLT!

EVERY DAY COMPANIES GET BLINDSIDED
by the future. Every day dozens of organizations
find themselves suddenly on the defensive,
struggling to adapt a decrepit business model to
someone else's business concept innovation. Yet the
future never arrives as a surprise to *everyone* in an
organization. Someone, somewhere, was paying
attention. For these heretics and novelty addicts,
tomorrow's opportunities are every bit as real and
inevitable as today's sunrise. But too often the seers
feel isolated and impotent. They don't know where
to begin in building a grassroots movement, even
though the principles of activism aren't classified
and there's no secret handshake. Over the decades,
social campaigners of all types have constructed a
highly practical theory of activism. How sad that the
principles of activism are virtually unknown to
citizens of the corporate realm.

Every senior executive claims to "embrace
change," and every CEO solemnly warns that
"change is the only constant." Isn't it rather odd,

then, that the principles of activism haven't been drilled into the head of every employee? After all, most social systems get changed by activists not by the elite. Yet I've never come across a company-sponsored training program that teaches the rank and file how to be activists. Let's end this strange omission, shall we? There's plenty we can learn from Dave Grossman, John Patrick, Ken Kutaragi, and Georges Dupont-Roc, profiled in the previous chapter, about how to organize a movement.

HOW TO START AN INSURRECTION

STEP 1: BUILD A POINT OF VIEW

As an activist, you need a point of view (POV), which includes the following:

- What is changing in the world?
- What opportunities do these changes make possible?
- What are the business concepts that would profitably exploit these changes?

If you understand the principles of business concept innovation, if you've learned how to be your own seer, then you're well on your way to developing your own POV.

It is rare to come across an individual who has a well-developed point of view about an opportunity for industry revolution. Most folks stand for nothing more than more of the same. This is much to your advantage. A sharply articulated POV is a sword that lets you slay the dragons of precedent. It's a rudder that lets you steer a steady course in a world filled with people blown about by fad and whim. And it's a beacon that attracts those who are looking for something worthy of their allegiance.

A point of view must meet four tests: it must be credible, coherent, compelling, and commercial. To be credible it must be based on unimpeachable data. A POV can be as bold and far-reaching as your aspirations, but it must have a foundation in fact. Georges Dupont-Roc demonstrated clearly and unequivocally that several renewable energy sources would become cost-efficient by the year 2020, if not before. He showed Shell's executive team that the cost per kilowatt-hour of renewable energy had been falling around 10 percent to 15 percent per year for several years. Project that forward, add in the cost of meeting stringent environmental standards for fossil fuels, and you can make a well-informed judgment about the point at which renewable energy sources will become a viable alternative to carbon fuels. It's also clear, given the technical hurdles involved, that any company that hopes to reap profits from renewable energy sources needs to start investing now.

John Patrick and David Grossman also had the tide of history on their side. Although the Internet was still a nascent phenomenon when they began agitating within IBM, there was plenty of hard data describing its rapid growth. There were also many analogies from history that suggested

Most folks stand for nothing more than more of the same.

the inevitable triumph of any technology that would allow people to better connect and communicate. They may have been in front of the curve, but there was a curve. Rhetoric isn't enough. You need to wade hip–deep in data to make sure you really understand what's going on. You have to be ready to back up your bold assertions. And you must clearly separate what can be known from what is unknowable—don't claim to know things you can't.

A POV must be coherent. The pieces of your POV must fit together and be mutually reinforcing. Corporate executives and their well–trained attack dogs will sniff out the slightest bit of inconsistency in your story line. Logic lapses are not allowed. This doesn't mean you have to have perfect perspicuity, but there's no excuse for muddled thinking. I often see would–be activists demolished when, in their enthusiasm, they defy logic. I witnessed one young activist in a large software company pitching a new product to his CEO. "This will be on everybody's computer. Everyone will use it every day," he gushed. The CEO's eyebrows moved closer together.

"Other than the browser, e-mail, and word processing, what applications get used by everyone, every day?" he inquired. The activist's balloon start-

IT'S NOT ENOUGH TO HAVE AN IDEOLOGY; YOU HAVE TO BE ABLE TO PASS IT ON, TO INFECT OTHERS WITH YOUR IDEAS.

ing hissing air. "Well, none," he had to admit. "And what is it about your application," the CEO pressed further, "that will create some new standard of ubiquity?" The balloon was now a flaccid bit of rubber. The would-be activist never got a second chance. Passion is no substitute for a coherent point of view.

Facts and logic are not enough, though. If you're going to enroll others in your dream, you must speak to their hearts as well as their intellects. You must be ready to tell people why your particular cause will make a difference in the world. If you can present your POV as a story (what happens to the world if we *don't* harness renewable energy sources) or as a picture (like the Web page featuring Grossman's six-year-old son), it will be that much more emotionally compelling. Many assume that only numbers talk. That's stupid. Only economists think we're perfectly rational. Beauty, joy, hope, justice, freedom, community—these are the enduring ideals that attract human beings to a cause. What is the ideal that makes your POV truly worthwhile?

If you want your company to *do* something, your POV must be commercial as well as emotionally compelling. If you can't describe how your business concept will generate wealth, you won't get far as a corporate activist. This doesn't mean you have to have a pro forma P&L accurate to two decimal places. It does mean your POV must point to a bona fide commercial opportunity. Anticipate the basic commercial questions: What's the value proposition for a customer? How will this create competitive advantage? What are the cost dynamics? Where is the flywheel of increasing returns? Your business concept may not yet be fully fledged, but you must demonstrate you are attending to these questions. Somewhere in all the enthusiasm and purpose must be the beginnings of a story about wealth creation.

A point of view that is credible, coherent, compelling, and commercial may rise to the standard of an *ideology*, which the *Random House Webster's Col-*

lege Dictionary defines as "a body of doctrine or thought forming a political or social program." Civil rights is an ideology. Democracy is an ideology. Christianity is an ideology. A vision of computers vested with the power and intelligence to display human emotion is an ideology. A belief in the power of renewable energy to sustain economic development without imperiling the planet is an ideology. As an activist, you must build your own ideology. Start your journey with a sense of destiny. Don't be afraid to dream big, like Kutaragi-san and Dupont-Roc. As one of my activist friends once put it, "If you're going to fish, use a big hook." Setbacks are inevitable. You will lose many battles in the process of winning the war. It is your ideology that will sustain you and from which you will draw courage. Know that you have a *righteous* cause—one that is in tune with what's changing, one that is inherently worthwhile, one that will help your company stay relevant in the age of revolution.

STEP 2: WRITE A MANIFESTO

These are the times that try men's souls. The summer soldier and the sunshine patriot will, in this crisis, shrink from the service of their country; but he that stands by it now, deserves the love and thanks of man and woman.

George Washington ordered these words read to his soldiers at Valley Forge, on Christmas Eve, shortly before crossing the Delaware. They are the first lines of a polemic written by Thomas Paine, the American revolutionary and pamphleteer. Paine's most famous work, *Common Sense*, was the manifesto for the American Revolution. Over the course of two centuries his powerful words and timeless principles have been used again and again to resist the authoritarian designs of despots and dictators.

You, too, must become a pamphleteer. It's not enough to have an ideology; you have to be able to pass it on, to infect others with your ideas. Like Thomas Paine, you have to write a manifesto. It doesn't have to be long. A contagious manifesto will do the following:

- Convincingly demonstrate the inevitability of the cause—here's why it is right, right now.
- Speak to timeless human needs and aspirations—here's why you should care.
- Draw clear implications for action—here's where to start.
- Elicit support—here's how you can contribute.

There are hordes of people in every organization who bitch and moan about what their company *should* be doing. But how many ever take the trouble to write a passionate and well-reasoned call to arms? Ideas that are flaky appear even more so when committed to paper. Conversely, ideas that are inherently strong get even stronger through the discipline of writing.

Think of your manifesto as a virus. What can you do to make it even more infectious?

- Search for "data bombs" that will explode upon reading—incontrovertible facts that challenge prejudices and create urgency.

- Find simple phrases and powerful analogies that people can use as "handles" to pick up your ideas and pass them around. (Don't you love the description of the PlayStation II as an "emotion engine"? Those two words say loads about Sony's view of the future of computing. They make a very complicated idea instantly portable.)

- Stay constructive. Don't criticize. Don't rehearse past failures. Don't look for culprits.

- Provide broad recommendations, but don't argue for a single, do-or-die course of action. Remember, you're launching a campaign that will need to go forward on several fronts. At this point you have to stay flexible on tactics.

- Keep your manifesto short. You're not getting paid by the word. Patrick's "Get Connected" was a simple 6-point treatise on how the Web would transform business and large-scale computing. Dupont-Roc's manifesto, "The Evolution of the World's Energy Systems," was only 7 pages. A 40-page white paper isn't a manifesto—it's a consultant's report, and it will never get read.

- Make it opportunity-focused. A manifesto is more likely to get passed around if it focuses on the upside rather than the downside. Where's the big win?

- Sometimes you need a stick. There are some whose love affair with the status quo borders on obsession. Like a reluctant Pharaoh, unwilling to free the Israelites from bondage, the only way they're going to change their minds is if you convince them that things are bad and getting worse. Every company sits on a burning platform. If you don't know where yours is burning, go find out. Maybe it's an online competitor that's about to rip your margins to shreds. Maybe it's just the hard fact that your company is underperforming and you've run out of ideas for propping up the share price. Maybe it's that you're living on Internet helium and you have no idea how to produce sustainable profits. Do a fast-forward—make it abundantly clear when and how the existing strategy is going to run out of steam.

Expect to hear dozens of reasons for *not* doing something. When timid, backward-looking souls go scrambling for an escape hatch, bolt it shut.

Escape hatch: "It's not happening as fast as you say."
    Bolt: "Oh yes it is, and here's the data to prove it."

Escape hatch: "You can't make any money with that kind of a business model."
    Bolt: "Someone already is, and here's how they're doing it."

Escape hatch: "We don't have the skills to do this."
    Bolt: "But we could get them, and here's how."

Escape hatch: "We don't have the bandwidth to deal with this right now."
    Bolt: "We have no choice. Here's what we should stop doing."

Escape hatch: "Someone already tried this, and it didn't work."
    Bolt: "They didn't try it *this* way."

Your manifesto must build a case for your *intellectual* authority. The depth of your analysis, the quality of your thinking, and the clarity of your reasoning must shine forth from every page. It must also wrap you in a cloak of *moral* authority. Moral authority comes from a cause that is both economically sound and undeniably in the best interests of the organization and its members. Your manifesto must contain nothing that would suggest your primary motivation is selfish. You're not some product champion trying to get your little widget built, or some corporate hack trying to defend a budget. You can't afford to be sectarian or parochial if you want to change the world. Martin Luther King spoke for African-Americans, but he called on all Americans to embrace justice and equality. Unlike Malcolm X, he was inclusive rather than exclusive. He understood that America could never live up to its promise if it relegated some to a permanent state of despair. It is no crime to be self-interested, but if you are *only* self-interested, your manifesto will be quickly and rightfully dismissed.

Your manifesto *must* capture people's imagination. It must paint a vivid picture of *what could be*. It must inspire hope. Your manifesto must challenge people to look the future in the eye, however disconcerting it may appear. It must deal forthrightly with the little lies that people tell themselves to avoid the discomfort of change. It must make inaction tantamount to corporate treason. But most of it all, it must ignite a sense of possibility.

STEP 3: CREATE A COALITION

You can't change the direction of your company all by yourself. This is a lesson that even corporate chairmen eventually learn. As founder and chairman of Silicon Graphics, Inc., Jim Clark fought a long–running and often bitter battle with SGI's CEO, Ed McCracken. Clark was eager that SGI go "down market" and produce workstations at the upper end of the PC price range. McCracken was loath to sacrifice fat margins to serve "out–of–scope" customers. Unable to change McCracken's mind, Clark eventually quit.

Even chairmen have to seduce, cajole, and convince to get things done. Granted, it's easier when you control capital budgeting and compensation, but it still ain't a walk on the beach. Most CEOs are good at exhortation and arm twisting, but this is seldom enough to re–vector a large company. To do that, you have to build a broad coalition. In building a coalition, you transform individual authority into collective authority. It is easy to dismiss corporate rebels when they are fragmented and isolated, and don't speak with a single voice. But when they present themselves as part of a recognizable coalition, speaking in a single voice, they cannot be ignored. This is the simple principle behind all collective action, be it a labor union organizing a strike or a trade association lobbying politicians. I have yet to see a company in which a few hundred or even a few dozen like–minded employees can't substantially impact corporate direction. The very fact that they *are* organized and *are* speaking from conviction is a powerful message to corporate leaders.

There is another reason to build a coalition. Most new opportunities don't fit neatly into any of the existing organizational "boxes." While there were scores of Netheads spread out across IBM, the Internet opportunity couldn't be shoehorned into any one division. Likewise, computer entertainment at Sony and renewable energy at Shell lacked natural organizational homes, at least to begin with. In creating a cross–company coalition, one is recognizing that the resources, brains, and passion needed to bring a new opportunity to fruition are broadly distributed. You are creating a magnet for people who harbor the same revolutionary tenden-

> **In building a coalition, you transform individual authority into collective authority. It is easy to dismiss corporate rebels when they are fragmented, isolated, and don't speak with a single voice.**

cies you do, wherever their current organizational home is. A movement is not a box on the organizational chart; it's an ink blot that has bled all over the formal org chart. It's a splat, not a department.

The first step in building a coalition is to recognize that you are not the only prescient, frustrated, yet ultimately loyal individual in your company. You're not the only one who "gets it." The second step is to begin to identify potential recruits. Start by asking these questions:

- Who is already in your orbit? Surely you've already been talking to some folks about your revolutionary ideas.

- Are there staff groups or task forces in the company that might be naturally inclined toward your point of view?

- Are there any cross–company initiatives you could tap into?

- Who across the organization might have a stake in the success of your campaign?

- What are the news groups or e–mail distribution lists you might hijack?

Maybe you can't write like Thomas Paine, but then he didn't have the Web. Put your manifesto up on an internal Web site. Build an e–mail list of those you think might share your views. Create an online forum where people can share their perspectives and help elaborate your manifesto. Locate outside experts who can lend your cause credibility. Invite network members to brown–bag lunches and after–hours soirees where you can scheme and plot and remind each other that you're not all crazy. Create opportunities to work together on some ad hoc project. Coalitions get stronger when they focus on a common task. Be inventive. Look for involvement vehicles like the Internet trade shows John Patrick used to mobilize IBM's early Internet converts.

Stay underground, at least initially. Use the network to help strengthen your business case and identify opportunities for early action. As your recruits start talking to colleagues in their own spheres of influence, the virus will spread. Don't be impatient. If you map the infection curve of a virus, it is initially flat. But at some point the exponential arithmetic of the network effect takes over, and the infection rate soars. Don't be overquick to present top management with a go/no–go decision. It's easy to shoot one pheasant out of the sky; it's a bit harder to bring down an entire flock. Keep building your flock.

And remember, you have an advantage that top management often doesn't. Most of the folks who report to them are conscripts, but you're building an all–volunteer army. Conscripts fight to stay alive, volunteers fight to win. Your goal is to enroll and embolden the latent activists. If you build strength from below, top management will ultimately come to you. Georges Dupont-Roc got his chance because a chorus of support for renewable energy was echoing off the walls of Shell's worldwide organization.

STEP 4: PICK YOUR TARGETS AND PICK YOUR MOMENTS

Sooner or later, the movement has to become a mandate. The "Get Connected" coalition became "IBM, the e-business company." Dupont-Roc's informal network of renewables fans turned into a $500 million commitment. In most companies, these commitments aren't made by the Birkenstock-wearing, Volvo-driving, ponytail brigade. Activists create movements, they don't create mandates. That's why activists always have a target—a someone or group of someones who can yank the real levers of power. You need to know who in your organization can say "yes" and make it stick. It may be a divisional vice president, it may be the CEO, or maybe it's the entire executive committee.

At Sony, Kutaragi knew his project was doomed unless he got the CEO onboard early. Sony's aristocracy was actively hostile to the idea of video games. After trying several approaches, Kutaragi established a relationship with Maruyama, who helped him lobby the CEO. At IBM Grossman managed to engineer an Internet demo for Lou Gerstner. Later, when Gerstner's likeness spoke from a Web page to a throng of IBM senior managers, the Internet die was cast. For Dupont-Roc, the pivotal moment came when he was asked to present to Shell's senior executive group.

All too often, corporate rebels are inclined to look at senior management as out-of-touch reactionaries, rather than potential allies. This is self-defeating. Their support is the object of the whole exercise. Few of them are stupid, and most are no more venal than you or I. Arrogant? Sometimes. Ignorant? Often. But that doesn't make them irredeemable. You must find a way to help them see what you see, to learn what you have learned, and to feel the sense of urgency and inevitability you feel.

So you've identified your targets. The next step is to understand them. What are the pressures they face—from Wall Street, from customers and competitors? What issues top their agenda? What objectives have they set themselves and the company? Which of them is searching for help and ideas? Be ready to bend your objectives to fit their goals. Sony had been struggling to demonstrate that hardware/software synergy was more than a concept. After Sony's initial debacle in Hollywood, Ogha was eager for another chance to justify Sony's foray into software and media. Kutaragi was ready to scratch Ogha's itch. Do you *really* know where the top guys itch? You gotta find out.

Often the top guy is easier to convince than the divisional barons one level down. Shareholder expectations hang over the head of the average CEO like Damocles' sword. With a corporate vantage point, the CEO is often less likely to be defensive and parochial than a divisional VP. In many companies, you find the "Gorbachev syndrome": there's a cautiously unorthodox leader at the top and a sea of discontent down below.

ACTIVISTS ALWAYS HAVE A TARGET—A SOMEONE OR GROUP OF SOMEONES WHO CAN YANK THE REAL LEVERS OF POWER.

Like Gorbachev, the CEO wants the organization to adapt and change. Likewise, ordinary citizens want a better life. It's all too obvious to them that the system doesn't work. The ones that are most difficult to convince are those in the middle—the city bosses, the *nomenklatura*, the vice presidents who feel most threatened by a new order of things. The recalcitrant middle can long resist the exhortations of an isolated and embattled CEO. But it's much more difficult for them to hold out when they are caught in the vise of a reform-minded CEO and a committed and revolutionary rabble. Savvy corporate leaders, such as Ogha and Gerstner, know this. They're more than willing to use the heat of the activists' passions to thaw the frozen middle in their own organizations.

Getting access to the top isn't always easy. "Invitations" often have to be engineered. Court the executive assistants, the adjutants, and the bag carriers. Find out who the top guy respects and relies on. Find out who writes the speeches. Know what customers the senior execs care most about—they may provide a back channel of influence. In other words, plot all the various avenues of influence that lead to your desired targets. Invite these people to your offsites, hook 'em up to your e-mail list, do a demo for them. Use your network to work all the approach routes simultaneously.

Make a list of all the events and occasions when you might get a chance to directly influence your targets. What are the meetings, workshops, or conferences that your targets regularly attend? See if you or one of your network members can get on the agenda. Keep your pitch short. Entice and intrigue, don't harangue. Think of the gatekeepers and high-profile events as "strategic infection points"—opportunities to educate, entertain, and enroll. To activists, the whole world's a stage. Every event is an opportunity to advance their POV. Patrick and Dupont–Roc gave dozens of speeches. As with skilled politicians, it didn't matter what question they were asked; they gave the answer they wanted to give. They were endlessly opportunistic. Every impromptu meeting, every hallway conversation was a chance to win another convert.

YOU ARE TRYING TO DISARM AND CO-OPT,

Sooner or later, you'll want to go one on one with your targets. Pick your moment carefully. You're waiting for the stars to align—you want the groundswell to have reached a critical mass; you want to catch your targets at a point when they're rooting around for a new idea; and, in an ideal

RATHER THAN DEMEAN AND CONFRONT. world, you'll time your big pitch to some external event that adds credibility and urgency to your case (such as the frenzy of environmental outrage produced by Shell's decision to sink an offshore platform). Get all this right, and top management won't think you're a rebel; they'll think you're a godsend.

TEMPER **YOUR INDIGNATION WITH RESPECT.**

Your big moment may not be planned. It may happen unexpectedly—in a company cafeteria, at a trade show. Always have your elevator speech ready. Know what you want to ask for—keep it small and simple. Make it easy to say yes.

STEP 5: CO-OPT AND NEUTRALIZE

Saul Alinsky was one of America's most accomplished twentieth-century radicals. His book on how to organize a movement, *Rules for Radicals*, is a classic.[1] In the mid–1960s he went to Rochester, New York, to lead a campaign on behalf of the city's black community. Mary Beth Rogers describes his approach:

> *Alinsky, in something of a self-parody of his own tactics, threatened to buy 100 tickets to one of Rochester's symphony concerts and feed the predominantly black members of the local organization a dinner of baked beans a few hours before they went to the concert. The resulting "stink-in" would be a surefire attention getter. . . . There was no law against it. It might be fun. And it would probably get action quickly because the social elite wouldn't want "those people" to invade their activities again.[2]*

Such tactics may work in the public sphere, but confrontation and embarrassment are seldom effective in a corporate setting. You are trying to disarm and co–opt, rather than demean and confront. Temper your indignation with respect.

John Patrick was extremely successful in drafting IBM's big guns into his cause. Given the scope of his ambition—to make the IBM Corporation Internet–ready—he realized that Gerstner's support would be necessary but hardly sufficient. With virtually no resources of his own, Patrick had little choice but to co–opt IBM's feudal lords. This took more than concerted lobbying. Patrick constructed a set of win–win propositions for key divisional leaders: Lend me some talent, and I'll build a showcase for your products. Let me borrow a few key people, and I'll send them back with prototypes for cool, new Internet–ready products. Patrick knew that reciprocity wins more converts than rhetoric.

Patrick didn't belittle, and he didn't berate. He worked hard to avoid an "us versus them" mentality. He wasn't trying to suck people and resources out of other divisions. He wasn't trying to build his own corporate fiefdom. He wasn't out there competing with the rest of IBM for customers. Divisional presidents saw him as a catalyst for change rather than as a competitor for resources and promotion. He wasn't cannibalizing their business; he was helping those businesses get ready for the future. In everything he did, it was clear that Patrick had the interests of the entire IBM Corporation at heart. In the beginning, he even lacked a formal organization. For all these reasons, he presented a very small target to his opponents.

Win–win propositions. Reciprocity. A catalyst not a competitor. Big impact, small target. These are vital principles for *your* campaign. Of course, it doesn't always work like this. The top brass at Sony saw Kutaragi's project as an impertinent challenge to their own MSX initiative. Companies have a finite number of resources, so expect a tug–of–war from time to time. But whenever you can, avoid expending political capital in highly charged head–to–head battles. At Shell, Dupont–Roc drew little fire because he never argued that renewables would replace fossil fuels. Indeed, he didn't think they would become fully competitive until 2020, long after the retirement of the existing divisional leaders. So yeah, you can stand on your soapbox and rant at the VPs. But to change your company, you're going to have to learn to co–opt at least some of the aristocracy into your revolutionary cause.

STEP 6: FIND A TRANSLATOR

You've been at it a while, and despite your best efforts you're having trouble getting heard. You talk, but you're not sure they comprehend. Don't be surprised. The very things that make you a revolutionary make it

difficult to build a base of common understanding with the disciples of orthodoxy. Imagine how a conservative dad might look upon a kid who comes home with green hair and an eyebrow ring. Well, that's the way top management is likely to view corporate rebels. Different experiences. Different languages. Different values. Different planets. This is why corporate revolutionaries need translators.

John Patrick was a translator for Dave Grossman—someone who could build bridges between the Internet cultists and IBM's corporate cardinals. Patrick was a translator between geekdom and officialdom. But he did more than explain the intricacies of HTML to guys still in love with Big Iron. He helped

Different experiences. Different languages. This is why corporate revolutionaries

to translate between the apparent chaos of the Web and the discipline of large-scale corporate computing; between the culture of "just enough is good enough" and the ethos of "zero defects"; between a half-baked technology and a zillion-dollar opportunity; between the agenda of the true believers (we just want to do "cool stuff") and the priorities of top management (those demanding shareholders, again). Patrick was also a credibility bridge. When top management asked, "Who *is* this guy, Grossman, and these kids in black?" he had an answer. "These guys care about IBM, they're not bomb throwers."

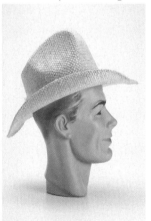

Patrick was also a translator between present and future. He found tangible ways of folding the future back into the present, starting with the Web sites built for sporting events. Each successive project gave long-term IBMers a better sense of what the new business model might look like in practice.

So if you're stymied, go find a translator—someone who is plugged into the future, who is naturally curious, and who may be shopping around for an interesting point of view to sponsor. Senior staff and newly appointed executives are often good prospects. Both are typically in search of an agenda to call their own.

STEP 7: WIN SMALL, WIN EARLY, WIN OFTEN

People can argue with position papers, but they can't argue with success. All your organizing efforts are worth nothing if you can't demonstrate that your ideas actually *work*. Start small. Unless you harbor kamikaze instincts, search for demonstration projects that won't sink you or your cause if they should fail—and some of them will. You may have to put together a string of demonstration projects before top management starts throwing money your way. You don't run pell-mell down an unfamiliar path on a moonless night. Nor do companies blindly throw resources at untested business concepts. Commitment to a new business concept should never be presented as all or nothing—

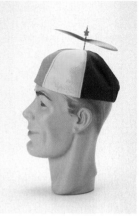

Different values. Different planets. need translators.

unless you're already way behind the change curve and some other company has taken all the risks. You have to help your company feel its way toward revolutionary opportunities, step by step.

Successful activists engineer a set of escalating experiments designed to test the new business concept and justify additional increments of investment. Without the original sound card he designed for Nintendo, Kutaragi would never have won the chance to do the PlayStation. Without Lillehammer, Deep Blue, and a dozen other small wins, Patrick and Grossman would have never pushed IBM out in front of the Internet curve. Without a success in his first $25 million demonstration project, Dupont–Roc would have never shaken half a billion dollars out of top management's pockets. Activists are not daredevils. Revolutionary goals, but evolutionary steps—that's the way to think.

Be careful not to overpromise. Patrick's team called its alpha projects "experimental applications" to clearly distinguish them from IBM's thoroughly tested market–ready applications. There will be some who will wish you to fail. If your early experiments are too grand or you claim too much for them, and you then falter, you will provide enormous satisfaction to the skeptics. Search for small projects that offer the greatest potential impact for the smallest number of permissions, projects that will engender maximum visibility with minimum investment risk. You may have a grand strategy in the back of your mind, but you need to start with some little "stratlets." Keep asking yourself, What would constitute an early win? What could we do, right now, with the limited resources available within our network to build our credibility? What could we do that would surprise the skeptics? What kind of success would others find compelling?

STEP 8: ISOLATE, INFILTRATE, INTEGRATE

Experiments that stay experiments are failures. The objective is to turn early experiments into radical, new wealth-creating business models with the power to change the direction of your company. For this to happen, you must eventually push your brood of baby projects out of the nest. In the early stages of your activist campaign, you may want to *isolate* your projects from the rest of the organization. Kutaragi moved himself and his team to a distinct precinct in Tokyo, out of the line of fire of hostile executives. With a similar logic, IBM's PC business was originally housed in Boca Raton, Florida, far from meddlesome corporate staff and antagonistic vice presidents. To grow, new opportunities need to escape bureaucratic controls and orthodox thinking. They need their own place—a place where new ideas, new values, and new teams can grow unmolested. This is the logic behind corporate "incubators," "internal venture divisions," and "skunkworks." Sadly, most projects never escape the incubator, which is often little more than an orphanage for unloved ideas. Malnourished and secluded, few projects ever find foster parents.

Companies are often advised to "protect" new initiatives from the overweening control of the old guard, particularly when the new projects are built around a competing technology. But extended isolation will kill any project that requires a significant input of talent or capital or that is in any way complementary to existing businesses. For example, while IBM succeed in "protecting" the PC business, that protection carried a stiff price. Physically cut off from the rest of IBM and from its broad base of capabilities, the PC development team had no choice but to turn to Microsoft and Intel for key software and hardware. The rest, as they say, is history. A similar fate befell many of the innovations spawned by Xerox's Palo Alto Research Center. Being 3,000 miles from headquarters guaranteed PARC a large measure of freedom, but it also made it difficult for Xerox to profit from PARC's endless stream of world-changing ideas. It's hard to drink through a straw that's 3,000 miles long.

Let's assume you are campaigning on behalf of something *big*. Sooner or later, a large-scale opportunity will require a large-scale resource commitment. This commitment is unlikely to be forthcoming if your project has been locked up too long in some business incubator. You will need to convince a broad cross-section of key executives that your new business concept is essential to your company's future. Only then do you have a chance at winning the battle over resources. To attract resources, you're going to have to make the leap from isolation to *infiltration*. A powerfully argued position paper, regular speech making, and high-profile demonstration projects helped Dupont-Roc to infect Shell with the renewable energy virus. He knew that if he couldn't get the rest of the organization to share his intellectual agenda, the renewables opportunity would never win the battle for resources within Shell. The resources that will make your dream a big commercial success have to come out of somebody's hide. Whoever's wearing that hide needs to be an ally. That will happen only if you've run a successful infiltration operation.

To attract resources, you're going to have to make the leap from isolation to infiltration.

Sometimes you need more than resources. Sometimes the opportunity is not a *new* business, but a dramatic reconfiguration of the *existing* business. If you're a drug company, you can't put genomics in solitary confinement. If you're a retailer, you can't relegate e-commerce to some offline business incubator. Here you need more than infiltration, you need integration. Patrick wanted to change the very essence of IBM—rather than simply launch a new business. To this end he courted executives from IBM's operating divisions, searched for projects they would find relevant, trained and returned their people, and put his alpha-stage projects up for early adoption. It wasn't enough for Patrick to infiltrate IBM with his POV about the Internet; he needed to *integrate* the early experiments of the Get Connected cohort into IBM's major business groups. He didn't want the Internet to be a pimple on IBM's backside; he wanted it to be a virus in its bloodstream.

Sometimes an innovation makes it out of the incubator, but never gets integrated. GM's Saturn division is more than just an experiment. Saturn's sponsors were successful in infiltrating GM with their POV about the need for a "fresh–start" small car brand. Yet it is unclear just how many of the lessons learned in Saturn have been woven into the fabric of Chevrolet, Oldsmobile, Pontiac, and GM's other brands. Indeed, in recent years it has appeared as if Saturn has become more like the rest of GM than the reverse. Integration requires more than a shared intellectual agenda. You are asking for more than capital and talent; you are asking the company to reinvent the core of who it is and how it competes. Your experiments must do more than attract resources away from incrementalist projects; they must take root throughout the organization and send out runners that will transform the landscape. It was John Patrick's hope that the Internet projects he transferred into IBM's operating divisions would ultimately seed a forest of local Web initiatives, and they have. This is the ultimate measure of success for a corporate activist.

Isolate. Infiltrate. Integrate. If you really want to change your company, you have to do it all.

ACTIVIST VALUES

Activists are the coolest people on the planet. They change big, complicated things with their bare hearts. They punch more than their weight. And when they fail, they fail nobly. To be an activist you need more than an agenda and a clever campaign. You need a set of values that will set you apart from the courtiers and the wannabes.

> *Honesty*: Activists are truth tellers. They are authentic. They don't sacrifice their integrity for personal political gain. Their views cannot be bought and sold in the marketplace for perks and prestige. They speak the "unspeakables."

> *Compassion*: Activists love the entire community. They are not interested in securing narrow sectarian advantage. Their goal is to create as big a legacy as possible for as many as possible.

> *Humility*: Activists are terribly ambitious for their cause, but personally humble. They are arrogant enough to believe they actually can change the world, but they're not glory hogs. Their egos never get in the way of making something happen.

> *Pragmatism*: Activists are more interested in action than in rhetoric. They're not searching for Utopia; they're trying to make stuff happen right here, right now. They prefer real progress to grand gestures.

Fearlessness: Activists are courageous. Their passion for the cause regularly overrides their sense of self-protection. They don't jump on land mines for the hell of it, but neither are they afraid to do battle with the defenders of the status quo.

Courage is, perhaps, the most important attribute of all.

Courage is, perhaps, the most important attribute of all. I have sat through hundreds of meetings where low-level employees soft-pedaled their convictions in an effort to protect the delicate sensitivities of top management. What came across as bold and uncompromising in a dry run presentation to their peers ended up as mushy and un-convincing when presented to top management. Afraid of bruising an ego or challenging a dogma, many would-be activists pull every punch and saw the sharp end off of every challenging point. In the end, every argument is so thoroughly padded with contingencies and qualifications that they might as well be firing cotton-ball bullets.

After Stalin's death, Khrushchev addressed the Supreme Soviet and denounced his predecessor's horrific crimes against the Soviet people. Many in the audience were stunned—the scale of Stalin's evil was mind-boggling. Finally, from the back of the hall, a voice rang out: "Comrade Khrushchev, you were there. You were with Stalin. Why didn't you stop him?" Momentarily flustered, Khrushchev's eyes raked the assembly. "Who said that?" he demanded. "Who said that?" he roared again. Those around the impertinent questioner sank lower in their seats. No voice was raised. No hand went up. After a terrible silence, Khrushchev said, "Now you know why." The questioner that day was no more willing to stand up to Khrushchev than Khrushchev had been willing to stand up to Stalin. The point was made. Luckily, there's no gulag in most companies. But activism still takes courage.

Listen, again to Thomas Paine:

> *Let them call me rebel and welcome, I feel no concern from it; but I should suffer the misery of devils, were I to make a whore of my soul.*

If you find yourself saying a quiet "amen," then you're an activist.

The burden of radical innovation is not yours alone. To survive in the age of revolution, companies must become places where rule-busting innovation flourishes. In the next chapter we'll dig deep into several companies that have reinvented themselves and their industries again and again. From their experiences we can identify the key design criteria for building companies that are activist-friendly and revolution-ready.

7
GRAY-HAIRED REVOLUTIONARIES

ACTIVISTS SHOULDN'T NEED THE COURAGE of Richard the Lion-Hearted, the patience of Job, or the political instincts of Machiavelli to make a difference in their organizations. Sincere but bumbling activists often find themselves outgunned and outmaneuvered by those who've sworn allegiance to the status quo. In the age of revolution we need organizations that celebrate activism. Is this possible? Can the fires of revolutionary fervor be made to burn brightly throughout an organization, rather than only in small pockets of insurgency? As you'll see, the answer is a resounding "yes."

It is possible to turn even tradition-soaked incumbents into gray-haired revolutionaries. Indeed, unless a company can institutionalize activism, it's unlikely to be able to meet the twin challenges of the age of revolution: reinventing itself and reinventing its industry. A company that can't re-imagine its deepest sense of what it is, what it does, and how it competes will be soon rendered obsolete.

And a company that can't proactively re-create its industry, as well as itself, will capture little of the future's financial bounty.

REVOLUTION AS A WAY OF LIFE

Consider a simple two-by-two matrix that reflects the dual challenges of reinventing core strategies and creating industry revolution:

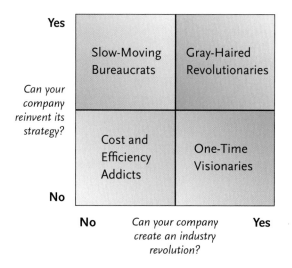

Companies that are incapable of changing either themselves or their industry are "efficiency addicts" at best. They are the dead and the dying, the no-hopers. They're acquisition fodder for more imaginative companies that will redeploy their skills and assets.

By contrast, the "slow-moving bureaucrats" may have been industry revolutionaries once but are now caught in catch-up mode. Think of Merrill Lynch and online trading, or Motorola and digital wireless technology, or SAP and the Internet. All too often, incumbents reinvent their strategies only under duress—only when it becomes patently and painfully obvious that they've missed a critical opportunity. When they finally get around to the business of transformation, they do little more than ape the strategies of irreverent newcomers. However successful the ensuing makeover, top management deserves little credit, and even less recompense, for tagging along at the end of someone else's revolutionary parade.

Most visionary companies won't be visionary more than once. Few of today's hot, young start-ups have any conception of how to reinvent themselves. Silicon Valley, that hotbed of innovation, is littered with the bones of one-strategy wonders—companies that ran to the end of their founders' headlights and then crashed. Of all the entrepreneurial upstarts spawned by the new economy, not 1 in 100 has any sense of how to repeat its own inaugural success.

The "gray-haired revolutionaries"—the rarest breed of all—are companies that have managed to reinvent themselves *and* their industry more than once. Their gray hair comes not from years, but from the experience of having lived through several strategy "lifetimes." They have done more than extend a legacy or enlarge a franchise. They have repeatedly turned themselves inside out and their industries upside down.

There is a myth at large in the land: companies that are big or old can't innovate in ways that transform industries. This is simply not true. Enron, Charles Schwab, GE Capital, Cisco, and other companies have again and again reinvented both themselves and their industries. There are even a few acne-faced revolutionaries—companies like AOL and Amazon—that change their business models faster than most companies change their product literature.

For every gray-haired revolutionary, there are hundreds of incumbents still living off momentum and thousands of start-ups that can't see beyond their IPOs. Even among the thin but vaunted ranks of gray-haired revolutionaries, there are no unqualified exemplars. There are no "excellent" companies. No company has totally cracked the code of the new innovation agenda. No company has yet fully internalized the new innovation regime with its focus on big, rule-busting ideas and radical entrepreneurship. But we can learn a lot from those that have made a start.

"Gray-haired revolutionaries" are companies that have managed to reinvent themselves and their industry more than once. Their gray hair comes not from years, but from the experience of having lived through several strategy "lifetimes."

ENRON: SEARCHING FOR FERTILE FIELDS

Since 1984, when it was formed out of a merger between two sleepy natural gas pipeline companies, Enron has invented a handful of radical new business concepts. In so doing the company has reinvented itself several times over. By the mid-1990s, Enron had transformed the wholesale natural gas business from an inefficient and highly regulated bureaucracy into an extraordinarily efficient market. It had changed electric power grids from stodgy old-boys' clubs into flexible energy markets that meet the ever-changing needs of energy-hungry customers. It had revolutionized international power plant development, creating entrepreneurial solutions to some of the most perplexing energy problems in the third world.

In the late 1990s Enron started selling electric power directly to commercial customers. But instead of just selling kilowatts as a commodity, Enron sold a total outsourcing solution, light and conditioned air at a predictable, low price. In another burst of innovation, Enron went live in November 1999 with one of the first online markets for all forms of energy. Just months after its launch, EnronOnline was doing a dollar volume far greater than Internet stars like Dell Computer, Cisco, or Amazon. Perhaps more astounding, the business was conceived and launched by a British employee of Enron who had not yet turned 30 when the business launched. The online business concept was developed, tested, and implemented in less than seven months, for less than $15 million. Enron's latest business innovation involves creating a wholesale market for bandwidth, so businesses will be able to buy as much bandwidth as they need, and no more, on a real-time basis. If Enron succeeds, it will increase the efficiency of Internet "plumbing," mostly fiber-optic cables, by up to 90 percent. Again and again, Enron has taken the seeds of its core competencies and planted them in new fields.

As much as any company in the world, Enron has institutionalized a capacity for perpetual innovation. No wonder *Fortune* magazine named Enron America's most innovative company for five years running.

"You cannot control the atoms within a nuclear fusion reaction," said Ken Rice when he was head of Enron Capital and Trade Resources (ECT), America's largest marketer of natural gas and largest buyer and seller of electricity. Adorned in a black T-shirt, blue jeans, and cowboy boots, Rice drew a box on an office whiteboard that pictured his business unit as a nuclear reactor. Little circles in the box represented its "contract originators," the gunslingers charged with doing deals and creating new businesses. Attached to each circle was an arrow. In Rice's diagram the arrows were pointing in all different directions. "We allow people to go in whichever direction that they want to go," Rice says. But around Enron's cowboys are constraints—boundaries to contain and harness their innovative zeal. Rice describes the boundaries as Enron's "risk-reward controls."

Enron's chief executive, Kenneth Lay, deserves much of the credit for Enron's ability to innovate. Lay, a former economics professor and Reagan administration official in the Department of the Interior, recognized earlier than most that deregulating energy markets would allow gas, and eventually electricity as well, to be traded nationally and, ultimately, globally. This momentous change has opened innumerable opportunities for innovators who think up ways to wrap financial products around energy commodities. But Lay dreams up few of Enron's rule-breaking business concepts. Instead, he has helped create an organization where thousands of people see themselves as potential revolutionaries.

Unleashing the Spirit of Innovation

Much of Enron's genius for innovation traces back to 1988, when Jeff Skilling, then an advisor to Enron and now president and chief operating officer, proposed an idea that laid the foundation for many of Enron's later business innovations. At the time, dereg-ulated gas prices were swinging wildly. In the spot market, prices might double one month, then crash the next. Nearly every producer, distributor, or large-scale customer feared disaster. Skilling suggested that Enron could help by cre-ating what he called a "gas bank." Con-ventional banks help customers hedge interest rates and currency fluctuations by selling products with intimidating names such as "swaps," "forward con-tracts," and "derivatives." In much the same way, Skilling proposed that Enron could help energy users protect them-selves from fluctuations in gas prices.

Enron hired "contract originators" who were bold, hungry, and creative.

Enron would buy gas from producers and make corresponding sales or hedging transactions at roughly the same time. Using techniques bor-rowed from the world of finance, it could offer buyers a predictable price if they wanted it, a low fluctuating price if they wanted that, or a price indexed to some external benchmark such as a wholesale price index. Sophisticated financial techniques would insulate Enron itself from almost all price risks.

To deliver the combinations of predictability and managed risk that Enron's customers wanted, without creating significant risk for Enron, the company had to build new core competencies in fields such as finance, law, insurance, credit analysis, and energy market analysis. It also had to create a sophisticated trading desk.

Enron hired "contract originators" who were bold, hungry, and creative. They were assigned a territory and/or a specialty, but their real assign-ment was simply to find ways to make money. When they had an idea for a deal, getting it approved was a matter of working with a variety of de-partments within Enron that provided either resources or approvals. A typical deal required approval from the finance department (for external funding), the portfolio management department (for portions of the deal that would remain on Enron's balance sheet), the risk management de-partment (for approval of the customer's credit risk and of risks of price

Controls form the cauldron in which Enron's innovative energies circulate. The heat comes from Enron's ambition to transform global energy markets and from the chance individual deal–makers have for personal wealth accumulation.

and interest–rate changes), and the legal department (for contracts and analysis of legal risks). Controls form the cauldron in which Enron's innovative energies circulate. The heat comes from Enron's ambition to transform global energy markets and from the chance individual deal–makers have for personal wealth accumulation.

Contract originators can put together sizable deals with relatively little participation from any senior executive. Ken Rice, a Skilling protégé, earned his originator spurs by conceiving and consummating a string of highly creative energy deals. One gave the New York State Power Authority predictable prices for decades—something that most gas traders would have considered absurd. Shuttling between New York and gas–supply experts in Enron's Houston headquarters, Rice worked out ways to hedge gas prices more than three decades into the future. The result was a contract for gas at fixed and indexed prices over the next 33 years.

Enron's early experience with the gas bank laid the foundation for Enron to become one of the largest energy traders in the world. More recently, Enron has developed one of the world's first online energy markets. The development of EnronOnline owes much to Louise Kitchin, who at age 29 was head of gas trading in Europe, a modest–sized Enron business. In the spring of 1999, Kitchin and others were chatting around the trading desk about the World Wide Web and how it might dramatically change the way Enron traded energy products. Kitchin thought online energy markets were inevitable, and she wanted Enron to take an early lead. "We started to say, 'We can do this. We should be doing it now,'" Kitchin recalls. So she made a decision. "I'm going to run with this," she told her boss, John Sheriff, the president of Enron Europe. Like many other

Enron entrepreneurs before her, Kitchin continued to hold her regular job while she built the new business. Others in her group took over many of her tasks to support her entrepreneurial efforts. "There were some really overworked people that year," she recalls.

In early May, Kitchin flew to Enron's Houston headquarters. She dropped in on the people who had been recommended to her as the best information technology specialists in the company. She called on the best lawyers, the best risk management people, the best tax specialists. Over and over again she made her pitch: online trading was going to happen, and Enron should lead the charge. Here she was, a 29-year-old trader based 7,000 miles from Enron's head office, and she was asking some of the busiest people in the company to carve out time for her project. But she had something that the people of Enron value—a powerful new idea.

And soon it was more than just an idea. Kitchin realized from the start that most of the firm would not take her seriously unless she could demonstrate a system that worked. By mid-August, she and her informal network had cobbled a demo site that allowed Enron's traders to participate in a simulated online energy market. Now she could approach skeptical traders not with a business plan but with a beta version of an electronic energy market: "Hey guys, this is your password; give the system a try." The prototype included a computerized "virtual trader" that Enron's real traders could compete against online, learning to be Web traders in the process. EnronOnline was designed to streamline many back-office functions, but it would not eliminate traders, since they would still set all prices. Other organizations had previously introduced electronic markets that matched buyers and sellers for highly liquid items like common stocks or petroleum products. But Enron's business demanded that it offer firm prices on gas, electricity, and other items at many different locations in the United States, Europe, and other parts of the world. This was a far more difficult task to do online. Enron would be a "principal" in its online market, in that it would both set and guarantee prices.

Soon lots of people were taking Kitchin and her vision seriously. By September she had 250 people in various parts of Enron working on her project, all of them on an ad hoc basis. "You bring in a tax lawyer, he brings in a financial lawyer, and that person finds us an Internet lawyer," she explains. Starting an e-business is cheap compared to many entrepreneurial efforts, and Kitchin got this far with few approvals from above because her work required minimal cash outlays other than the purchase of a few server computers and some plane tickets. Indeed, Kitchin was coordinating a global project, yet neither Enron's president or chairman had yet heard even a word about the online effort. John Sheriff, Kitchin's boss, didn't see any reason to ask Skilling about the project till late in the summer—when the new trading system was just a few months away from going live.

Six months later Skilling would tell the story as a joke on himself. "Finally, I got a call in September from John Sheriff," Skilling recounts. "'He said, 'Hey, John, I've really got to talk to you about something. This idea of an online trading system, it's really interesting.'"

Skilling's response was cool at first. "You know, we've looked at this before," he demurred. Sheriff explained some of the details of the system Kitchin was proposing, and Skilling conceded that the idea might be worth exploring.

"So John says to me," recalls Skilling, "'Actually, we're almost done.'" Skilling goes on, "I was never asked for any capital. I was never asked for any people. They had already purchased the servers. They had already started ripping apart the building. They had started legal reviews in 22 countries by the time I heard about it." Skilling insists he wasn't shocked and soon became a strong supporter of the project. He calls Kitchin's entrepreneurship and Sheriff's nurturing role "exactly the kinds of behavior that will continue to drive this company forward."

EnronOnline was launched November 29, less than six months from Kitchin's first flight to Houston. By the end of February 2000 it was processing 1,000 transactions a day, worth approximately $450 million. In three months it had become one of the highest volume e–commerce sites in the world and was driving nonlinear efficiencies in Enron's trading system. The clarity and ease of the new trading process for Enron's customers was generating increased volume in many commodities. In the process, Louise Kitchin was made a managing director, one of Enron's youngest.

Kitchin's story is not as unique as one might expect. Even new hires fresh out of college or an M.B.A. program are challenged to find a field in which they'll take a personal interest, then create a new business in that field. A contract originator still in her twenties, Lynda Clemmons was working on trading emissions credits—rights owned by power companies that pollute less than the law allows, which can be sold to firms that pollute more heavily. In meetings with utilities she learned they needed something else, too. One of their biggest concerns was weather—a heat wave in summer could force them to buy high–priced power or restart high–cost generators, demolishing their profits, while a warm winter could cause demand to fall far below budget. Clemmons began putting together products that allowed utilities to essentially buy insurance against the "wrong" kinds of weather.

Initially, utility executives were skeptical. "You're younger than my daughter. Why should I listen to you?" they asked. But ultimately they listened, and Clemmons had soon written $1 billion in weather hedges. But that's only a start. Clemmons notes that weather-dependent businesses have more than $1 trillion in annual revenues.

Everyone knows that the champions of business concept innovation get handsomely rewarded.

From Skilling to Kitchin to Clemmons, everyone at Enron knows that business concept innovation is central to the company's success. Ken Rice, now head of Enron's broadband business, speaks for thousands at Enron when he says:

We view the way we do things as making fundamental changes in a business, where a lot of our competition looks at doing things on the margin. This is what sets us apart from our competition. There's no business, no matter how boring and dry, that can't be structured in a fundamentally different way to create new value.

Likewise, everyone knows that the champions of business concept innovation get handsomely rewarded. Enron has typically given entrepreneurs phantom equity in the new business they are helping to create. The team that conceived and launched Enron's energy outsourcing business benefited substantially from this far-sighted compensation system.

BETTING BIG

Offering commercial customers a total energy management solution proved even more complicated, and costly, than developing EnronOnline. Lou Pai, who left Enron's gas trading business in 1992 to start its power (electricity) trading business, believed that deregulation would soon allow Enron to serve industrial customers directly, rather than merely trading energy in wholesale markets. Such a retail business, focused primarily on large commercial-energy users, would be less a trading-based business and more a relationship business. Indeed, Lou Pai borrowed heavily from

At Enron, failure—even of the type that ends up on the front page of The Wall Street Journal—doesn't necessarily sink a career.

the IT outsourcing business models of
IBM, EDS, and others in designing Enron's energy
outsourcing business.

Pai summarizes the conceptual innovation behind EES:

> As we talked to companies about their energy needs, we quickly realized that there
> was a private utility owned by these companies—the energy conversion assets, boil-
> ers, substations, chillers, and so on. The margins on the commodity side were pretty
> narrow and wouldn't allow us to profitably develop a sales force to go after these com-
> mercial customers. So I started to look at other industry models for insights into how
> to sell business-to-business. Information technology outsourcing was a good parallel.
> It was difficult for industrial customers to keep up with changes in IT, so it made
> sense for them to outsource. As we talked to big energy users, it became clear that
> what these clients wanted wasn't cheap gas or cheap chillers, but light and condi-
> tioned air—reliably and inexpensively. So we came up with a product that let them
> outsource not the public utility, but the private utility. We could upgrade inefficient
> assets, help them negotiate better energy rates, and so on.

This thinking led Enron to launch Enron Energy Services in late 1997.
Pai realized that to become an energy outsourcer, Enron would have to
develop new competencies, including managing the physical heating and
cooling assets for hundreds of companies across the United States. As a
start, Enron bought a large heating, ventilation, and air conditioning company with 4,000 employees. Most of these employees wore blue coveralls
and were entirely different than the traders who regularly put together
complex energy deals. Yet Enron also brought substantial competencies of
its own to the new business. Large, nationwide energy users typically buy
their power from hundreds of local electric and gas utilities, each with its
own complex tariff structure. Local facility managers typically have neither the time nor the economic incentive to push for the very best possible rates. Enron's deep understanding of tariff rates across the country, and
its ability to aggregate local energy demand in order to obtain better rates,
meant that it could usually offer its commercial customers instant energy
savings.

Building a nationwide energy outsourcing business has been an expensive undertaking for Enron. In 1998, the year in which many states finally

deregulated local electricity markets, Enron Energy Services signed $3.5 billion in energy supply contracts with commercial customers. Most of these contracts were for three years and covered nothing more than the supply of energy. In 1999 EES wrote $8.5 billion of contracts, most of which were 10-year contracts involving the full outsourcing of customers' energy needs and infrastructure. After several years of losses, the business was expecting income of around $70 million in 2000, a $150 million swing from the year before. More impressively, when Enron sold some shares in EES in 1997, before a single dollar of revenue had been booked, investors gave the business a valuation of $1.9 billion. A little more than two years later, Pai figured that analysts would value EES at nearly $10 billion.

Yet before this spectacular success, Pai's group had suffered a humiliating setback. In 1997, the power trading group committed considerable capital to an effort that was supposed to make it the nation's leading marketer of electricity to residential customers. New Hampshire, California, and several other states had passed bills to allow homeowners, as well as businesses, to buy their electricity from firms other than their local power companies. And Enron was one of the first companies to set itself up as an alternative energy provider. Despite spending tens of millions of dollars on marketing, Enron managed to sign up only a tiny handful of customers. It turned out that the states that were opening their markets to competition were still setting rules designed to give their traditional utilities big advantages, and Enron's deal makers had little experience in consumer marketing. Enron killed the project and promptly gave Pai the chance to build the commercial outsourcing business. Enron's leaders know that you can't pioneer new markets without taking some risks, and that if you put all those risks on one person's shoulders, you'll soon have few entrepreneurs left who are willing to bet their careers on "the next big thing." At Enron, failure—even of the type that ends up on the front page of *The Wall Street Journal*—doesn't necessarily sink a career.

PUSHING THE BOUNDARIES

Enron's pro-entrepreneurship culture induced Ken Rice, formerly the chairman of Enron's biggest business, to take on the challenge of building Enron Communications, which he confidently predicts will become the "dominant network services provider" for business. But in an industry that moves on "Internet time," a key challenge was not just building a new business concept, but to rapidly assemble an enthusiastic team. That depended on the willingness of top-notch Enron people to uproot their careers almost overnight for the chance to strike off in search of unexplored lands and yet more wealth.

It pays to hire the best.
You can't build a forever restless,
opportunity-seeking company
unless you're willing to hire
forever restless, opportunity-seeking
individuals.

While EnronOnline and Enron Energy Services were extensions of Enron's existing energy businesses, Enron Communications emerged after Enron bought an electric utility in Oregon that owned a tiny business linking the Portland-area offices of Intel and other high-tech firms with fiber-optic cable. A close look persuaded Rice and others that the provision of broadband capacity on the Internet was amazingly like the markets for gas and electricity prior to deregulation. A thicket of regulations in energy markets had locked producers, transporters, and users into long-term contracts that resulted in extraordinary inefficiency. The Internet's management of bandwidth was almost equally inefficient, though the reason was not regulation.

Network companies like AT&T and others forced large corporations to buy bandwidth in enormous chunks sufficient to meet peak needs. As a result, the buyers filled their communication "pipelines" only a tiny fraction of the time. The waste was vast. Solving the problem called for trading and legal skills much like those Enron had developed in the gas and electric businesses. In fact, Enron would not only trade bandwidth, the company decided, it would use its knowledge of how to rationalize markets to rationalize much of the Internet network. It would stitch together the world's leading broadband network, while owning only a relatively small physical network itself, something Enron had managed to do in gas and electricity markets.

Upon landing in his new role, Rice immediately held a "draft" in which he picked some of the best players from the rest of Enron to join him, including 15 people at the managing director or vice president level. Initially, 70 people in other Enron businesses were identified as potential contributors to the new business. Within one week, 64 had signed up to join Enron's broadband brigade. No one was required to sail with Rice into the uncharted waters of Internet bandwidth. Enron is proud of the fact that, for the most part, its employees have "self-directed careers." But at the same time, all of the 15 who opted to join the new venture knew that Enron had a track record of creating new industries, would be willing to bet big when that became necessary, and would generously reward the

pioneers. Whether Enron can ultimately compete with companies that have managed bandwidth for decades remains to be seen. Yet the fact that Enron sells 20 times more natural gas than Exxon, and bested companies like Duke and PG&E in the energy outsourcing business, suggests that incumbency is not always all that it is cracked up to be.

Enron could still fail in Enron Communications, but the lure is a $400 billion market. Enron knows it must build on its traditional competencies, but it also realizes that defining itself strictly as an "energy company" and staying out of an opportunity like Communications could destroy the company's capacity for revolution. After all, Enron isn't in the business of eking the last penny out of a dying business, but of continuously creating radical new business concepts with huge upside.

Enron is a successful revolutionary for many reasons. It has the out-sized aspiration that I've often called "strategic intent." Skilling recalls that when the newly launched "gas bank" held its first Christmas party in 1988—a group of eight people gathered together in a living room—they already knew they would become the world's largest seller of gas. "We knew we would conquer the world, because we had a better idea."

Enron believes that radical ideas come from radical people. Ken Lay recalls that his highest priority when he became chief executive was to get a "game-breaking player"—someone who could transform an industry—into every key job. He recalls his enormous frustration as chief operating officer at another pipeline company when he would lose good people he wanted to hire because the his chairman didn't think it necessary to meet their compensation demands. Lay has proved at Enron that it pays to hire the best. You can't build a forever restless, opportunity-seeking company unless you're willing to hire forever restless, opportunity-seeking individuals.

Lessons from a Gray-Haired Revolutionary

The essential elements of Enron's innovation style are these:

- A *passion* to make markets of all kinds more efficient.
- A *broad definition of business boundaries*, based on core competencies such as trading and arbitrage, that encompasses a wide range of market opportunities—from gas to electricity to bandwidth and beyond.
- A vibrant *internal market* for new, wealth-creating ideas where *new voices* have the chance to get heard.
- An *open market for talent* that makes it easy for company's most creative and energetic staff members to work on its most exciting new opportunities.
- Highly motivated entrepreneurs who get to *share in the wealth* they create.
- *Fluid organizational boundaries* that allow skills and resources to be creatively and endlessly recombined.

While Enron's approach to innovation may seem unique, even idiosyncratic, it is not. GE Capital's spectacular success has also been based on cauldron-style innovation. GE Capital's business development buccaneers

roam across the world looking for opportunities to reinvent large segments of the financial services industry. Senior executives act more like the hands-on board of a venture capital fund than the control-oriented bean counters that typically run large conglomerates. Each new venture is subjected to a rigorous risk control process, divided into two parts: a set of

GE Capital's business development buccaneers roam across the world looking for opportunities to reinvent large segments of the financial services industry

strict rules for approving capital spending and an aggressive monitoring system. Since GE Capital's charter is so open-ended (Gary Wendt, GE Capital's former chairman, described GE Capital's business boundaries as "not manufacturing and not broadcasting"), its tight operational controls are crucial to keeping the company from wandering into risky businesses it doesn't understand.

The similarities with Enron's broad control systems are notable. When entrepreneurial–minded managers come to GE Capital or Enron, they find more financial resources and fewer rules than almost anywhere else. "Any organization," said Wendt, "that is very old has come up with a long list of things it doesn't want to do. Over time, this becomes a book. We wanted to keep our book very, very short."

No wonder GE Capital's success has been as spectacular as Enron's (Capital accounts for about 40 percent of GE's total profits). Just how big is the cauldron in your company? Is it boiling over with business concept innovation?

CHARLES SCHWAB: A SPIRAL STAIRCASE OF INNOVATION

David Pottruck, president and co–CEO at Charles Schwab, puts it this way: "We're change junkies. We're addicted to change." Born a rule–breaker, Charles Schwab & Co. led its first revolution when it helped to create the discount brokerage industry by undercutting the steep fees of traditional brokers such as Merrill Lynch and PaineWebber. Its second revolution came with OneSource, a mutual fund supermarket that eventually let investors choose from more than a thousand different funds. Before OneSource it was difficult for investors to move assets between funds, and anyone with more than a few investments received a bewildering array of statements every month. By the late 1990s, Schwab's convenient one–stop shop for mutual funds had accumulated 10 percent of America's mutual fund assets in no-load funds and the company no longer relied so heavily on trading rev-enues. Between 1993 and 1998, the percentage of Schwab's revenues coming from commissions on stock trading had declined from 75 percent to 58 per-cent, attesting to the revolution in Schwab's business concept.

Schwab's metamorphosis from discount broker to mutual fund power-house is only one of several strategy transformations Schwab has accom-plished. Each metamorphosis has threatened to undermine historic sources of profitability, yet each has ultimately paid off by bringing cus-tomers fundamentally new benefits. Before OneSource, Schwab charged its clients a fee for the convenience of buying mutual funds in one place. Customers could avoid the fee by buying their no–load funds directly from the issuing investment companies. Irked that customers should have to pay more at Schwab than elsewhere, David Pottruck, then an executive vice president, was one of those who argued for doing away with the fee. Others at Schwab protested that this would cut the profitability of the company's mutual fund business in half. Ultimately the interests of the customer prevailed, and Schwab was able to recoup the lost fees by charging a small processing fee to the companies whose mutual funds Schwab was selling.

Schwab fought the cannibalization demon a second time when the company morphed itself into the nation's leading online broker. Deciding to make cheap Web trading available to all its customers was a gut-wrenching decision that slashed the company's commission for those trades by more than half. But by late 1999, Schwab boasted 3 million Internet customers with more than $260 billion in online assets (rival E*TRADE's assets were only one-tenth that size). With its Web offerings, Schwab recast itself as a new kind of full-service broker and entered the Age of Advice, coming full circle from its early days when it thought "advice" was a dirty word. "We are reinventing the full-service investing business and ourselves at the same time," says Pottruck.

Schwab's conception of who it serves has also been a moving target. During its first decade, for instance, Schwab thought of itself as a no-frills broker that catered to sophisticated traders. Yet even within the discount brokerage industry, Schwab bucked conventional wisdom. Instead of sticking to a low-overhead, phone-based business, it started to build a network of branches. Chuck Schwab figured that people wanted to feel physically close to their money. This insight paid off handsomely when the company began to broaden its target audience. As investing became democratized—first through mutual funds, then via the Web—Schwab found that its branches were terrific for capturing neophyte investors because they gave Schwab bricks-and-mortar credibility. In 1999 customers opened more than one million new accounts at Schwab. Many of these investors had never had a broker before. In the process Schwab became one of the first "clicks-and-mortar" companies, with a business concept that optimized both its online and its offline presence.

Schwab's knack for reinvention and finding new business models has allowed it to thrive where others have foundered. It long ago zoomed past Quick & Reilly, its toughest competitor in the 1970s. From 1993 to 1998, Schwab's revenues grew at an average annual rate of 23 percent to $2.7 billion, and its earnings grew at an average annual rate of 24 percent to $350 million. During the same period, its stock price zoomed up 1,072 percent, as compared with 218 percent for Merrill Lynch and 164 percent for the S&P 500. In December 1998, Schwab's market capitalization surpassed that of Merrill Lynch for the first time ever. No one in the brokerage industry doubts that Schwab has been a revolutionary more than once.

IN LOVE WITH CUSTOMERS

Schwab has never let itself become trapped in any one particular business model. Jeff Lyons, head of mutual fund marketing, says, "We have a

Schwab has never let itself become trapped in any one particular business model.

hard time defining ourselves. We're uncomfortable with any of the labels." Rather, Schwab has always defined itself in terms of its cause, which is to serve investors by doing whatever it takes to help them secure and improve their financial lives. "When Chuck Schwab started the company," says John McGonigle, who runs the mutual funds group, "his goal was to make it a place where he would feel comfortable doing business as an investor. Chuck is the voice of the customer."

One of the company's widely communicated and deeply held values is customer empathy, and Chuck Schwab is its foremost apostle. Says Bob Duste, CEO of Schwab Europe:

> *I have never heard Chuck raving on about returns, profits, or the share price. He is always talking about customers. He believes we need to do more to teach people how to invest—not for us, but for them. If we do right by the customer, he knows profitability will take care of itself. Chuck goes once a month to serve soup to old people at a Salvation Army kitchen. He says, "If they would have started early and planned, they could have avoided this, and it just breaks my heart. We have to have better products and reach more people."*

Schwab's rank and file see their jobs not just as processing transactions, but as protecting some of the most precious things in a customer's life: the ability to send a kid to college, to support an elderly parent, or to retire stress-free. "We think we're curing cancer," says chief strategist Dan Leemon.

Schwab has repeatedly found the courage to challenge industry dogmas by working from the customer backward. While other parts of the financial services industry seem to look on customer ignorance as a profit center, Schwab always assumes it is serving a very discerning customer—even when it is not. Comments McGonigle: "Something that distinguishes Schwab from most of the other financial services companies is that we presume that our customers are really smart and we're not going to pull anything over on them. We don't think we can fool them on fees or execution."

Schwab's unconventional strategies have often left competitors scrambling. It took Fidelity six years to fully embrace the idea of a mutual fund supermarket like OneSource because it was loath to carry competing products and surrender some of its management fees to other companies.

Schwab complements its customer worship with bold growth targets.

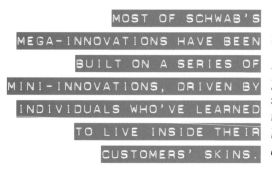

MOST OF SCHWAB'S MEGA-INNOVATIONS HAVE BEEN BUILT ON A SERIES OF MINI-INNOVATIONS, DRIVEN BY INDIVIDUALS WHO'VE LEARNED TO LIVE INSIDE THEIR CUSTOMERS' SKINS.

Says Art Shaw, a senior VP:

Every year we feel we have to grow 20 percent. Every year we have to say that last year is over, and we're starting from zero. This creates an incredible desire to innovate. Only about 10 percent of large companies have grown both their revenues and earnings 20 percent per year for five years in a row.

Schwab sees itself as addressing a nearly limitless market. Of America's $15 trillion in savings, only 4 percent sits in discount brokerage accounts, and Schwab itself holds only about $600 billion. Its goal is to grab $1 trillion worth of assets before 2005 and nearly double its number of active customers to 10 million.

Besides its ardor for customers and ambitious growth goals, there are two other forces powering innovation at Schwab. The first is the opportunity that every employee has for wealth creation. Every employee at Schwab is a shareholder. Says CFO Steve Scheid, "One of the best financial disciplines is having your largest shareholder walking the halls thinking about serving customers." McGonigle, who previously worked at a giant bank, says, "At Schwab, the customer and the shareholder are preeminent. At my bank they were theoretical constructs."

The other spur for innovation is a meritocracy that welcomes new ideas. At Schwab the champions of innovation have been consistently promoted out of rank and out of order. Jeff Lyons, John McGonigle, and Bob Duste were all activists who got early passes to an executive suite. "Everyone in top management had a big idea when they were more junior," says Susanne Lyons, Jeff's wife and another innovation activist at Schwab. She adds, "Each of us did something with our idea and got rewarded for it." Around Schwab, Susanne Lyons is known as the "Queen of Segmentation." When she first arrived at Schwab in 1992 from Fidelity, Schwab's approach to customers was pretty much one size fits all. Every customer had to call the same 1–800 numbers and got the same plain-vanilla service, whether they had $3,000 in their account or $300,000. But Lyons noticed that an elite group of customers known as the "Schwab 500," which included some of Chuck Schwab's friends and acquaintances, was getting special, personalized service from a small team of eight account representatives. She thought, "Why not replicate this on a much bigger scale? We could have these small teams serving affluent investors." Her enthusiasm ran headlong into a wall of resistance because most folks at Schwab thought the notion of a premium service conflicted with the company's core value of treating the small investor well and every investor alike. So she started collecting data on Schwab's more affluent customers and its most active traders. She discovered that although they represented only 20 percent of Schwab's customer base, they accounted for an astounding 80 percent of its trading revenues. Now she had the ammunition to argue for the expansion of the Schwab 500 and to help her colleagues rethink their definition of "fairness." Why shouldn't investors who brought more value to Schwab get more value in return? Wasn't that simply fair? This logic won most people over.

Starting with the customers already in the Schwab 500, Lyons launched the service in 1994. It was targeted at investors who traded more than 48 times a year (later reduced to 24 and then to 12) or people with more than $100,000 in assets. Schwab started using Caller ID technology to automatically route calls from high-asset individuals to the special teams. A live person was available 24 hours a day, thus providing a level of round-the-clock personal service unmatched by traditional brokerages. Each eight-person team was given responsibility for a specific set of accounts, so that a customer could be assured of always talking to someone who really did understand his or her particular situation. Each team comprised individuals representing a broad spectrum of investment expertise. By 1999, around 750,000 customers were enrolled in Schwab 500, which had been renamed "Signature Services."

LEAPING ONTO THE WEB

Susanne Lyons's story is not unique. Most of Schwab's mega–innovations have been built on a series of mini-innovations, driven by individuals who've learned to live inside their customers' skins. Dramatic business concept breakthroughs such as Signature Services and schwab.com are more often the product of a string of rule–bending experiments than some grand strategic leap—more like a tireless climber bounding up a spiral staircase than Superman leaping over tall buildings in a single bound. In the same way that Schwab 500 prepared the way for Signature Services, a long string of technology–oriented experiments helped Schwab beat many of its traditional competitors to the Web.

A few of Schwab's early experiments with technology, such as its StreetSmart dial–up trading software, were modest successes, but most were dismal failures. In 1982, for instance, Schwab came out with the PocketTerm, a bulky, portable contraption that could receive stock quotes over the airwaves. In 1985, it unveiled SchwabLine, a device that, when connected to a phone line, would spit out quotes on an extra–wide roll of adding machine tape. Schwab also developed a slew of stock-trading software programs that bombed. Nevertheless, the young innovation addicts at Schwab were encouraged to build these early flying machines.

Every so often, Schwab's penchant for experimentation would turn up a winner. TeleBroker was an idea that came from outside Schwab. In 1989, a small start-up came to Schwab and demoed a technology that would allow investors to check quotes and trade stocks using the keypad on a Touch-Tone telephone. Schwab's call centers were constantly busy, and here was an inexpensive way to increase the number of calls it could handle without hiring more people. Duste, who was head of software engineering at the time, took the idea to a senior VP in the retail service group. He ran straight into trouble. Recalls Duste: "The business people thought this was a terrible idea. They thought customers would reject it because customers want to speak with a real person, or wouldn't be able to use the keypad. They couldn't understand it, because they couldn't imagine how it would be used."

Schwab's relentless pursuit of a better customer experience had once again paved the way for a radical rebirth of the company's strategy.

Instead of arguing with them, Duste had two of his developers build a demo and roll it out in a pilot test. Customers found its deep, automated voice soothing and telephone trading highly convenient. Within six months, TeleBroker was available to all of Schwab's customers. As one Schwab manager puts it, "Around here the pilot is the first week of the rollout."

By 1995, about a fifth of Schwab's trading volume was going through TeleBroker and StreetSmart. And with the promise of the Internet glistening on the horizon, Duste worked with a few passionate technologists to build another demo to show Pottruck and Chuck Schwab that they could do TeleBroker on the Web. When Schwab saw the demo, he was dumbfounded. "I fell off my chair," he later told *Fortune*.[1] Duste and his colleagues didn't write an elaborate strategy paper on how the Web would transform investing. Instead they gave Schwab and Pottruck a first-person, hands-on experience of Web trading. Pottruck immediately set up a Web-trading unit called e.Schwab. It was up and running on the Web by mid-1996 and attracted 25,000 customers in its first two weeks.

But as the Web blossomed, cracks in the e.Schwab business model started to appear. Customers who used e.Schwab were given a 40 percent discount off the company's usual charges, but Schwab was still twice as expensive as E*TRADE. And there was another catch: Schwab's online clients were not allowed to call Schwab's phone representatives or visit its branches—they had to agree to do all their business over the Web. A traditional Schwab customer who wanted to trade online had to set up a new account.

Pottruck wanted to do away with this dual structure, but there was a lot of concern among the senior officers that doing so would hammer profits. They thought that encouraging traditional customers to trade online would cannibalize transaction fees. Conversely, it was feared that the fees generated by new online customers wouldn't be sufficient to cover the cost of in-person service at Schwab branches or phone help from Schwab's call centers.

But once again, the desire to do right by the customer overcame the initial concern over cannibalization. As one senior executive put it:

> We asked ourselves whether Internet trading was the right thing to do for the customer—and the answer was "yes." It would mean better information, more timely information, quicker access to their account, and so on. Once this was clear, we knew we had to make the move sooner rather than later. We couldn't wait until we had an ironclad business case. It's our responsibility, not the customer's, to figure out how to make money in the new Internet business model.

In January 1998, Web trading was opened up to all Schwab customers and e.Schwab was rechristened schwab.com. By the end of the year, 61 percent of all Schwab's trades were being completed over the Web. Between the first quarter of 1998 and the first quarter of 1999, Schwab gained nearly one million new customers (almost all of them online), commissions increased 60 percent, online assets doubled, and total assets were up 33 percent.

Could Schwab have beaten Merrill Lynch and other traditional brokers to the Web without a succession of earlier mini-innovations? Most at Schwab doubt it. Customer behavior and business concepts seldom get changed in one fell swoop. Schwab's relentless pursuit of a better customer experience had once again paved the way for a radical rebirth of the company's strategy.

OVERCOMING ORTHODOXY

Success typically turns beliefs into unquestioned orthodoxy. Yet unlike most companies, Schwab has again and again challenged its deep-seated beliefs. For example, since the company's founding, Schwab has had an aversion to giving advice and hawking proprietary products. As a result, the company has avoided the kind of conflict-of-interest dilemmas that have bedeviled other investment firms. Schwab's image of studied neutrality has long been highly valued by customers. But a wave of newbie customers, who are far less sophisticated than Schwab's original high-volume traders, has forced the company to revisit this particular bit of dogma.

forever in flux.

Explains Pottruck:

For a long time we thought advice was a self-serving path. That was the reality we saw in the rest of the investing industry. Advice always had a self-serving motive, whether it was to push proprietary products or to get paid for the trade. So we said, "We don't give advice." We no longer have that luxury. Today, in excess of 50 percent of our new customers have no investing experience. They don't want us to just give them a brochure.

Schwab was able to move beyond the advice/neutrality impasse only once it realized that this was a false dichotomy—that values and habits could be separated. Says Art Shaw:

Giving advice has nothing to do with our values, but avoiding conflict of interest does. Advice had a lot of connotations from the world we left behind—we had an allergic reaction to advice. So we had to ask a new question: "How do you give advice without a conflict of interest?"

So in 1994, Schwab launched AdvisorSource, a network of some of its independent money managers to which it began to refer customers who felt they needed counsel. The company has also launched several index-linked funds under the Schwab brand name, a move that lets Schwab keep more mutual fund profit in-house, but keeps the firm out of the stock-picking game. And it provides investment research tools on the Web as a form of self-directed advice.

LESSONS FROM A GRAY-HAIRED REVOLUTIONARY

As in the case of Enron and GE Capital, business concept innovation at Charles Schwab rests on a few foundations:

- _Outrageously ambitious growth objectives_ that are simply unattainable without business concept innovation.

- _Working from the customer in,_ rather than from your existing processes and offerings out.

- An _innovation meritocracy_ where great ideas win out, no matter where they come from.

- _Rapid experimentation and prototyping_ that lets innovators test and define new ideas at a speed that leaves traditional competitors breathless.

- A _loose and evolving definition of the service offering,_ which ensures that Schwab doesn't get boxed in by its own orthodoxies.

CISCO: PAC-MAN OF THE INTERNET

Cisco Systems is still a teenager, but gray hair comes early when you're

Cisco's markets for networking and Internet equipment are

living on Internet time. Less than nine years after going public in 1990, its market capitalization reached the $100 billion mark–a quicker run to that stratospheric valuation than any other company before it. By early 2000, it boasted a market cap of more than $500 billion, making it the most valuable company in the S&P 500 (ahead of Microsoft and GE). Not bad for a company formed by a husband and wife team at Stanford University.

Cisco's experience with accelerated strategy life cycles is a precursor of what many other companies will face as frenetic change sweeps through their industries as well. At a December 1998 investment conference, Cisco CEO John Chambers warned a roomful of CEOs and portfolio managers of the Internet's business challenges:

> *The Internet's pace is so fast. Changes here that take one or two years . . . used to take decades in other industries. You have to make change a part of your culture. Those that don't will simply be left behind. The market is going to change so quickly that if you don't have your finger on the pulse of the customer, what you thought was added-value will quickly become commoditized.*

He speaks from experience. Cisco's markets for networking and Internet equipment are forever in flux. No matter how much money Cisco pumps into R&D ($1.5 billion in fiscal 1999), its internal efforts can generate only two–thirds of the products that it needs. There is just too much innovation going on *outside* in the world of Internet communications for Cisco to cover all the bases *inside*. So out of necessity, Cisco has perfected the art of using acquisition as an engine of strategic renewal. It's made more than 45 acquisitions since 1993. Disproving the old adage that you can't buy your way to prosperity, probably as much as half of Cisco's $12 billion in revenues is derived from the products of companies it has acquired. Cisco constantly refreshes its products and strategies by gobbling up companies, Pac–Man-like, that possess complementary business concepts and leading–edge technologies. Cisco doesn't fight the revolutionaries, it buys them.

FROM ROUTER TO INTERNET ARMS MERCHANT

Cisco holds the number one or number two market share spot in nearly all the product areas in which it competes—such as routers, switches, remote access devices, and other networking equipment. Yet Cisco started as a one–product company selling routers that acted as electronic mailmen in large corporate computer networks. It then broadened into other areas, mostly by acquiring hot start–ups and pushing their products through its finely honed distribution channels. It also grew with the Internet, which was built with Cisco routers. Today nearly 85 percent of Internet traffic travels over Cisco hardware at some point. Indeed, if the Internet revolution is akin to the industrial revolution, then routers and switches are the steam engines of the new economy. Cisco's transformation from a one-product company to a data communications kingpin has placed it in elite company—only a handful of Silicon Valley start-ups, Intel and Hewlett-Packard among them, have managed to outlive their first strategy.

Michelangelo (Mike) Volpi, Cisco's 34-year-old head of business development, explains the company's evolution:

> *We've redefined this company many times over. We were a router company, then we were a networking company, and now, fundamentally, we are a communications company. I think one of the competencies of Cisco is to deal with that type of change pretty regularly. We don't compete today with the same people that we competed with 10 years ago, or even 5 years ago.*

Like other gray-haired revolutionaries, Cisco has been willing to cannibalize its existing revenues. Says one executive: "If we don't make it easy for our customers to replace our own products with newer technologies, our competition will do it for us."

Before Cisco could challenge the likes of Lucent and Nortel, it had to fend off a rabble of smaller competitors, that, like Cisco, specialized in hardware for data communications. The first router was built in 1982 by a company called Bridge Communications, which later was bought by Cisco's rival, 3Com. Fortunately for Cisco, 3Com was too preoccupied with its existing network adapter card business to pay much attention to the nascent router market, giving Cisco the chance to steal the show. When two other Cisco rivals merged to form Bay Networks in 1994, Bay had more revenue than Cisco and was the leader in the hot new market for devices called switches. Yet by the time Bay was acquired by Nortel in 1998, Cisco's revenues were nearly four times as large as Bay's, and it had usurped the top spot in switches. Despite starting with similar advantages in one of the most dynamic industries in history, Cisco's competitors have fallen short. How does Cisco repeatedly avoid the stumbling blocks that have given others bloody knees? Simple: it doesn't allow itself to fall in love with any particular technology.

A TECHNOLOGY AGNOSTIC

Despite the fact that Cisco bills itself as a high-tech superpower, it is fundamentally not a technology company. Unlike most of its competitors in Silicon Valley, Cisco isn't trying to promote one technology at the expense of others or to build some quasi monopoly around a unique standard. Explains Volpi:

We've let go of the belief that our core asset is having two photons that do this or that. Our core assets are our ability to move fast, satisfy customer needs, be first to market, and leverage our distribution channel. Once those assets are in place, then much of technology development can effectively be outsourced, just like we might outsource some basic manufacturing.

When you're a technology agnostic like Cisco, there's no such thing as a "disruptive" technology. Every technology is simply and honestly evaluated on its merits.

OUTSOURCING INNOVATION

Cisco's Pac-Man-like acquisition process has played a central role in allowing the company to stay relevant in the midst of revolutionary change. Cisco's acquisition strategy was born as a reaction to an industry–wide technology shift. Besides routers, the other main component of corporate networks in the early 1990s was the hub. Hubs are the boxes in office wiring closets to which all the computers on a floor or in a particular location get connected. Cisco made the routers and worked in partnership with companies that made hubs. But then along came switches, which had half the intelligence of a router but were twice as fast as a hub and threatened both. A 1995 magazine article recounts Cisco losing a $10 million order to an upstart switch company. When Chambers asked the customer what he could do to get back that business, the reply was, "Start making switches."[2] All of a sudden, Cisco realized it needed to get into this new market, even if it meant competing with its hub partners. It could no longer be just a router company.

While Cisco had the engineering talent to build a switch on its own, it didn't have the time. The technology was moving so fast that in the two years it would take Cisco to develop its own switch someone else would undoubtedly run away with the market. So Cisco decided to do something it had never done before: buy instead of build. In 1993 Cisco made its first acquisition for $95 million in stock. Crescendo Communications was a switch company with 100 employees at the time (while Cisco had 1,000). In effect, Cisco was saying that its loyalty was to customers and profits, not products, and that its future lay with whatever technology could bring in the most revenue. With the purchase of Crescendo, the outlines of Cisco's approach to innovation began to take shape: control the customer interface, be technology–neutral, and outsource (or, more accurately, import) innovation by acquiring young companies with new technologies and business concepts.

Cisco's offer to the management and shareholders of target companies was simple: we'll double or triple your underlying growth rate by pumping your products and technology through our well–oiled distribution channels. In return you'll get a chunk of rapidly appreciating Cisco stock. This was an increasing returns game for Cisco. As its product line broadened through acquisitions, the company became a one–stop shop for networking gear. This strengthened the company's position with major customers who were happy to have someone else wrestle with the Byzantine problems of equipment integration. Cisco's pole position with customers allowed it, in turn, to get better leverage out of its acquisitions than could its competitors. Hence, Cisco could afford to outbid competitors for hot, young companies, thus ensuring that it always had the latest and best technology to offer customers.

s routine as product development might be in other companies.

Rather than try to predict which of several technologies might finally win out, Cisco tried to keep a finger in every pie. In the mid-1990s, for instance, there was a rancorous debate about which technology would be used by switches in the future. The two candidates were gigabit Ethernet and ATM (asynchronous transfer mode). Regular Ethernet was the standard transmission protocol for most corporate networks. The hubs from networking's earliest days were based on Ethernet technology, as were the switches that replaced the hubs and the fast Ethernet switches that were beginning to replace first-generation switches. Gigabit Ethernet would be 1,000 times faster than regular Ethernet. The only problem was that the entire networking industry was obsessed with a completely different technology invented by the telephone companies, called ATM.

ATM had been the early odds-on favorite because it, too, was faster and more reliable than regular Ethernet, as well as being compatible with the voice networks owned by the telcos. So one of Cisco's early acquisitions was a small company that was developing ATM switches for corporate networks. But by 1996, ATM was starting to look like the wrong technology, at least for corporate networks. So Cisco hedged its bet by ponying up $220 million for Granite Systems, a three-month-old gigabit Ethernet start-up formed by Andy Bechtolsheim, co-founder of Sun Microsystems.

Like many other founders who had sold their companies to Cisco, Bechtolsheim realized the power of Cisco's customer-oriented business model. As he puts it, "It is easier for a customer to buy a network from one supplier than to guess which start-up is going to survive." And it is easier for Cisco to let the market sort out the "right" technology and then make a speedy acquisition than to make irreversible bets years earlier about which technology might ultimately win in which markets.

Cisco knows that the price for being late to market is often permanent foreclosure. The firm learned that lesson the hard way when its competitor Ascend Communications (now part of Lucent) came out with an ISDN product several months ahead of Cisco and never ceded its leadership. "Given the speed with which new markets take off," says Bechtolsheim, "if you are six months late you can lose half-a-billion dollars." Indeed, in 1998 the size of the gigabit Ethernet market was just $100 million. The following year, it was more than 10 times bigger!

For all these reasons, Cisco has worked to make acquisition a routine process, as routine as product development might be in other companies. Cisco's business-buying group goes by the name "Acquisitions and Devel-

When compared with its geek-filled, technology-worshipping competitors,

Cisco's business model is contrarian to the core.

opment," or "A&D," and it is treated as a complement to R&D. Volpi, the head of A&D, started working at Cisco when he was 26 and has been involved in all but two of Cisco's acquisitions. He reflects on A&D's role:

In a constantly changing market, acquisitions give us a tremendous amount of flexibility because we do not have to play a guessing game about what products we will need. We don't have to plan 18 months ahead of time to determine that we need to be in a market segment, then start product development, and hope we have the right one. But rather we can decide in three weeks that we want to be in that market segment.

In this way, Cisco is able to readily tap into Silicon Valley's abundant market for innovative start-ups and bring the best ones inside. The company does not care where innovation comes from. "There is no 'Not Invented Here' syndrome at Cisco," says Bechtolsheim. "If they want to get into an area, they buy a company."

The time between initial contact and the closing of a deal is usually less than three months. "It takes longer to print the agreements at this point than to negotiate them," Volpi once told *Corporate Finance*.[3] There is a set of well-rehearsed procedures for selecting acquisition candidates, negotiating the deals, and then integrating the companies into Cisco. Leads can come from salespeople, venture capitalists, investment bankers, or even customers. Once an agreement is reached, Cisco sends in an experienced team to manage the integration process. One team member will create a blitzkrieg program for training the acquired company's sales force. Another will focus on integrating the customer support organizations, and others will focus on engineering, marketing, manufacturing, e-mail systems, and back-office functions.

The integration process is made easier by the fact that the acquisitions are friendly, and the CEO of the acquired company almost always stays on with Cisco. Senior VP Howard Charney, the former CEO of Grand Junction Networks, a Cisco acquisition, remembers how he was seduced to sign on:

Even though at moments it was painful, what saved it was that they wanted us to become bigger by two orders of magnitude. Our engineers could see we really had the potential to go from 5 percent market share to 25 percent. And Chambers treated me like a peer. He asked me what I thought and never talked down to me. Despite differ-

ences in size, Cisco treats every acquisition like a merger of equals. Cisco delivered on its promise.

Cisco's Pac–Man approach to innovation helps the company import entrepreneurial talent as well as new technologies. About 20 percent of Cisco's 24,000 employees come from acquisitions, so the company is littered with experienced entrepreneurs who serve as a healthy source of genetic diversity. Many of Cisco's senior executives and thought leaders—including Bechtolsheim, Charney, chief technology officer Judy Estrin, and two of the four major division heads—come from acquired companies. In its acquisition of StrataCom, Cisco paid over $3 million for each of its 1,200 employees. When you pay this much for new people, you're inclined to listen to them.

The sheer fact that Cisco is hiring so many new people every year also reinforces a culture of change. In 1996, when Cisco was still adding more than 50 percent to its head count annually, Chambers told *Upside*:

> *Here at Cisco we have a culture [that] is evolving regularly. [When] you're adding a 50 to 60 percent increase in people per year, it's fairly easy to evolve your culture in that environment because you're bringing in a lot of new ideas and a lot of new approaches. It's much more difficult for the majority of people who have been with [a] company for a very, very long period of time. Your organization is not expanding and your leaders are the same leaders who led through a different era."*[4]

To the extent there is an "old guard" at Cisco, it regularly gets overwhelmed by the new guard, thanks to the company's many acquisitions.

An absolute devotion to customers is another critical element of Cisco's approach to innovation. "At Cisco we work to get purchase orders from our customers," says Volpi, "not to build fantastic technology." Regular and intense communication with leading–edge customers helps Cisco define its own innovation agenda. Adds Bechtolsheim:

> *One of the fundamental advantages at Cisco is that we always order our most urgent priorities based on customer demand and engineering feedback. There is less need for visionaries because we are responding to customer needs. If our beliefs as engineers intersect with what we are hearing from customers, we know we have a home run.*

How very odd that a company born in Silicon Valley and filled with engineers should not describe itself as a technology company. How strange that those engineers should humble themselves and listen, really listen, to customers. When compared with its geek–filled, technology–worshipping competitors, Cisco's business model is contrarian to the core.

Being the world's leading data networking company isn't enough for Cisco. The company is intent on transforming itself yet once again, from a builder of data networks to a constructor of communications networks that combine data, voice, and video. In doing so, its goal is to move from being the leader of the $30 billion data networking market to a major contender in the $300 billion telecommunications equipment market dominated by the likes of Lucent Technologies, Siemens, Alcatel, and Nortel Networks. And as networking invades the home, Cisco wants to play there too. Says CEO Chambers, "I want Cisco to be a dynasty. I think it can be a company that changes the world."[5]

LESSONS FROM A GRAY-HAIRED REVOLUTIONARY

As a stock market supernova and one of the companies at the heart of the new economy, Cisco's Pac–Man style of innovation is rife with lessons for other companies intent on staying relevant in a topsy–turvy world:

- Recognize that however successful your company is as an innovator, *much of the innovation that will shape the future of your industry will occur outside the boundaries of your organization.*

- View the thousands of start–ups that get created every year *not as competitors* to be feared, *but as potential sources of innovation to be exploited.* Co–opt the insurgents.

- Understand that the ultimate value of an acquisition may not be in its technology or products, but in the *contribution it makes to genetic diversity and entrepreneurial energy.*

- Remember that in a fast–changing world, *an allegiance to a single technology or to one particular business concept will stifle innovation and ultimately kill the company.*

Cisco is not alone in in–sourcing innovation through acquisitions. But although companies such as Intel, Microsoft, and Amazon.com have used acquisitions to fill product gaps and enter new businesses, none have used acquisitions to constantly redefine their core business concepts as successfully as Cisco.

STYLE AND SUBSTANCE

Enron, Schwab, and Cisco have all shown the ability to continually reinvent both themselves and their industries. Yet, while there are many common elements to their successes as revolutionaries—outsized aspirations, a willingness to seek out and listen to new voices, flexible organizational boundaries—there are also unique differences in their innovation *styles.*

In Enron's fertile-fields style of innovation, the seeds of its core competencies are regularly planted in new markets. Top management sees its job as cultivating the growth of entirely new markets and industries. Talent naturally flows to where crop yields (the potential for wealth creation) are

Schwab's spiral-staircase style of innovation is based on the never-ending pursuit of better solutions for its investor-customers.

highest. Like independent farmers who sell through a co-op, individual entrepreneurs benefit personally from their wealth-creating efforts, yet can also exploit the scope of a large organization. Organizational structure is loose and evolves organically. There is only a loose conception of what "business" the company is in.

Schwab's spiral-staircase style of innovation is based on the never-ending pursuit of better solutions for its investor-customers. Relentless innovation carries the company round and round the spiral staircase as it climbs toward ever-higher levels of customer satisfaction and delight. While innovation is more focused at Schwab than it is at Enron, Schwab's head-over-heels love affair with its customers has spurred a string of medium-scale innovations that have dramatically changed the company's underlying business model. In spiral-staircase-style innovation, most innovations get integrated into the company's existing service delivery system. There is a culture of constant tinkering and experimentation. Any idea for radically improving the customer experience finds a ready audience, and the most innovative customer champions are visibly rewarded.

Cisco's Pac-Man model of innovation is equally distinct. Given the speed at which technology changes in the world of the Internet, Cisco has had little choice but to learn how to import innovation. Indeed, Cisco has been as good at exploiting the *external* market for innovation as Enron has been at exploiting its *internal* market for new ideas. For this style of innovation to work, a company must itself be located near a hotbed of innovation and must pay close attention to the trajectory of tiny start-ups.

Fertile fields, the spiral staircase, Pac-Man—these innovation styles are not entirely distinct. In each case, rule-busting ideas are the most respected currency of the realm.

But the hard work of turning incumbents into gray-haired revolutionaries is not just about picking an innovation style but also about building a radical, revolutionary impulse deep within the organization. Gray-haired revolutionaries have many qualities in common. These qualities suggest that there is a set of "design rules" for building companies capable of radical, perpetual innovation. It is to these design rules that we now turn our attention.

MAKE NO MISTAKE, INCUMBENTS CAN BE REVOLUTIONARIES.

DESIGN RULES FOR INNOVATION

WATCH A FLOCK OF GEESE TURNING
and swooping in flight, undeterred by wind, obstacles, and distance. There is no grand vizier goose, no chairman of the gaggle. They can't call ahead for a weather report. They can't predict what obstacles they will meet. They don't know which of their number will expire in flight. Yet their course is true. And they are a flock. Complexity theorists describe this, and the many other examples of spontaneous harmony in the world around us, as *order without careful crafting* or *order for free*. The intricate play of the many markets that make up the global economy, the vibrant diversity of the Internet, the behavior of a colony of ants, that winged arrow of geese—these are just a few instances in which order seems to have emerged in the absence of any central authority. All of them have something to teach us about how revolutionary strategies should emerge in a chaotic and ever-changing world. Complexity theorists have demonstrated that by creating the right set of preconditions, one can provoke the emergence of highly ordered things—maybe even things such as revolutionary business concepts.

Order emerges out of deep but simple rules. Craig Reynolds has shown that with three simple rules, one can simulate the behavior of a flock of birds in flight.[1] Too many executives have been trying to design flight plans for their far-flung flock rather than working to create the conditions that would help their brood get off the ground and on their way to new and distant shores. They have spent too much time working on "the strategy" and not enough time working to create the preconditions out of which new wealth-creating strategies are likely to emerge.

Assembling grand strategies in the corporate tower is a futile undertaking in the age of revolution. This doesn't mean that top management is irrelevant. Far from it. But top management's job isn't to build strategies. Its job is to build an organization that is capable of continuously spawning cool, new business concepts. Its contribution is to design the context rather than invent the content. Its role is to operationalize the design rules for creating a deeply innovative organization—the design rules we see at work in our gray-haired revolutionaries.

So what are the rules for building habitually and perpetually innovative organizations?

DESIGN RULE #1: UNREASONABLE EXPECTATIONS

Listen to senior executives from some gray-haired revolutionaries:

> *GE Capital:* It is expected that we will grow our earnings 20 percent per year or more. When you have objectives that are that outlandish, it forces you to think very differently about your opportunities. If one guy has a 10 percent target and the other has a 20 percent target, the second guy is going to do different things.

> *Charles Schwab:* We are a growth company. This is our charter. Every year we feel we have to grow 20 percent. Every year you have to say that last year is over, and we're starting from zero. This creates an incredible desire to innovate.

> *Enron:* We are always looking for the next elephant—the next huge business we can create. That's what keeps us awake at night. Every new thing we do starts out with a completely unrealistic expectation.

NO COMPANY OUTPERFORMS ITS ASPIRATIONS.

Here's an experiment. Do a quick poll of 25 people in the middle of your organization. Ask them this question: "What do you believe would be a reasonable expectation for top-line growth this year?" Compute the average answer—is it 20

BELIEFS
SET THE UPPER LIMIT
ON WHAT'S POSSIBLE.

percent, 30 percent, or something substantially less ambitious? It is tautological but true: no company outperforms its aspirations. If most of your colleagues believe you are in a 5 or 10 percent growth business, you are. Their beliefs set the upper limit on what's possible. No wonder Enron, GE Capital, and Schwab are radical rule breakers—they subscribe to radical goals.

I meet few individuals who truly believe their organization should be able to grow three or four times as fast as the industry average. Research across 20 industries over the past 10 years shows that only 1 company out of 10 managed to grow at double its industry average. I'm willing to bet that no more than 1 company out of 10 has set itself the *goal* of growing at twice the industry average. And although a bold aspiration won't by itself produce a multitude of nonconformist strategies, its absence always yields bland, me–too strategies.

Whether the objective is growth in revenue, earnings, or efficiency, nonlinear innovation begins with unreasonable goals. Likewise, strategy convergence, that pernicious margin killer, is the product of expectations convergence across an industry. I'll bet there aren't many people at American Airlines who believe their company can grow three times faster than United Airlines. In most companies, the majority of individuals believe there is some preordained, and typically uninspiring, "industry" growth rate. Growing as fast as one's mediocre peers is deemed good enough. Only when people subscribe to unreasonable goals will they start searching for breakthrough ideas.

Convincing people in an organization that it is reasonable to strive for unreasonable goals is tricky. Mere exhortation is not enough. You have to demonstrate that it's actually *possible* to dramatically outperform the average—and you have to do this with real examples. Otherwise, the aspiration has no credibility. For example, ask your colleagues what they would do if they were in the lettuce business. You can't put a Pentium chip in a head of lettuce. It's not easy to digitize green leaves and send them zipping over the Internet. Yet thanks to Fresh Express and a few other pioneers, the market for prewashed, precut, prepackaged lettuce (a salad in a bag) grew from nothing in the late 1980s to $1.4 billion by 1999. Send an e-mail to everyone you know in your com-

> ## "Table-ready lettuce. $1.4 billion. If someone can do this with a vegetable, what the hell is our excuse?"

pany: "Table-ready lettuce. $1.4 billion. If someone can do this with a vegetable, what the hell is our excuse?" Never, ever believe you are in a mature industry. There are no mature industries, only mature managers who unthinkingly accept someone else's definition of what's possible. Be unreasonable!

One caveat: if you push for unreasonable growth goals, some folks in your organization will search for shortcuts—a mega-acquisition, deep price cuts, rebates. Don't let them get away with it. Only nonlinear innovation will drive long-term wealth creation.

DESIGN RULE #2: ELASTIC BUSINESS DEFINITION

Gray-haired revolutionaries aren't bound by a narrow self-concept. Their opportunity horizon is expansive and forever changing:

> *GE Capital:* We don't talk about market share because when people talk about market share it means they are defining their business too narrowly.

> *Charles Schwab:* There are very few people here who feel they have a narrow business charter and have to defend their business against new models that will undermine those businesses.

> *Enron:* We've never viewed Enron as just an energy company. We're pretty good at creating new products and services around our high-tech trading and risk management skills.

Who are we? This is, perhaps, the most fundamental question a company's employees and executives can ask themselves. How they answer it determines whether or not the company searches for unconventional opportunities. Too many companies define themselves by what they *do,* rather than by what they *know* (their core competencies) and what they *own* (their strategic assets). A business school that views itself first and foremost as a degree–granting institution will never take seriously the opportunity to use the Internet for on–demand training of midcareer executives. But if the august professors define their institution by its competencies (curriculum development and knowledge transfer) and its assets (a respected brand name), new opportunities open up.

Virgin spans industries as diverse as air travel, packaged holidays, music retailing, banking, and radio broadcasting. Says Virgin's Gordon McCallum, head of business development, "There is no assumption about what business Virgin should be in or shouldn't be in." Yet Virgin will enter an industry only if it believes it can (a) challenge existing rules, (b) give customers a better break, (c) be more entertaining, and (d) put a thumb in the eye of complacent incumbents. Says McCallum, "The culture is one of why not, rather than why."

Like Virgin, Disney owns a brand that transcends any particular business. Judson Green, chairman of Disney Attractions, doesn't define his business as "theme parks" but as "three–dimensional entertainment." Disney's success with cruise ships, Broadway shows, mini–theme parks, and a host of other ventures evinces an elastic business definition.

An elastic business definition helps to reduce the protectionist instincts of executives worried about cannibalization. At GE Capital, the senior executives who run the company's major business spend as much as 50 percent of their time looking for opportunities *outside* the boundaries of the business they're managing. Every business leader is assumed to be a business development officer for the entire company. Is that how divisional vice presidents feel in *your* company? Is that how *you* feel? Parochialism is one of innovation's most deadly enemies. It's not only the CEO who needs an elastic definition of business boundaries—so does every single employee.

To drive this point home, chairman and CEO Jack Welch has asked GE's business heads to redefine their markets so that each business has less than a 10 percent share of its market. After spending years driving home the message that a business needs to be number one or two in its industry to survive, GE's top management is now telling its business leaders that only companies with expansive business boundaries will grow faster than their competitors. In a similar way, Schwab's employees don't see their company as the undisputed leader in discount brokerage, but as having captured only about 1 percent of the accumulated savings of American investors.

An elastic business concept isn't a license for ill-conceived diversification. Entering a business where one's competencies don't count for much is a recipe for a big write-off. Disney's Judson Green notes, "You can look back over time at everything Disney has done and put it into two buckets: the stuff that leverages the Disney brand and the stuff that isn't really related to the Disney franchise. We haven't done very well in the latter stuff." In the absence of a clear plan for leveraging competencies and assets, an elastic business definition is an accident waiting to happen.

So start asking your colleagues, Who are we? Where does our opportunity horizon begin and end? What do we currently regard as "out of scope"? Get a few people together and start redefining your company in terms of what it knows and what it owns, rather than what it does. This will help you stitch some elastic into your company's sense of self.

DESIGN RULE #3: A CAUSE, NOT A BUSINESS

Gray-haired revolutionaries draw much of their strength from their allegiance to a cause that goes beyond growth, profits, or even personal wealth accumulation—a cause that goes beyond themselves, a cause that is truly noble. Listen to what they say:

> *Charles Schwab:* Around here, we think we're curing cancer.

> *Virgin Atlantic:* Our business is about creating memorable moments for our customers.

> *Enron:* We always felt we were on a mission. We were morally outraged that so much of the energy business was a government-mandated monopoly. You were hostage as a customer. We were always on the side the angels. The people who were against us were always the entrenched interests.

Without a transcendent purpose, individuals will lack the courage to *behave* like revolutionaries. Gray-haired revolutionaries must periodically shed their skin. Every time they abandon a decaying strategy or jettison an out-of-date belief, they leave a bit of themselves behind. The most unsettling thing about business concept innovation is the need to write off one's own depreciating intellectual capital. To a great extent, an individual's worth in an organization is determined by what he or she knows. Business concept innovation changes the price tag on every bit of knowledge in the firm. Some knowledge becomes more valuable, and other knowledge less so.

Perhaps even more distressing is that business concept innovation often undercuts the value of an individual's accumulated social capital. Think, for example, of a car company bigwig who's spent years schmoozing with car dealers. Countless boozy dinners, boondoggles in Hawaii with star dealers, a few hundred rounds of golf—and now you're going to tell this person that, in some brave new world, traditional dealers may be a handicap rather than an asset? Good luck. It's hard enough to write off some of what we know; it's even harder to watch social relationships fray under the strain of a radical new strategy.

Any individual poised between a familiar but tattered business model and a lustrous but untested business concept is bound to ask a few questions: Will my skills and my relationships be as valuable in this new world as they were in the old? How much will I be asked to unlearn? How much effort will it take for me to adapt myself to a new order of things? These are genuine, heartfelt questions. And, for the most part, they can't be answered in advance. The courage to leave some of oneself behind and strike off for parts unknown comes not from some banal assurance that "change is good" but from a devotion to a wholly worthwhile cause.

Where did Schwab get the courage to migrate its business model to the Web, knowing that the move would force it to slash prices by up to 60 percent and more? Think about how your company would react if it were faced with this kind of decision. (We know how Merrill Lynch reacted. It denied, denied, denied, then debated, debated, debated, and, finally, decided.) In most companies there would be months, perhaps years, of savage debate. Factions would form, positions would harden. The specter of cannibalization would roam the hallways, striking fear into fainthearted executives. All this was avoided at Schwab for a single, simple reason—online trading was the right thing to do for customers.

When asked to describe the cause that imbues his colleagues with their revolutionary fervor, David Pottruck, president and co-CEO of Charles Schwab, says this: "We are the guardians of our customers' financial dreams." Think about that. When was the last time a bank teller looked like the guardian of *your* financial dreams? It's not surprising that Schwab regularly turns itself inside out on behalf of customers. After all, how many companies do you know that list "empathy" as one of their core values?

However mundane a company's products or services, they must be infused with a sense of transcendent purpose. This can't be a thin coating of sickly sweet sentiment; instead, it must come from the part of every human being that yearns to make the world a bit better off. Roy Disney, Disney's vice chairman, knows why his company is in business:

> *You go talk to anyone who works in the parks, and they're all moved by the chance to make a difference in people's lives. We all feel very much the same. You do a good movie and you watch people walk out of the theatre with more hope in their lives. I get letters every once in a while from folks who just say, "Thanks for what you have done in my life."*

What we need is not an economy of hands or heads, but an economy of hearts. Every employee should feel that he or she is contributing to something that will actually make a genuine and positive difference.

For most of the industrial age, employees were valued only for their muscle power. Henry Ford is reputed to have once asked, "Why is it that whenever I ask for a pair of hands, a brain comes attached?" Henry wanted robots, but they hadn't yet been invented. Today, we celebrate our enlightenment. We live in the "knowledge" economy. We *want* employees to bring their brains to work. Yet if we rob them of the chance to feel they are working on something that really *matters*, are we really so enlightened? Brainpower versus muscle power, neurons versus tendons—is that really such a big leap forward? Is that what distinguishes us from machines—our slightly more advanced cognitive abilities? What we need is not an economy of hands or heads, but an economy of hearts. Every employee should feel that he or she is contributing to something that will actually make a genuine and positive difference in the lives of customers and colleagues.

For too many employees, the return on emotional equity is close to zero. They have nothing to commit to other than the success of their own career. Why is it that the very essence of our humanity, our desire to reach beyond ourselves, to touch others, to do something that *matters*, to leave the world just a little bit better, is so often denied at work? After all, most people devote more of their waking hours to work than to home, family, community, and faith combined. To succeed in the age of revolution, a company must give its members a reason to bring *all* of their humanity to work. Viktor Frankl, the great Austrian psychiatrist, said it well: "For success, like happiness, cannot be pursued; it must ensue . . . as the unintended side–effect of one's personal dedication to a cause greater than oneself."[2]

So ask yourself, What are you actually working *for*? What kind of difference would you like to make? Who will thank you, I mean *really* thank you, if you succeed? Do you have a calling, or do you just have a job?

DESIGN RULE #4: NEW VOICES

If senior management wants revolutionary strategies, it must learn to listen to revolutionary voices:

GE Capital: We put together a young team—all of them under 30—and asked them to come back and tell us where the opportunities were.

Virgin: We typically pick people from outside an industry. The basic recruiting model is bright graduates who come from outside the industry.

Look at Ted Turner and broadcast news (CNN), Anita Roddick and cosmetics (The Body Shop), Sir Richard Branson and the airline business (Virgin Atlantic), Jim Clark and health care (Healtheon), Jeff Bezos and retailing (Amazon.com), and Pierre Omidyar and auctions (eBay). More often than not, industries get reinvented by outsiders—by newcomers free from the prejudices of industry veterans. Yet in most companies strategy is the preserve of the old guard. Strategy conversations have the same 10 people talking to the same 10 people year after year. No wonder the strategies that emerge are dull as dishwater.

What, after all, do the top 20 or 30 executives in a company have to learn from each other? They've been talking at each other for years—their positions are well rehearsed, they can finish each other's sentences. What is required is not a cohort of wise elders or a bevy of planners, but a tap-root sunk deep into the organization. Put simply, without new voices in the strategy conversation, the chance for industry revolution is nil.

There are revolutionaries in your company. But all too often there is no process that lets them be heard. They are isolated and impotent, disconnected from others who share their passions. Their voices are muffled by layers of cautious bureaucrats. They are taught to conform rather than to challenge. And too many senior executives secretly long for a more compliant organization rather than a more vociferous one.

Maybe you think I'm being too hard on top management. Consider this: A disaffected employee in one of America's largest companies recently showed me a simple chart that had been distributed throughout the firm as part of a major cultural change program. He pointed out the fact that only "senior executives" were accountable for "creating strategy." Not a word about thinking strategically appeared in the performance criteria for "managers" and "associates." With a single chart, the company

managed to disenfranchise 99.9 percent of its employees, relieving them of any responsibility for business concept innovation and of any involvement in their own future. Ironically, the company expects executives to be "open to learning," unless, of course, it involves a suggestion for a new strategy or business concept. You may wince at this example, but don't kid yourself: this is the reality in all too many companies.

For a company to become or remain the author of industry revolution, top management must give a disproportionate share of voice to three constituencies that are typically underrepresented in conversations about destiny and direction.

The very group with the biggest emotional stake in the future—young people— is typically most likely to be prevented from contributing to the process of strategy creation.

LET YOUTH BE HEARD

The first constituency is young people or, more accurately, those with a youthful perspective. There are 30-year-olds who qualify as "old fogies" and 70-year-olds who are still living in the future. On average, though, young people live closer to the future than those who have more history than future. It is ironic that the very group with the biggest emotional stake in the future—young people—is typically most likely to be prevented from contributing to the process of strategy creation.

While at Siemens Nixdorf, Gerhard Schulmeyer instituted a process of "reverse mentoring" where twenty-somethings got the chance to teach senior executives a thing or two about the future. A few years ago Anheuser-Busch set up a "shadow" management committee whose members were a couple of decades younger than the executives on the "real" management committee. The youngsters get to second-guess their elders on key decisions—from acquisitions to ad campaigns. What's more, they were given their own reporting channel to the board. If you want to get close to the future, listen to someone who's already living there.

LISTEN TO THE PERIPHERY

A second constituency that deserves a larger share of voice is those near the geographic edges of the organization. The capacity for radical innovation increases proportionately with each kilometer you move away from HQ. For an American company, the periphery might be India or Singapore or even the West Coast. For a Japanese company, it might be the UK or the United States. In the late 1990s, pretty much everyone at the top of GM

would have pointed to Brazil as the most innovative place in the GM empire.

At the periphery, people typically have fewer resources. They are forced to be more creative. They are less easily "controlled." Orthodoxy doesn't hold the same sway it does inside the corporate heartland. Freethinkers on the periphery understand well the rationale traditionally offered by rebels in the Chinese hinterland—the emperor is far away and the hills are high. But again, in many companies, the periphery has a scant share of voice in the strategy–making process.

LET NEWCOMERS HAVE THEIR SAY

The third constituency is the newcomers. Particularly useful are newcomers who have arrived from other industries or who have so far managed to escape the stultifying effect of corporate training. Again, they deserve a disproportionate share of voice in any conversation about business innovation. Perhaps your company has looked outside for senior executives with fresh, new perspectives. But how systematically has it sought out the advice of newcomers at all levels who've not yet succumbed to the creeping death of orthodoxy?

Newcomers deserve a disproportionate share of voice in any conversation about business innovation.

It is ironic that companies so often pretend to celebrate "diversity" while systematically stamping it out. The kind of diversity that really counts is not gender diversity or racial diversity or ethnic diversity. It is, instead, a diversity of thinking. An organization that mimics the United Nations in its diversity is of little practical use if corporate training, "best practices," "alignment," and "focus" have destroyed intellectual diversity. In many companies, what could be a rainbow is instead monotonously monochromatic.

Here's a benchmark: the next time someone in your organization convenes a meeting on "strategy" or "innovation," make sure that 50 percent of those who attend have never been asked to attend such a meeting before. Load the meeting with young people, newcomers, and those from the far–flung edges of the company. Do this, and you'll quadruple the chances of coming up with truly revolutionary business concepts.

DESIGN RULE #5: AN OPEN MARKET FOR IDEAS

If you want to free the entrepreneurial spirit inside your company, you're going to have to create a dynamic internal market for ideas. In gray–haired revolutionaries, new ideas are the currency of the realm.

GE Capital: Every week the senior leadership gets together for a half day to talk about new business ideas. Anyone can get on the agenda.

Virgin: Everyone has the chairman's phone number, and he probably gets three calls a day from people wanting to try something new.

SILICON VALLEY IS NOTHING MORE THAN A REFUGEE CAMP FOR

Enron: We've taken down as many of the physical walls as we can. Even if someone isn't on the management or executive committee, they can corner you in the hall and pitch an idea, and this happens all the time. Where we have walls, we've covered them with whiteboards. We just said to people, "Anytime you have an idea, put it on the whiteboard."

Many corporate leaders envy the success of Silicon Valley's entrepreneurs, and dozens of big companies have established venture funds to invest in Silicon Valley start-ups. Yet few executives have thought about how they might bring the creative ethos of the Valley inside their own organizations—how they might ignite the entrepreneurial passions of their own people. They assume the Valley is filled with brilliant visionaries, while their own organizations are filled with witless drones.

What makes Silicon Valley a hothouse of business concept innovation is not some super-race of entrepreneurial visionaries, but the existence of three tightly interconnected "markets": a market for ideas, a market for capital, and a market for talent. Ideas, capital, and talent swirl through Silicon Valley in a frenetic entrepreneurial dance, melding into whatever combinations are most likely to generate new wealth. In most large companies, by contrast, ideas, capital, and talent are inert and indolent. They don't move unless someone orders them to move. Where Silicon Valley is a vibrant market, the average big company is a centrally planned economy. It's no wonder that many Silicon Valley entrepreneurs are corporate exiles. Silicon Valley is nothing more than a refugee camp for revolutionaries who couldn't get a hearing elsewhere.

An average-sized venture-capital firm in Silicon Valley gets as many as *five thousand* unsolicited business plans a year. How many unsolicited business plans does a senior vice president in *your* company get every year? Five? Ten? Zero? There's not much chance of catching the next wave when your corner of the ocean is as placid as a bathtub. So what's the difference between Silicon Valley—or Virgin or GE Capital or Enron—and your company?

For starters, everyone in Silicon Valley understands that radical new ideas are the only way to create new wealth—both corporately and individually. New-economy billionaires such as Jerry Yang, founder of Yahoo!, and Pierre Omidyar, chairman and founder of eBay, didn't get rich by wringing the last ounce of efficiency out of dying business models. Until employees believe that rule-breaking ideas are the surest way to wealth creation, both for their companies and themselves, the market for ideas will remain as barren as a Soviet supermarket in the Brezhnev era.

REVOLUTIONARIES WHO COULDN'T GET A HEARING ELSEWHERE.

There's another difference between Silicon Valley and the corporate hierarchy. In most companies, the marketplace for ideas is a monopsony—there's only one buyer. There's only one place to pitch a new idea—up the chain of command—and all it takes is one *nyet* to kill it. In the Valley, there's no one person who can say no to a new idea. It's rare to find a successful start-up whose initial business plan wasn't rejected by several venture capitalists before finding a sponsor.

What's more, in Silicon Valley there's no prejudice about who is capable of inventing a new business concept. Silicon Valley is a meritocracy. It matters not a whit how old you are, what academic degrees you've earned, where you've worked before, or whether you wear denim or Armani. All that matters is the quality of your thinking and the power of your vision. In the Valley, no one assumes that the next great thing will come from a senior vice president running the last great thing. This is yet another reason the marketplace for ideas is more vibrant in Silicon Valley than in most companies.

Ailsa Petchey was a young flight attendant at Virgin Atlantic Airways. This unlikely entrepreneur got her brain wave when she was helping a friend plan a wedding. Like most brides-to-be, her friend was overwhelmed by a seemingly endless list of to-dos: find the church and a reception hall, arrange the catering, hire the limousine, pick out a dress, outfit the bridesmaids, choose the flowers, plan the honeymoon, send out the invitations, and on and on. Suddenly Ailsa was struck by an idea—why not offer brides-to-be a kind of one-stop wedding planning service?

Petchey took her idea to Sir Richard Branson, who encouraged her to go for it. The result: a 10,500–square–foot bridal emporium, which is Britain's largest, and an array of bridal coordinators who will help arrange everything for the big day. The name of the new business? Virgin Bride, of course. Could this happen in *your* company—could a twenty–something first–line employee buttonhole the chairman and get permission to start a new business? Or, like Louise Kitchin at Enron, could she assemble a team of several hundred to work on a dramatic new business concept without even informing the chief executive?

DESIGN RULE #6: AN OPEN MARKET FOR CAPITAL

Does this sound like the way capital budgeting works in your company?

Virgin: In terms of new projects, we're not in the business of calculating hurdle rates. We don't have hurdle rates. The questions we ask are, Is it sustainable? Is it innovative? Can we make money? If the answer is yes, we'll go into a business. If you think something's off the page as an opportunity, there's no point in saying it's two times off the page.

Venture capitalists are not financially stupid people, but they sure don't think like CFOs. While both may be in the business of funding projects, the market for capital in Silicon Valley isn't anything like the market for capital in large companies. The first difference is access. How easy is it for someone seven levels down in a large company to get a few hundred thousand dollars to try out a new idea? Whether the sum is half a million or $50 million, the investment hurdles usually appear insurmountable to someone far removed from top management.

Historically, roughly two–thirds of Silicon Valley start–ups received their initial funding from "angels"—wealthy individuals who pool their investments to fund new companies. The average angel puts in around $50,000, and the average first–round investment for a start–up is $500,000. That's a rounding error in the annual report of a medium–sized company. Yet how easy would it be for an ardent entrepreneur in your company to find 10 angels willing to invest $50,000 each?

Creative new business ideas seldom make it through traditional financial screens. If financial projections can't be supported with reams of analysis, top management takes a pass. But does it really make sense to set the same hurdles for a small investment in a new experiment as for a large and irreversible investment in an existing business? Why should it be so difficult for someone with an unconventional idea to get the funding needed to build a prototype, design a little market trial, or merely flesh out a business case—particularly when the sum involved is peanuts?

The market for capital works differently in Silicon Valley. Talk to Steve Jurvetson, who funded Hotmail and is one of the Valley's hottest young VCs. Ask him how he evaluates a potential business idea, and this is what he'll tell you:

> The first thing I ask is, Who will care? What kind of difference will this make? Basically, How high is up? I want to fund things that have just about unlimited upside. The second thing I ask is, How will this snowball? How will you scale this thing? What's the mechanism that drives increasing returns? Can it spread like a virus? Finally, I want to know how committed the person is. I never invest in someone who says they're going to do something; I invest in people who say they're already doing something and just want the funding to drive it forward. Passion counts for more than experience.

A VC has a very different notion of what constitutes a business plan than the typical CFO. Again, listen to Jurvetson:

> The business plan is not a contract in the way a budget is. It's a story. It's a story about an opportunity, about the migration path, and how you're going to create and capture value.
>
> I never use Excel at work. I never run the numbers or build financial models. I know the forecast is a delusional view of reality. I basically ignore this. Typically, there are no IRR forecasts or EVA calculations. But I spend a lot of time thinking about how big the thing could be.

The point is this: in most companies the goal of capital budgeting is to make sure the firm never, ever makes a bet–the–business investment that fails to deliver an acceptable return. But in attempting to guarantee that there's never an unexpected downside, the typical capital–budgeting process places an absolute ceiling on the upside.

Venture capitalists start with a very different set of expectations about success and failure. Out of 5,000 ideas, a five–partner VC firm may invest in 10, which it views as a portfolio of options. Out of 10, 5 may be total write–offs, 3 will be modest successes, 1 will double the initial investment, and 1 will return 50 to 100 times the investment. The goal is to make sure you have a big winner, not to make sure there are no losers.

In most large companies someone with a vision of a radical new business model has to go to the defenders of the old business model to get funding. All too often the guy running the old thing has veto power over the new thing. To understand the problem this creates, imagine that every innovator in Silicon Valley had to go to Bill Gates for funding. Pretty soon everyone in the Valley would be working to extend the Windows franchise. Goodbye to the network computer. Goodbye to Java and Jini. Goodbye to PalmPilot. Goodbye to application service providers. And goodbye to most anything else that would challenge Microsoft's current business model.

A VC doesn't ask how one venture plays off against the success of another. Nobody asks, Is this new venture consistent with our existing strategy? Now, consistency is a virtue, but in a world where the life span of the average business concept is longer than a butterfly's but shorter than a dog's, one needs the chance to consider a few opportunities that are *inconsistent* with the current strategy. One of those opportunities might just turn out to be a whole lot more attractive than what you're already working on. But how will you ever know unless you're willing to create a market for capital that puts a bit of cash behind the unorthodox?

DESIGN RULE #7: AN OPEN MARKET FOR TALENT

Every Silicon Valley CEO knows that if you don't give your people truly exhilarating work—and a dramatic upside—they'll start turning in their badges.

> *Enron:* The culture is that if a person wants to move to a new opportunity, they can. The message we've always sent is that the best people belong to the corporation, not a single business leader. Managers can't hang on to people who want to try new things. When it comes to people, possession is definitely not nine-tenths of the law.

Imagine what would happen if 20 percent of your best people up and left in a single year. It happens all the time in Silicon Valley. Valley workers change employers with less angst and anguish than most people change jobs *within* companies. Sure, they jump for money, but more than that, they jump for the chance to work on the *next great thing.* Companies pursuing killer opportunities attract the best talent. As one venture capitalist bluntly put it, "'A' people work on 'A' opportunities."

The market for talent works with a brutal efficiency in Silicon Valley. In the early 1990s, companies such as Apple and Silicon Graphics hemorrhaged talent, while up-and-comers like Cisco and Yahoo! were magnets for the cerebrally gifted. In old economy companies, employees are still viewed as something akin to indentured servants. Divisional vice presidents think they own their key people. And if those people work in South Bend, St. Louis, Des Moines, Nashville, or a hundred other cities that don't have the kind of superheated economy that exists in Silicon Valley, they may not find it so easy to jump ship. But that's no reason to chain ambitious and creative employees to the deck of a slowly sinking business model.

When Enron set out to create a business focused on trading bandwidth, the new management team identified 70 commercially experienced people in other parts of Enron who would be critical to getting a fast start. Of those 70, 64 moved across to the bandwidth business—within one week! If talent isn't this mobile in your company, there's not a chance in hell that it will be able to capture new markets in the age of revolution. There are a couple things that lubricate the market for talent at Enron. At senior levels, job titles are portable—they are attached to individuals, not positions. A vice president in an existing business who moves to a new business is still a vice president, even if he or she spends the first few months reporting to a more junior person. There's also a chance for some serious wealth accumulation, since the founding team in a new Enron business is typically given phantom equity whose value is tied to the venture's success.

Employees have to believe that the best way to win big is to be part of building something new.

At Enron, the market for talent is so fluid that top management uses it as a guide on where to invest. Jeff Skilling, Enron's president and chief operating officer, explains: "If all of a sudden people start moving into a new business area, that's a signal we ought to pour in more resources. Our people search out and find opportunities. People are smarter than we are at the top. They vote with their feet."

In too many companies there's a sense of entitlement among divisional vice presidents and business heads. "Hey, we make all the money; we ought to have the best people," they'll say. But the marginal value a talented employee adds to a business running on autopilot is often a fraction of the value that individual could add to a venture not yet out of the proverbial garage. Why not create an internal auction for talent, where SVPs would have to bid against internal venture managers to attract the best talent? Talent that had been locked up inside moribund businesses could be induced to join swashbuckling venture teams with a combination of attractive salary and phantom equity. After all, if your best people are going to leave for a big upside, why not let them leave for a big upside inside your own company?

A market for talent is more than a list of job openings. Employees have to believe that the best way to win big is to be part of building something new. That means providing incentives for employees who are willing to take a "risk" on something out of the ordinary. It means cele-

Silicon Valley in Royal Dutch/Shell

Royal Dutch/Shell, the Anglo–Dutch oil giant headquartered more than 6,000 miles from Silicon Valley, is seldom mistaken for a lithe and nimble upstart. Shell's globe-trotting managers are famously disciplined, diligent, and methodical; they don't come across as wild-eyed dreamers. But a band of renegades, led by Tim Warren, the director of research and technical services in Shell's largest division, Exploration and Production, has been intent on changing all this. Warren and his team have been working hard to free up the flow of ideas, capital, and talent—to make E&P an innovation-friendly zone. Their initial success suggests that it is possible to imbue a global giant with the kind of damn-the-conventions ethos that permeates Silicon Valley.

By late 1996, it had become apparent to Warren and some of his colleagues that E&P was unlikely to meet its earnings targets without radical new innovation. Looking to stir up some new thinking, Warren had encouraged his people to devote up to 10 percent of their time to "nonlinear" ideas, but the results were less than he'd hoped for. His frustration was the genesis for an entirely new approach to innovation, one both simple and slightly deviant. He gave a small panel of freethinking employees the authority to allocate $20 million to game-changing ideas submitted by their peers. Anyone could submit an idea, and the panel would decide which deserved funding. Proposals would be accepted from anywhere across Shell.

The GameChanger process, as it came to be known, went live in November 1996. At first, the availability of venture funding failed to yield an avalanche of new ideas. Even bright and creative employees long accustomed to working on well-defined technical problems found it difficult to think revolutionary thoughts. Hoping to kick start the process, the GameChanger panel enlisted the help of a team of consultants from Strategos who designed a three-day "Innovation Lab" to help employees develop rule-busting ideas. Seventy-two enthusiastic would-be entrepreneurs showed up for the initial lab, a much larger group than the panel had anticipated. Many were individuals no one would have suspected of harboring entrepreneurial impulses.

In the Innovation Lab, the budding revolutionaries were

encouraged to learn from radical innovations from outside the energy business. They were taught how to identify and challenge industry conventions, how to anticipate and exploit discontinuities of all kinds, and how to leverage Shell's competencies and assets in novel ways. Groups of eight attendees were then seated at round tables in front of networked laptop computers and encouraged to put their new thinking skills to work. Slowly at first, then in a rush, new ideas began to flow through the network. Some ideas attracted a flurry of support from the group; others remained orphans. By the end of the second day, a portfolio of 240 ideas had been generated. Some were for entirely new businesses, and many more were for new approaches within existing businesses.

The attendees then agreed on a set of screening criteria to determine which of the ideas deserved a portion of the seed money. Twelve ideas were nominated for funding, and a volunteer army of supporters coalesced around each one. The nascent venture teams were invited to attend an "Action Lab." Here the teams were taught how to scope out the boundaries of an opportunity, identify potential partnerships, enumerate sources of competitive advantage, and identify the broad financial implications. Next, they were coached in developing 100–day action plans: low-cost, low-risk ways of testing the ideas. Finally, each team presented its story to a "venture board" consisting of the GameChanger panel, a sampling of senior managers, and representatives from Shell Technology Ventures—a unit that funds projects that don't fall under the purview of Shell's operating units.

Since the completion of the labs, the GameChanger panel has been working hard to institutionalize the internal entrepreneurial process. It meets weekly to discuss new submissions—320 were received in the first two years of the panel's existence, many through Shell's intranet. An employee with a promising idea is invited to give a 10–minute pitch to the GameChanger panel, followed by a 15–minute Q&A session. If the members agree that the idea has real potential, the employee is invited to a second round of discussions with a broader group of company experts whose knowledge or support may be important to the success of the proposed venture. Before rejecting an idea, the panel looks carefully at what Shell would stand to lose if the opportunity turned out to be all its sponsors claim. Ideas that get a green light often receive funding—on average, $100,000, but sometimes as much as $600,000—within 8 or 10 days. Those that don't pass muster enter a database accessible to anyone who would like to compare a new idea with earlier submissions.

Some months later, each project goes through a proof-of-concept review in which the team has to show that its plan is indeed workable and deserves further funding. This review typically marks the end of the formal GameChanger process, although the panel will often help successful ventures find a permanent home inside Shell. About a quarter of the efforts that get funded ultimately come to reside in an operating unit or in one of Shell's various growth initiatives, others get carried forward as R&D projects, and still others are written off as interesting, but unproductive experiments. Of Shell's five largest growth initiatives in early 1999, four had their genesis in the GameChanger process. Perhaps even more important, the GameChanger process (depicted in the drawing) has helped convince Shell's top management that entrepreneurial passion lurks everywhere and that you really can bring Silicon Valley inside.

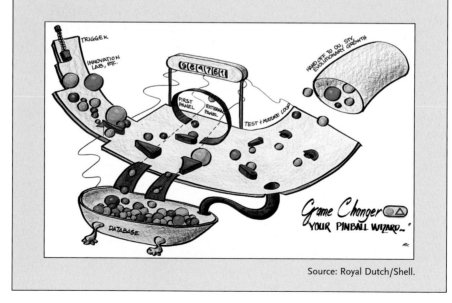

Source: Royal Dutch/Shell.

brating every courageous employee who abandons the security of a legacy business for an untested opportunity.

What's the payoff for creating internal markets for ideas, capital, and talent? Well, consider this: Silicon Valley has about 2 million people. Let's say 50 percent of them are at work in the private sector—the rest are kids, retirees, government employees, and the like. Of that million in the private sector, let's say half are of the caliber you'd find in your company—people who haven't spent their entire careers working at 7-Eleven or Jiffy Lube. That makes 500,000 people. Let's call that the Silicon Valley gene pool. In 1998, that gene pool produced 41 IPOs, which by January 1999 had a combined market cap of $27 billion. If you divide $27 billion by 500,000, you get $54,000. That's $54,000 in new wealth creation per capita—in a single year. In the superheated IPO market of 1999, there were approximately 90 IPOs with a market value of $245 billion in early 2000. But let's stick with the more conservative 1998 data.

Multiply $54,000 by the number of employees in your organization. Did your company create that much new wealth last year out of your employee gene pool? Let's see. At the end of 1998, General Motors had 594,000 employees. That's $32 billion in potential new wealth—if only GM could engender the passion and imagination of Silicon Valley. Sears, Roebuck had 324,000 employees—that's $17 billion in potential new wealth. Motorola had 113,000 employees—that's $6 billion.

Okay, so maybe it's unreasonable to aspire to match the heady performance of Silicon Valley. Maybe you can create new wealth at only half that pace. But ask yourself this: Would the potential payoff for bringing Silicon Valley inside be any less than what you're getting with supply chain management, enterprise resource planning, or some other stewardship program? If not, doesn't it deserve at least the same attention? Let's be clear, what matters in the new economy is not return on investment, but return on imagination. And there's no way of raising your company's return on imagination unless you can bring Silicon Valley inside.

The last bastion of Soviet-style central planning can be found in Fortune 500 companies—it's called *resource allocation*. Big companies are not markets, they're hierarchies. The guys at the top decide where the money goes. Unconventional ideas are forced to make a tortuous climb up the corporate pyramid. If an idea manages to survive the gauntlet of skeptical vice presidents, senior vice presidents, and executive vice presidents, some distant CEO finally decides whether or not to invest.

In contrast, Silicon Valley is based on *resource attraction.* If an idea has merit, it will attract resources in the form of venture capital and talent. If it doesn't, it won't. There's no CEO of Silicon Valley. There's no giant brain making global allocation decisions. Resource allocation is well suited to investments in existing businesses. After all, the guys at the top built the business, and they're well placed to make judgments about investments aimed at perpetuating existing business models. But management veterans are not usually the best ones to judge the merits of investing in entirely new business models or making radical changes to existing models.

It's not that top-down resource allocation has no place in companies. It does. But it can't be the only game in town. If the goal is to create new wealth, something much more spontaneous and less circumscribed is required—something much more like resource attraction. For this reason every company must become an amalgam of disciplined resource allocation *and* impromptu resource attraction. Can it be done? Yep. Take a minute to read the story of Shell's GameChanger process (see the sidebar "Silicon Valley in Royal Dutch/Shell"). If Shell can do it, so can you.

Enron's Jeff Skilling believes his company has gone a long way toward bringing Silicon Valley inside:

> *There are all kinds of innovation and ideas percolating within Enron, and people and capital flow to the good ones. I would hope that if you put a circle around Silicon Valley, you would have something that looked a lot like Enron. But it should be easier to create new business models inside a company than it is in the Valley, because there is less friction. People don't have to negotiate new jobs every time they move to a new business, and we can leverage our core competencies. We also have huge financial resources.*

So ask yourself, Does your company feel more like Silicon Valley or the Soviet Union?

DESIGN RULE #8: LOW-RISK EXPERIMENTATION

Being a revolutionary doesn't mean being a big risk taker:

> *GE Capital:* We go for things where the barriers to entry are small. You won't find us doing many mega-mergers. We do hundreds of acquisitions. But it's very unusual for us to do a big transaction. Big transactions bring you big risks. Have you timed the market right? Are

you buying a business because the other guy thinks it's the right time to get out?

Virgin: We're very adept at managing the downside. We usually take someone else's skills and someone else's money.

There is an implicit assumption in many companies that it is less risky to be incremental than to be revolutionary. Many believe that it is best to let a foolhardy competitor take the risk of testing a new business concept, that the safe bet is to be a fast follower. There are others, a minority in most companies, who will argue that to capture new markets a company must be bold. They will argue that if you're not first off the blocks, you will never win the race to tomorrow's riches. "We need more risk takers around here" is an oft-heard plea in companies that have missed exciting new markets.

Yet there is a false dichotomy here. The choice is not between being a cautious follower on one hand and a rash risk taker on the other. Neither of these approaches is likely to pay off in the age of revolution. For example, Motorola got caught behind Nokia in the move to digital phones and paid a heavy price for its ambling pace. The company learned that you can't play catch-up with a competitor that moves at light speed. On the other hand, Motorola took a huge gamble with its participation in Iridium, the satellite-based communication business, and was ultimately forced into a big write-off when expectations about the rate of customer adoption turned out to be wildly overoptimistic. It is possible, though, to find a way between these two extremes. Gray-haired revolutionaries are prudent *and* bold, careful *and* quick.

Again, the venture capital community provides a useful analogy. Venture capitalists are risk takers, but they're not *big* risk takers. AT&T buying into the cable TV industry, Monsanto spending billions on seed companies, Sony betting a billion on a new video game chip—these are big risks. VCs look for opportunities that don't need a lot of cash to get started. The initial investment in Hotmail was $300,000; the company was sold to Microsoft for something north of $400 million. Historically, Silicon Valley was fueled by nifty new ideas, not zillions of greenbacks. VCs worked hard to enforce a culture of frugality in the companies they backed. And because they were intimately involved in those companies—helping to appoint the management team, sitting on the board, plotting strategy with the owners—they were well positioned to know when to double their bets and when to cut and run. Compared to VCs, the average CFO is a spendthrift. Yet VCs also know that speed is everything. They have no tolerance for talking about doing, for getting ready to get ready. They know that the only way you resolve the inevitable uncertainty around new opportunities is to actually dangle something in front of customers and see if they bite.

VCs live by Virgin's motto of "Screw it, let's do it." Indeed, Virgin has shuttered more businesses than most companies have ever created. Virgin has an exit plan for every business it enters—one that minimizes the potential damage to the Virgin brand. This kind of forward planning doesn't evince any lack of commitment to new opportunities, it simply recognizes that what is true for Silicon Valley is also true for Virgin: most start-ups will fail (though Virgin claims a better track record than the average VC fund).

There is an important mind-set here: *most new ventures will fail.* Do people in your company understand this? A VC could have 5 or 6 failures in 10 starts and still be a hero. Could anyone survive that kind of ratio in *your* company? What matters less than the success rate is the number of new experiments you get started. It is perverse that in many companies billion-dollar commitments to moribund businesses can be thought of as "safe," while Lilliputian experiments are viewed as risky. Risk is the product of investment multiplied by the probability of failure. A $100,000 experiment with an 80 percent chance of failing is substantially less risky than a $100 million investment with a 1 percent chance of failure. Assuming no residual value for either project in the event of failure, the expected downside for the "risky" venture is $80,000 ($100,000 × 80%) and $1 million ($100 million × 1%) for the "sure thing." Yet which would be quicker to win funding in your company? Most companies fail to grasp this simple arithmetic. If they did, they'd be doing fewer big mergers, for example, and would instead be spawning dozens upon dozens of radical low-cost, low-risk experiments.

It is important to make a distinction between project risk and portfolio risk. The risk that any single new experiment fails may be high—say, 80 percent. Yet in a portfolio of 10 such experiments, each with a 1-in-10 chance of success, the likelihood is that 1 of them will pay off. And while the best possible rate of return on large, incremental investments is typically modest, the same is not true of small investments in radical new business concepts. VCs look for opportunities with enormous upside potential, on the order of 10:1, 100:1, or even 1,000:1. If most of the ventures in a portfolio have this kind of upside potential, the "expected value" of the portfolio can be stratospheric, even though each project is far more likely to fail than succeed. A prudent investor would not want to invest in any single project but would be delighted to invest in the entire portfolio. This, of course, is the logic behind companies like CMGI and ICG, Internet

Make a distinction between project risk and portfolio risk.

incubators that manage a portfolio of Web-based start-ups. Again, many companies fail to grasp this simple portfolio logic. This is why most companies *don't* have dozens upon dozens of new-rule experiments bubbling away. But to find a breathtaking breakout opportunity, every company must build a portfolio of business concept experiments.

By the way, if you treat the person who just blew a 20-percent "sure thing" the same way you treat the guy who just blew a 99-percent "sure thing," you're going to end up with a company full of timid little mice. The guy who is managing a highly speculative project in a portfolio of such projects is almost expected to fail. But the gal who has an incremental project in a long-established business should never fail. Yet again, this distinction is seldom made. It's a bit like treating the person who fails to get a hole-in-one on a 300-yard, par-4 golf hole the same way you treat the person who just missed a two-foot putt. Do this, and you'll end up with a company full of two-foot putters—nervous souls who will congregate in "safe" businesses. And there's not a chance in the world your company will join the ranks of the wealth creators. Personal risk must be divorced from project risk. Celebrate the individual or the team that leads an expedition into the unknown.

Companies don't need more risk takers; they need people who understand how to de-risk big aspirations.

Companies often overestimate the risk of doing something new for the simple reason that top management is too distant to make an informed assessment—too far from the voice of the customer and too far from the voice of the future. There is an important difference between actual risk and perceived risk. Actual risk is a function of irreducible uncertainty: Will the technology work? Will customers value this new service? What will they be willing to pay for it? and so on. Perceived risk is a function of ignorance. The farther you are from a hands-on, first-person understanding of the new opportunity, the greater the perceived risk. For years Detroit designed dependably boring automobiles—cars like the Chevrolet Lumina and Ford Contour. Was this because these were the only kind of cars that Americans wanted to buy or because Detroit's designers weren't in touch with the leading edge of customer demand? Cars like the New Beetle and the Dodge Viper looked risky only to those who weren't in tune with trendy young buyers and wild-eyed enthusiasts. The point is simple: you can't let people who couldn't see the leading edge with a pair of binoculars make judgments about what is and isn't risky.

In the end, though, companies don't need more risk takers; they need people who understand how to de-risk big aspirations. There are several ways to do this. Like Virgin, you can pass off risk to strategic partners. When Virgin launched its financial services business, Virgin Direct, it relied on an Australian insurance company for the majority of the initial capital and on a British bank for back–office support. Like GE Capital, you can buy small "popcorn stands," little businesses that will help you learn about bigger opportunities. Once GE understands the basics and the opportunity to reinvent the business, it pours in capital. In the early stages of any new business concept experiment, the goal is to maximize the ratio of learning over investment.

Reconnoitering a broad new opportunity is a bit like trying to shoot a game bird in a fast–flying flock. If you use a rifle, you'll almost certainly miss. A rifle is fine if the target is big and slow. If the target is small and swift, a shotgun is your only hope. Too often a company makes a single, premature bet when confronting a new and underdefined opportunity. The greater the initial uncertainty about which customers will buy, what product configuration is best, what pricing scheme will work, and which distribution channels will be most effective, the greater the number of experiments that should be launched.

Many large companies feel that it is virtually a waste of time to pour scarce management talent into pint–sized experiments. After all, the thinking goes, how big would these experiments have to be in order to make an appreciable impact in a company with $10 billion, $20 billion, or $50 billion in revenue? This isn't the way they think at GE Capital. To qualify as a "bubble," the name GE Capital gives to its major operating units, a business has to be able to generate $25 million in profits per year. That may sound like a lot, but it's significantly less than 1 percent of what GE Capital earns in a good year. "Popcorn stands" are even smaller. GE Capital's senior managers spend a lot of time searching for popcorn stands and trying to grow them into pre–bubble "ventures." And remember, the new economy is filled with young businesses that have stratospheric valuations. Yet these towering redwoods were but seedlings a few years earlier.

All too often there is a 1:1 ratio between the amount of management attention a project or business receives and its current revenues. This is a misapplication of management attention, and it is recipe for maintaining the status quo. Small things need to be nourished by top management attention. Without the fertilizer of top management interest, they will re-main small things.

Inevitably, the time will come when a fledgling business needs to bor-row some critical resource from somewhere else in the organization, to win some argument around channel conflicts, or to double up its invest-ments. If top management's attention has been elsewhere, it will lack the confidence to "go for it." GE Capital's ventures and popcorn stands don't languish in some isolated "new ventures division." Instead they are nurtured and guided by line executives who know that the only way to keep growing is to keep starting a lot of small experiments.

Make small bets. Make a lot of small bets. Think of your experiments as a portfolio of options. Pass off risk to your partners. Accelerate learning. Celebrate the pathfinders. This is the ethos of low–risk experimentation. And it is a critical design rule for building organizations that are consistently revolutionary.

DESIGN RULE #9: CELLULAR DIVISION

Gray–haired revolutionaries are not monoliths. They are big companies that have been divided into a large number of revolutionary cells.

> *Virgin:* We don't run an empire, we run a lot of small companies. We call it a big, small company. We want to be a substantial business with a small company feel so people can see the results of their own efforts.

> *Enron:* We haven't been able to start new businesses within existing businesses. Big businesses will scratch their itch first. When we started our wholesale electricity business, we physically segregated the start–up team. These people had been working within the wholesale gas business. We told them, "There's no going back."

A human embryo grows through a process of cell division: a single cell becomes 2, then 4, then 8, then 16, and so on. Some cells become lungs, others fingernails, bones, tendons, and all the other organs and structures of the body. Division and differentiation—that's the essence of growth. The

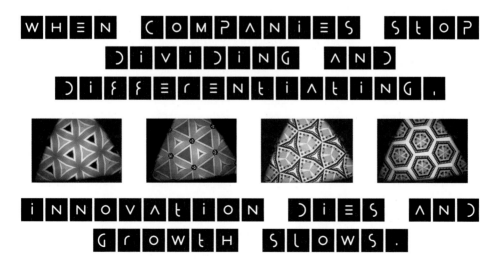

WHEN COMPANIES STOP DIVIDING AND DIFFERENTIATING, INNOVATION DIES AND GROWTH SLOWS.

same is true for organizations. When companies stop dividing and differentiating, innovation dies and growth slows.

For example, when Virgin Records showed the first signs of lethargy, Sir Richard Branson took the deputy managing director, deputy sales director, and deputy marketing director and made them the nucleus of a new company—in a new building. Suddenly, they were no longer deputies, they were in charge. Collectively, Virgin became the largest independent record company in the world, but nowhere, Branson claims, did it feel like a large company.

Virgin's not the only believer in cellular division. The last few years have seen a record number of de-mergers, divestitures, and spin-offs (AT&T and Lucent, Hewlett-Packard and Agilent, 3M and Imation, Rockwell and Conexant, and dozens more). Yet much of this is too little too late. The real champions of cellular division practice a much more radical version of corporate mitosis.

Illinois Tool Works is a $6 billion company you've probably never heard of. Yet between 1994 and 1999, its earnings growth was twice that of the S&P 500. ITW is broken into nearly 400 business units, with average revenues of just $15 million each. Each unit has its own general manager, who has all the authority of a CEO—as long as the unit is outperforming the competition. When a business gets to $50 million in revenue, it is split into 2 or 3 units. For example, the company's Deltar business, which sells plastic fasteners to the auto market, took seven years to hit $2 million in sales. After being split off from the Fastex division and getting its own manufacturing facility and dedicated sales force, its revenues grew 700 percent in four years. Since then, Deltar itself has been split again and again. The original business now has 26 "children" with combined sales of $300 million. An $800 million acquisition made in 1998 was soon split up into more than 30 units. Here's what some of ITW's executive team say about the company's penchant for cellular division:

> We love competing against a big company, because their management teams don't have the same feel that our people have. It's not that we're smarter. It's that our people are only concentrating on one small part of the market. They are like entrepreneurs—it's not an exaggeration.

> We develop managers so rapidly that a person can start running a business when he is in his 20s. Some segments start out very small, perhaps $5 million to $8 million. That's a great place to try a young person. If they fail, we just pick up the pieces and move on. If they worked for another company, they would be trapped in some function. Here they get a chance to do everything.[3]

The advantages of cellular division for business concept innovation are many. First, it frees human and financial capital from the tyranny of any single business model. You've heard it said that size is the enemy of innovation. That's wrong. Size is not the issue. Orthodoxy is the issue. A business unit, whether $1 million or $10 billion in size, typically corresponds to a single business model. It is the allegiance to that business model that inhibits innovation, not the size of the business per se. Cellular division creates space for new business models. Lou Pai of Enron, who left the wholesale electricity trading business to start a business that sells energy outsourcing directly to commercial clients, puts it simply:

A lot of times if you are running an existing business and are responsible for a new business as well, you're not really accountable for the success of the new business as long as your old business continues to do well. We want everyone building the new business to be involved 100 percent.

Second, cellular division provides opportunities to nurture entrepreneurial talent. It reduces the number of stewards minding someone else's store and increases the number of entrepreneurs running their own businesses. Third, by keeping units small and focused, cellular division keeps general managers close to the voice of the customer. And fourth, by dispersing power, it undermines the ability of strong divisions to kill projects that might cannibalize their revenue streams. For example, Hewlett-Packard's decision to put its ink jet printer unit and its laser jet printer business in separate divisions helped both businesses to sidestep the cannibalization debate that so often cramps the style of new initiatives. The benefit for HP was that it became the world leader in two printing businesses.

Sure, cellular division forces companies to forgo some shared economies, but scale's not quite the advantage it used to be, and fragmentation is not quite as expensive as it used to be. Speed, flexibility, and focus have never been more important. That's why cellular division is a critical design principle for innovation. So does your company have any $1-billion-plus divisions? Give W. James Farrell, the CEO of Illinois Tool Works, a carving knife, and he'll turn it into 66 independent businesses, more or less!

DESIGN RULE #10: PERSONAL WEALTH ACCUMULATION

You can't reward entrepreneurs like you reward stewards. Companies that fail to understand this simple fact will hemorrhage entrepreneurial talent.

Enron: If we've broken a paradigm, it's the compensation paradigm. We pay people like entrepreneurs. A lot of companies talk about intrapreneurship and ask people to take risks, but if those people succeed they get nothing more than a small bonus and if they fail they get fired.

Enron understands that if you want people to create wealth, you have to share the wealth—not just with a few privileged executives, but with successful revolutionaries at all levels.

Consider two data points that are indicative of a much broader trend:

In 1999, 25 percent of the Harvard Business School M.B.A. class went to work for companies with fewer than 50 people. Twenty-five percent of the Stanford M.B.A. class went to work for companies with fewer than 25 people. M.B.A.'s have a nose for wealth, and they know their best chance for accumulating wealth is to go work for entrepreneurial companies that reward people for wealth creation.

Andersen Consulting is hardly stingy when it comes to compensating its senior partners. Yet three of the firm's top partners left in 1999 for entrepreneurial start-ups.

Entrepreneurs won't work for peanuts, but they'll work for a share of the equity. A recent study by Strategic Compensation Research Associates found that the average Internet company had issued options to employees that, if exercised, would dilute current shareholders by 24 percent.[4] Entrepreneurs demand a piece of the action. And who can blame them? The energy it takes to create something out of nothing is a multiple of the energy it takes to polish someone else's legacy.

INDIVIDUAL ENTREPRENEURS MUST BE GIVEN THE CHANCE TO WIN BIG— TO REAP REWARDS ALL OUT OF PROPORTION TO THEIR ROLE OR TITLE.

Radical business concepts and entrepreneurial energy are the real "capital" in the age of revolution. No wonder *idea capitalists* expect to be rewarded on a par with other "shareholders." Sure they want to do something "insanely great," but they also want to see a 1:1 correlation between contribution and net worth.

In the past, employees would often trade away the chance for big bucks in a risky start-up for the promise of a lifetime sinecure at a staid but secure company. Now, after a decade of downsizing, employees know that there's no more job security at Incumbent, Inc., than there is at Upstart.com. So why, they ask themselves, should we stick around when the upside has so much more "up" to it somewhere else? After all, how many revolutionaries do *you* know who want to wait around for 20 years to collect their corner office and stock options?

Take just one case in point. In 1998, when Hasso Plattner, co–CEO of SAP, the German software company, refused to create a stock option plan for his top management team in America, he set off a wave of defections. Said Plattner at the time, "We have a different philosophy in Germany. I wasn't going to sacrifice the company for a few American managers."[5] This despite the fact that Plattner's own stake in SAP was worth billions. Within two months of this decision, SAP's head of global accounts, who had first raised the issue of options with Plattner, had moved to Ariba in exchange for a rich package of options. Over the next 18 months, SAP America saw more than 200 of its senior managers leave for less–stingy companies. It's simple, really: in the age of revolution, it's going to become increasingly difficult to create wealth unless one is willing to share it.

Listen to Jim Taylor, the noted futurist: "You need to have a tradition of spectacularly rewarding the people who make a nonlinear change in the business. It has to be clear to people that a spectacular innovation is the surest way of reaping spectacular economic rewards."

Charles Schwab credits its broad–based stock ownership plan with keeping everyone focused on serving customers in ways that create new wealth. Said one senior executive at Schwab: "All employees own shares. Everybody is on the same page and there is harmony in the agenda. We all know we can get wealthy if we serve the customer better than someone else does."

Employee stock ownership plans are a beginning, but they don't go far enough. Innovators need more than a stake in the company. They need a stake in their own ideas. Without it, they will lack the perseverance and courage that is so often the difference between a brilliant insight and a viable new business concept. Individual entrepreneurs must be given the chance to win big—to reap rewards all out of proportion to their role or title. There's a quaint notion in many companies that rank correlates with wealth creation—how else could one explain the strictly pyramidal compensation structure that predominates in most companies. Yet senior executives are more often caretakers than rule breakers. At best, they create a climate in which radical innovation can flourish. To be a gray–haired revolutionary, a company must disconnect compensation from rank, grade, job titles, and hierarchy. Enron has done this. Within Enron's gas trading business there are four levels: junior commercial, senior commercial, vice president, and managing director. Every year a few junior commercial people make more than a managing director, and quite a few senior commercial folks make more than the average vice president.

Of the eight overarching themes in Enron's "vision" statement, four are focused on spurring revolutionary strategies: innovation, creativity, diversity, and change. No surprise, then, that Enron believes in rewarding entrepreneurs on a scale commensurate with their accomplishments.

Here's how this simple principle helped Enron get to where it is today. Each time Enron has created a new business, be it Enron International, Enron Energy Services (energy outsourcing), or Enron Communications (bandwidth trading), the company has given the start-up team a significant chunk of phantom equity. The value of the equity is determined by the growth in the valuation of the new business, which can be calculated using a multiple on revenue or profits, or by an outsider investment bank. Enron uses the phantom equity to attract talent from other companies, in the same way a hot, young start-up might. Once the new business becomes a significant profit generator, the original phantom shares in the particular venture are traded in for actual Enron shares. In the case of Enron Energy Services, around 40 people on the start-up team received phantom equity. No wonder ambitious entrepreneurs at Enron are eager to go off and start new things. The system focuses Enron's most ambitious and most creative people on creating new wealth that drives the company's market capitalization ever higher.

Enron executives believe that salary alone is unlikely to motivate folks to search tirelessly for unconventional projects and unconventional approaches. Enron has been able to attract high-end financial talent, of the sort that might have gone to work for Goldman Sachs or Salomon Smith Barney, because it gives individuals a sizable stake in the wealth they create. One year, Enron took more hot, young graduates from the Wharton Business School than any consulting company or investment bank. Enron knows you can't win the war for talent if the talent doesn't feel as if it has a chance to swing for the fences.

A decade ago, would-be entrepreneurs had few options. But in a world awash in VC money, their choices are virtually limitless. Ask venture capitalists in Silicon Valley to name the scarcest resource in the wealth creation value chain, and they'll all give you the same answer: someone with entrepreneurial passion and operational experience who could be an effective CEO. You have dozens of people in your company who meet this job spec. Must they leave to find their fortune? One of the oldest maxims in business is this: You get what you pay for. If your company isn't willing to pay for entrepreneurship and innovation, it's not going to get them.

IS YOUR COMPANY BUILT FOR INNOVATION?

Step back for a moment and reflect on the design rules for innovation—on the qualities that imbue gray-haired revolutionaries with their revolutionary fervor. Your company may pretend to be serious about innovation but has it fully committed itself to embodying the design rules in every way, every day?

Ask yourself these questions:

Is your company ready to pump up its aspirations to the point where anything less than radical innovation won't suffice?

Is your company ready to throw out its definition of "served market" and define its opportunity space more broadly?

Is your company ready to begin searching for a cause that will be so great, so totally *righteous*, that it will turn a bunch of apprehensive cubicle dwellers into crusaders?

Is top management in your company ready to shut up for a while and start listening, *really* listening, to the young, the new hires, and those at the geographic periphery?

Is your company ready to throw open its strategy process to every great idea, no matter where it comes from?

Is your company ready to start funding ideas out on the lunatic fringe even if 80 percent of them return precisely zilch?

Is your company ready to emancipate some of your best people so they can get to work on building tomorrow's business models?

Is your company ready to start paying attention to the tiny seeds of innovation that are right now struggling to break through the topsoil?

Is your company ready to take on the imperialists who would rather preside over a big but slowly crumbling empire than give self–rule to eager young business builders?

Is your company ready to de–couple compensation from hierarchy and experience and share the wealth with the radical thinkers and courageous doers?

More than likely, your company has not fully embraced the new innovation agenda. To thrive in the age of revolution, it must commit itself fully to making business concept innovation a deep capability. This is the challenge we will take up in the next and final chapter.

THE NEW INNOVATION SOLUTION

FOR ONCE, YOU ARE NOT STARTING from behind. Yeah, there are companies that embody some of the design rules for innovation, but none of them will claim to have made innovation as ubiquitous as six sigma, cycle time, rapid customer service, or any of a dozen less essential capabilities. That's the good news. The bad news is that by the time you read fawning stories in *Business Week* or *Fortune* about companies that have bolstered internal activism, baked the "design rules" into their organizations, and declared radical innovation to be a core competence, it's going to be too late.

Just how long will it take your company to embrace the new innovation agenda? Are you willing to start now, long before the principles and practices of business concept innovation have been reduced to the kind of prosaic manuals of "best practice" so beloved by consultants and the bottom–quartile companies on which they feed? Take a moment before you respond. After all, your share of the future's wealth depends on how you answer.

It took companies such as Ford, Xerox, and Caterpillar a decade and more to regain the ground they lost when they fell behind their Japanese competitors in the march toward quality. This time, you're not going to get 10 years to catch up. This time you're not even going to see the warning lights come on. Industry revolutionaries are like a missile up the tailpipe. Boom! You're irrelevant!

SHAKING THE FOUNDATIONS

To embrace the new innovation agenda you are going to have to challenge every management tenet you inherited from the age of progress. Belief by belief and brick by brick, you must examine the philosophical foundations that undergird your convictions about leadership, wealth creation, and competitiveness. Whenever you find a brick that is old and fractured, kick it out and push a new one in. By now you should have a few ideas on where to start:

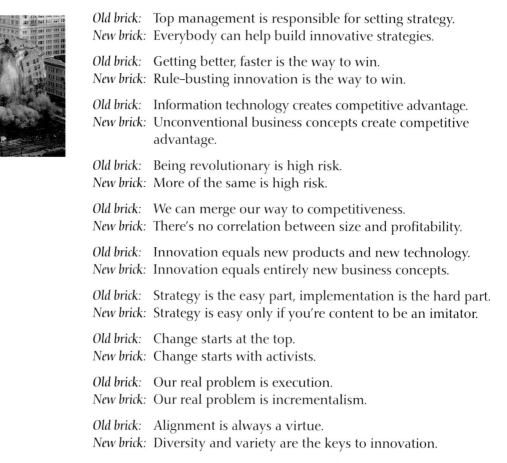

Old brick: Top management is responsible for setting strategy.
New brick: Everybody can help build innovative strategies.

Old brick: Getting better, faster is the way to win.
New brick: Rule–busting innovation is the way to win.

Old brick: Information technology creates competitive advantage.
New brick: Unconventional business concepts create competitive advantage.

Old brick: Being revolutionary is high risk.
New brick: More of the same is high risk.

Old brick: We can merge our way to competitiveness.
New brick: There's no correlation between size and profitability.

Old brick: Innovation equals new products and new technology.
New brick: Innovation equals entirely new business concepts.

Old brick: Strategy is the easy part, implementation is the hard part.
New brick: Strategy is easy only if you're content to be an imitator.

Old brick: Change starts at the top.
New brick: Change starts with activists.

Old brick: Our real problem is execution.
New brick: Our real problem is incrementalism.

Old brick: Alignment is always a virtue.
New brick: Diversity and variety are the keys to innovation.

Old brick:	Big companies can't innovate.
New brick:	Big companies can become gray-haired revolutionaries.

Old brick:	Incumbents will always lose to entrepreneurial start-ups.
New brick:	You can bring the disciplines of Silicon Valley inside.

Old brick:	You can't make innovation a capability.
New brick:	Oh yes, you can, but not without effort.

If you want your company to be revolution-ready, no belief can go unexamined.

Industry revolutionaries are like a missile up the tailpipe. Boom! You're irrelevant!

GETTING COMMITTED

You have to believe three things in order to commit your organization to building a capability for radical innovation.

- An investment in making innovation a capability will yield huge dividends.
- There is a wealth of latent imagination and untapped entrepreneurial zeal in your organization.
- It's actually possible to make innovation a systemic capability.

THE RETURN ON INNOVATION

If you've ever worked in a company where quality has become a religion, you know how much time and effort were devoted to institutionalizing quality as a capability. Quality may be free, but building quality as an advantage is an expensive undertaking. Yet it is universally deemed worth the effort. Given the potential payoff to industry revolution—a payoff that's reflected in the wealth creation of rule-breaking companies—I believe the case for investing in business concept innovation as a capability is at least as sound as the case for investing in quality.

If you agree, then you must also agree that many companies have been misdirecting their energies: they've been moving heaven and hell to eke out the last bit of wealth from a dying business model while largely ignoring the chance to create new wealth from new business concepts. Maybe your company has held a few brainstorming sessions. Maybe top management has hosted a two-day conference in a bucolic resort to consider the challenges of innovation and growth. But if you're honest, you're going to have to admit that there is a huge disparity in the amount of energy your

> While you can't bottle lightning, you can build lightning rods.

company has devoted to getting better and the amount of effort it has expended in getting different—in getting revolution-ready. The implicit belief seems to be that incremental improvement is backbreaking work, while nonlinear innovation is easy. This is, of course, nonsense. Building any woof-and-warp capability is difficult and expensive. But the return on an investment in innovation will beat the return on any other capability one can imagine.

REVOLUTIONARIES EVERYWHERE

Despite the lesson of Silicon Valley, where the most unlikely sorts of people have created new fortunes, there's still a prejudice in most companies that first-line employees are unlikely to be sources of wealth-creating innovation. Thirty years ago, few people believed that blue-collar workers with no more than 12 years of formal education could take responsibility for improving quality. In a few years, the notion that "ordinary" employees are the wellspring for business concept innovation will be no more remarkable than the proposition that everyone is responsible for quality. Yet unless you and your colleagues are ready *right now* to accept the fact that there are revolutionaries everywhere in your company, you will lose. There is no place for elitism in the age of revolution.

MAKING SERENDIPITY HAPPEN

Can something as effervescent as innovation be *systemized*? Again, the analogy with quality is useful. In times past, quality of the sort offered by Rolls-Royce, Tiffany, or Hermes required the unerring eye and skilled hands of an artisan. Who would have believed that a Toyota could be made as reliable as a Bentley or that a Swatch could keep better time than a Rolex? Yet this was the singular contribution of the quality movement: to make what had been unique, ubiquitous. It goes without saying that eureka moments cannot be programmed in advance. Innovation will always be a mixture of serendipity, genius, and sheer bloody-mindedness. While you can't bottle lightning, you can build lightning rods. Nonlinear innovation can be legitimized, fostered, celebrated, and rewarded.

To create a hotbed of business concept innovation, you have to start with the design rules. But you can't stop there. It's not enough to create a *climate* for radical innovation and it's not enough to venerate the activists. You must create a positive *capability* for business concept innovation. What follows is an agenda for anyone who would like to get a head start on building the pivotal source of competitive advantage in the age of revolution.

THE NEW INNOVATION SOLUTION

While the 10 design rules and the principles of activism are parts of the innovation solution, there are other equally important components:

- Skills
- Metrics
- Information technology
- Management processes

Each of these is a critical component of the *new innovation solution*. Each has an essential role to play in creating a deep capability for business concept innovation (see the figure "Innovation as a Capability").

INNOVATION AS A CAPABILITY

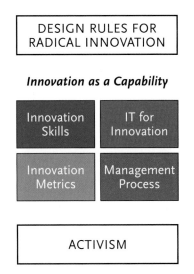

SKILLS

Your company has virtually no chance of leading the revolution if it is populated by industrial–age mind–sets. Every mind in your company must be retooled for the age of revolution. Training is tedious, and learning is hard work, but there's no other way to embed capability. Ask yourself these questions:

- How many people in your company understand the role industry revolution plays in wealth creation?
- How many know how to calculate the decay rate of current business models?
- How many know how to identify and deconstruct industry and company orthodoxies?
- How many are able to distill proprietary foresight out of an ocean of information on "discontinuities"?
- How many are adept at inventing new business concepts and reinventing old ones?
- How many feel personally responsible for business concept innovation?
- How many understand the principles of activism and would know how to launch a grassroots innovation campaign?
- How many would know how to build a low–cost experiment to test a radical new idea?
- How many are working to apply the design rules for innovation to their parts of the company?

If you didn't answer "the majority," your organization isn't yet revolution–ready. If you've read the other eight chapters in this book, you've already taken a substantial step in "re–skilling" yourself for the age of revolution, but that's not enough. To thrive in the age of revolution, companies will need thousands, not tens of individuals who are revolution-ready. It's not enough to have little islands of capability—a few individuals here and there who are sources of nonlinear innovation. In most companies, it took systematic, cross–company training to firmly embed quality as a capability. The same will be true for business concept innovation. Forget all that blather in your company's mission statement about creativity and innovation. Unless it's running boot camps for industry insurgents, it's still substituting rhetoric for action. Radical innovation must become the next agenda item for every corporate university. So get on the phone to your HR VP or the person who runs corporate training. Tell them you have a few ideas for some curriculum changes.

METRICS

Did you ever read the classic article "On the Folly of Rewarding A, While Hoping for B?"[1] There's a lesson in there for every company that wants to fuel the fires of innovation and create new wealth. Most companies have dozens of measures focused on cost, efficiency, speed, and customer satisfaction— and pay people for making progress against these metrics. Yet in my experience, there are few companies that have any metrics that focus on radical innovation. If you have any doubts about this, take the following quiz:

- How many measures do you have in your company that focus explicitly on innovation (versus optimization)?

- How many individuals in your company could say as much about your company's innovation performance as they could say about your company's cost efficiency?

- How many people in your company have any personal performance metrics related to innovation?

- Does your company systematically benchmark other companies on innovation?

Traditional metrics don't force a company to consider how it is performing against new and unorthodox competitors.

Most companies use a decidedly unbalanced scorecard—one that is heavily weighted toward optimization rather than innovation. Measures like RONA, ROCE, EVA, and ROI often encourage managers to beat a dead horse even harder. How often have you heard an entrepreneur boasting about capital efficiency? The fact that you haven't should tell you something. It's not that industrial-age metrics are *anti*-innovation; it's just that they're not *pro*-innovation. And in a world where innovation is the surest route to wealth creation, that's a fatal flaw. Without strong pro-innovation metrics, the default setting in most organizations is "more of the same."

Traditional metrics don't force a company to consider how it is performing against new and unorthodox competitors in the quest for wealth creation. What does it matter to an investor if a company is earning its cost of capital if its rivals are capturing the lion's share of new wealth in an industry? Companies need a way of measuring their *relative* capacity to invent new business concepts and create new wealth. One such measure is the *wealth creation index*, or WCI. It is currently being used by a number of companies that are eager to focus attention on the challenge of new wealth creation. The WCI lets a company determine how it has performed against a relevant set of "competitors" in creating new wealth. The process of determining your company's WCI involves two steps: defining the domain and calculating changes in the market value of your company versus the value of the entire domain.

Defining the Domain

The first step in calculating a company's WCI is to specify a competitive domain. I use the word "domain" rather than "industry" because measuring wealth creation within an "industry" often leads to an overly narrow definition of a company's potential opportunity horizon. The domain should include all the companies that are positioned either upstream or downstream from your own company in a vertical "value chain." It should also encompass companies that supply complementary products or services within a broader "value network." For example, an auto manufacturer would need to include the new Internet auto retailers as well as the providers of ancillary services such as body shops and oil change shops.

Further, the definition of domain should include companies that possess similar core competencies or those that satisfy the same deep customer needs. For example, Tower Records must include in its definition of domain all the new Web-based businesses where consumers can download music. An oil company should define its domain as "energy." An insurance company would define its domain as "financial services," and so on. If the definition of domain includes companies with similar competencies or serving the same broad class of needs, there is little chance of being surprised by a "disruptive technology."

Calculating Changes in Market Value versus Domain Value

The next step is to measure changes in a company's market value versus changes in the market value of *all* the companies within its domain. This lets you answer an important question: Has my company created more or less than its "fair share" of new wealth? To calculate a company's share of wealth creation, simply divide its share of total domain value at the end of a period by its share at the beginning of a period. If a company's market capitalization represented 5 percent of total domain value in Year 1, and 10 percent in Year 5, the company would have a WCI of 2.

A company's market value is the net present value of its expected future net earnings—based on the collective assessment of investors. In a world of diminishing returns to incrementalism, it is unlikely that any company can dramatically grow its market capitalization in the absence of business concept innovation. Incremental efficiency programs are seldom capable of producing a step-function change in investor expectations about a company's profit potential. Aside from acquisitions and mergers, it is virtually impossible for a company to dramatically raise its market cap without inventing new profit streams.

Likewise, if a company's market value is stagnant or collapsing, it suggests a decrepit strategy. For all these reasons, changes in market cap are a reasonable proxy for strategic innovation. (Of course one must make adjustments for de-mergers and disposals, as well as for acquisitions and mergers.) Changes in a company's market capitalization *relative* to other companies in the same domain provide an even better proxy for strategic innovation. If a company is a division of a much larger company or privately held, one must calculate an implied market cap for that particular division using well-known valuation techniques. Don't expect to derive wealth creation measures straight out of the *Wall Street Journal*. Defining the relevant domain and establishing valuation numbers is hard work. But in my experience, the discussion engendered and the insights derived always justify the effort. When the value of the entire domain is increasing, only companies that achieve *above average* growth in market cap can claim to be true strategy innovators. It is nearly tautological: in the absence of acquisitions or mergers, any company that achieves a big jump in its share of domain value is an industry revolutionary.

Let's take one example. The value of the nonfood retailing domain grew 6.3 times over the last decade (only U.S. companies were included in the calculation). The table "The Nonfood Retailing Domain" summarizes changes in wealth share between 1988 and 1998. Already number one in 1988, Wal-Mart continued to grow its share of wealth over the next decade. The Home Depot was another awesome wealth creator. Sears, Kmart, J. C. Penney, and Toys "R" Us were big WCI losers. They failed to reinvent themselves or their industries.

A WCI score of less than 1 is a sure sign of nostalgia for an out-of-date business concept. All too often, the bonds of misplaced loyalty are severed only when the company suffers some catastrophic earnings failure. Instead of looking back over a decade and bemoaning a failure to grab new opportunities, track share-of-wealth data on an ongoing basis. A WCI that is edging lower suggests that the company is falling behind in the search for new business concepts.

The percentage of new wealth created by newcomers is a simple way of judging the susceptibility of incumbents to nonlinear innovation. Upstarts captured fully 27 percent of the new wealth in the computer domain over the past 10 years. In retailing, companies that didn't even exist in 1988 captured 16 percent of the new wealth created. This means that despite all their advantages, retailing incumbents surrendered $107 billion of new opportunities to agile and innovative upstarts.

THE NONFOOD RETAILING DOMAIN

	Share of Wealth (% in 1988)	Share of Wealth (% in 1998)	Wealth Creation Index (1988–1998)
The Home Depot	1.8	13.9	7.7
Wal-Mart	20.0	28.0	1.4
Gap	1.7	4.9	2.9
Amazon.com	0.0	2.6	∞
Costco	0.0	2.4 [A]	∞
Walgreens	2.1	4.5	2.1
Sears	17.1	2.5 [B]	0.15
Kmart	7.9	1.2	0.1
J. C. Penney	7.3	1.8	0.2
Toys "R" Us	5.4	0.7	0.1

[A] 0.3 percent of Costco's gain reflects market cap added from Costco's 1993 $1.7 billion all-equity acquisition of Price Co.

[B] During this period Sears spun off two large holdings with a combined market value of $16.8 billion. Without these disposals, Sears PSW would have been higher by about 2.6 percent.

Source: Standard and Poor's COMPUSTAT; Strategos calculations.

If new entrants can capture billions of dollars of new wealth in an industry without the resources and accumulated experience of an established player, imagine the possibilities if the energy and resources of an already successful company could be focused on the challenge of inventing new opportunities for new wealth creation. Actually, you don't have to imagine; just look at Gap, Inc.

Over the past decade Gap built a powerful casual clothing brand that has surpassed Levi's in market value. Yet Mickey Drexler and his restless colleagues haven't been content to rest on their khaki–clad butts. Alert to the danger that Wal–Mart and Target might start siphoning off budget-conscious consumers, Gap launched Old Navy, a hip, new retailing format aimed at value–focused consumers. Bright and funky, an Old Navy store feels nothing like a warehouse superstore. Old Navy was up and running in less than a year and grew to $1 billion in sales faster than any other bricks–and–mortar retail format, ever. Given Gap's outsized ambitions, concerns about potential cannibalization of the Gap brand were given short shrift. The urge to continue creating new wealth was stronger than the urge to defend the past.

Calculate your company's WCI over the past year, or two, or five. Get a discussion going over the appropriate definition of domain. Challenge the definitions of "industry" and "served market" that prevail in your company. Ask yourself: Are these definitions broad enough? Do they blind us to nontraditional competitors? What opportunities have we missed? Then look at the companies that have created a disproportionate share of new wealth and ask, How did they define their opportunity horizon? Why did they see opportunities we didn't? What was their implicit definition of domain? How did they exploit our myopia? Answering these questions will expose the biases and beliefs that have aborted innovation in your own company.

Use the new metrics to challenge complacency. Redefine "acceptable" performance so it includes not only good stewardship but also an above-average WCI score. Look for companies that have excelled in the wealth creation sweepstakes, and use their example to reset aspirations in your own company. The distilled essence of entrepreneurial energy is the quest for new wealth. When widely discussed and understood, metrics like WCI can help you bring that energy inside your own company.

Of course, no single metric, on its own, can endow employees with imagination, make management responsive to new ideas, and bestow the courage needed to abandon comfortable orthodoxies. But be sure of this: if you don't get the metrics right, none of the other needed behaviors are likely to follow.

INFORMATION TECHNOLOGY

Intranets. E-mail. Newsgroups. Instant messaging. The fact is so obvious, it's hardly worth noting: information technology has been dramatically changing the way organizations work. Digital communication drills through layers of bureaucracy, undermines hierarchy, makes much of middle management redundant, enables globe-spanning collaboration, unites far-flung supplier networks, makes 24/7 tech support available worldwide—and that's just for starters. Odd, then, that IT vendors and professionals have contributed so little to the cause of radical innovation. There are few companies where IT has helped to turbocharge business concept innovation.

Imagine a corporatewide IT system—an *innovation network*—designed to support radical innovation. Any employee with a germ of an idea, or just an urge to create, could go online and find a wealth of innovation tools— here's how you discover industry orthodoxies, here's how you build a business concept, here's how you develop a 100-day new-rules experiment, and so on. The tyro entrepreneur could toss his or her idea into a corporatewide "Ideaspace"—essentially an online market for radical ideas. An "innovation editor" would group similar ideas together and post them on the company's intranet. Anyone visiting the site could build on the ideas submitted—"Have you thought about this?" or "Here's another way of going to market." It would be easy to host real-time online discussions for particularly hot ideas. Ideas that attracted attention and thoughtful inputs would flower and grow, while those that didn't would wither.

Individuals across the company could register their interest in working on a particular idea—"Yeah, I'd be willing to spend six months helping you get this launched," or "I'll loan you one of my team members to help you build the prototype." There could also be an internal market for funding. Anyone in the company with a budget could decide to sponsor a radical new idea. Ordinary employees might even be able to buy "options" in the nascent venture—whether in the form of phantom equity or a share of some future profit stream. A divisional vice president might say, "Okay, I'll put $100,000 in so you can take this idea to the next stage," or an individual might say, "I'll invest $5,000 for a quarter-percent of equity." Conversely, innovators could bid for talent and capital, using phantom options in return. If the new idea is a reinvention of an existing business concept, rather than an entirely new business with its own P&L, the valuation problem gets more difficult, but the providers of talent and capital might be given a share in the profit growth of an existing business. In any case, ideas that attracted talent and money would get implemented; those that didn't, wouldn't. Of course, top management could monitor the innovation marketplace and put big money and topflight talent behind ideas that showed great promise.

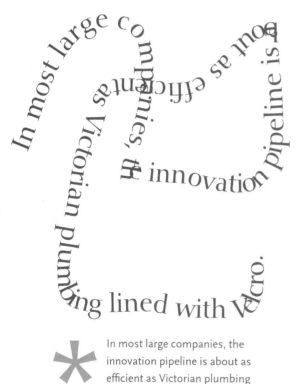

In most large companies, the innovation pipeline is about as efficient as Victorian plumbing lined with Velcro.

To institutionalize radical innovation, companies will need to build highly efficient electronic markets for ideas, capital, and talent. As they do so, it will no longer be the knowledge management function that constitutes the leading edge of corporate IT, but the innovation marketplace. Are you ready for this?

MANAGEMENT PROCESSES

Many companies have spent a decade reinventing their core business processes for efficiency. The goal has been to straighten out the kinks in the supply chain—from suppliers through incoming logistics through work-in-progress through outbound logistics and customer fulfillment. Dell Computer is the poster child for supply chain integration. To a customer, Dell Computer's delivery pipeline appears both short and slick. While supersmooth business processes are great for efficiency—Dell operates with negative working capital—they don't do squat for innovation. In most large companies, the innovation pipeline is about as efficient as Victorian plumbing lined with Velcro. Radical ideas get hung up in the Byzantine complexity of the strategic planning process, the capital budgeting process, the staffing process, or the product development process.

Companies that have reengineered their core business processes for efficiency are now going to have to reinvent their core management processes for innovation. If supply chain integration was about minimizing the time between an order and delivery, reinventing management processes for innovation is about accelerating the payoff for radical ideas.

There are several ways in which management processes are inimical to innovation. First, most of them are *calendar-driven*—there seems to be an implicit assumption that you can count on new opportunities to wait patiently for the arrival of the October planning round. Budgets are set on a quarterly or annual basis and, once set, are inviolable.

Second, most management processes are *biased toward conservation rather than growth*. They tend to put a premium on efficiency and undervalue experimentation aimed at exploring new competitive space. Ideas for trying something new and out of bounds are implicitly viewed as dangerous diversions from the central task of driving down costs and building market share in the core business. I have seldom seen a management process that explicitly challenges managers to develop and test a portfolio of unconventional strategic options. In general, management processes are focused on minimizing variances rather than maximizing opportunities.

Third, most management processes *take the existing business model as the point of departure*. Traditional definitions of market structure, traditional ways of describing the value chain, traditional assumptions about the cost structure, traditional beliefs about where you take your profits—all these are woven into the form and substance of management processes. In ways subtle and not so subtle, management processes perpetuate the status quo. Champions of business concept innovation will, invariably, find themselves working against the grain of key management processes.

Most management processes are *focused on existing customers and markets*. Again, there is a subtle bias toward serving existing customers better, rather than finding entirely new types of customers. Even worse, it is the articulated needs of customers that get all the attention, rather than their unarticulated needs. Most management processes have a place to plug in the banalities produced by market research, but have no way of accommodating the highly impressionistic but infinitely more profound insights that come from experiential, out-of-bounds learning. And, of course, market share gets a lot more discussion than wealth share.

Most management processes are *controlled by the defenders of the past*. The senior staff who "own" corporate training, planning, and capital budgeting view their role as serving the barons who run today's big businesses. Any redesign of

Most management processes are controlled by the defenders of the past.

the management process usually begins by polling the executive vice presidents. Seldom is any attention given to the needs of struggling entrepreneurs and would-be activists.

Finally, most management processes are *implicitly risk averse*. The burden of proof is on those who would like to change the status quo. Seldom is the risk of over-investing in a decaying business model made explicit. In countless ways, internal revolutionaries are given the message that incrementalism is safe and radicalism is risky, when of course the reverse is more often true.

Interview successful revolutionaries in large companies, and you'll hear a familiar refrain: "I succeeded despite the system." All of them know that "the system" is there to frustrate the new, the unconventional, and the untested. Management systems are designed to enforce conformance, alignment, and continuity. We would be horrified if employees said they managed to deliver quality products and services "despite the system." We should be horrified that employees have to produce innovation "in spite of the system."

So here's what you do. Identify the four or five most pervasive and powerful management processes in your company: compensation, succession planning, leadership training, strategic planning, capital budgeting, product development, whatever. For each core process, assemble a review team, comprising a diagonal slice of your company. Make sure you have a senior staff person, a VP, a couple of middle managers, and a mix of successful and unsuccessful corporate rebels on each team. Ask a proven revolutionary to chair each team. Give each team one management process to redesign. Have them pull together all of the documentation used to support that process. Have them map the process across time and across the organization by asking, What are the milestones? Who gets to participate? What are the inputs? What are the outputs? What kinds of decisions does the process produce? Have them interview a couple dozen process "users": in what ways does the process hinder business concept innovation and in what ways does it foster it? Have the team go back and review the purpose behind the process—what was it originally designed to do? Is that goal still valid? Is it possible to design a process that will meet that goal without killing innovation? Ask them to review each component of the management process for any evidence that the process is any of the following: inappropriately calendar–driven; biased toward conservation and efficiency rather than experimentation and growth; too tightly intertwined with the existing business model; overfocused on existing customers and markets; controlled by and run for the benefit of those defending large, established businesses; inherently risk averse.

Finally, have the team suggest ways in which each component of the process could be redesigned to make it less backward–looking and more innovation–friendly. The team will need to write a new mission statement for the process—one that explicitly includes nonlinear innovation and wealth creation.

THE WHEEL OF INNOVATION

So you're baking the design rules into your organization, you're offering succor to the activists, and your working to make business concept innovation a systemic capability. But there's still more to do. Innovation is a *dynamic process*, with the following elements:

- Heretics and novelty addicts *imagine* new possibilities.
- Using the principles of business concept innovation, they *design* coherent business models around those ideas.
- They launch small–scale *experiments* to test the viability of their business concepts and then adapt them.
- Having conducted an experiment or two or three, they *assess* what has been learned.
- Depending on what has been learned, they decide whether to *scale up* or go through another experiment cycle.

Imagine, Design, Experiment, Assess, Scale. (By now you've spotted the helpful mnemonic.) This is the wheel of innovation, and it is the next critical component in the innovation solution (see the figure "The Wheel of Innovation").

THE WHEEL OF INNOVATION

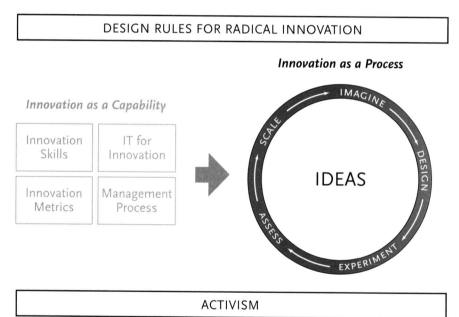

Making the Wheel Spin Faster

The speed at which a company gets the wheel of innovation turning determines the amount of new wealth it creates. The first stumbling block is often an inability of potential innovators to go from the fragment of an idea to a reasonably holistic business concept design. Senior executives often tell me, "Our problem isn't a lack of ideas—we have too many ideas." But when I ask them whether they have a too many truly compelling and coherent strategic options, the answer is always "no." This is why the skills needed to design a new business concept

COMPANIES ARE GOING TO HAVE TO LEARN TO RUN AT MORE THAN ONE SPEED. YOU CAN'T WIN A FORMULA 1 RACE WITH A JOHN DEERE TRACTOR.

around the shard of an idea must be widely distributed. Would-be entrepreneurs must be able to do some initial quality assessment on their own ideas—is this a brainwave or a brainfart? If you can't imagine a coherent, profitable business concept supporting your idea, send it aloft with all the other greenhouse gases.

Successive Approximation

Once there is a potential business concept, it must be tested experimentally, in much the same way an aeronautical engineer tests the flight characteristics of a high-performance fighter on a computer before strapping a pilot into the cockpit. Experiment, assess, adapt. Experiment, assess, adapt. The faster a company can go through this cycle, the faster it can resolve the uncertainty that inevitably surrounds a new and unconventional business concept, and the faster it can get to a viable, cash-generating business concept.

When every little new-rules experiment is scrutinized and reviewed as if it were a $100 million investment, the wheel of innovation comes to a grinding halt. Companies are going to have to learn to run at more than one speed: at "all deliberate speed" for big investments in capital-intensive projects where assets last for 20 years and at "light speed" for experiments in imagination-intensive opportunities. You can't win a Formula 1 race with a John Deere tractor. If you can't get your internal wheel of innovation turning as fast as it does in Silicon Valley, you lose.

Listen to a couple of speed demons from our cast of gray-haired revolutionaries:

> *Charles Schwab:* We have a learning mentality: it's better to start early and learn more than to wait around and try to get the thing perfect before you start.

How diverse

GE Capital: We deal with short cycle times. We'll have a dinner, study something, and then do a transaction within weeks.

These companies understand that developing great new business concepts, or reinventing fading business concepts, is often a process of successive approximation—a succession of fast-paced experiments, each designed to test some particular aspect of a novel business concept.

Customers as Co-Developers

In the age of revolution, there is simply no way to stay ahead of the innovation curve unless your customers are your co-developers. The larger the community of co-developers, the quicker problems and opportunities for improvement are identified. Listen to Bill Gross, the ebullient founder of idealab!:

Is your company's

We have the ability to test what customers would really like in a way that we've never had before. In my previous business, we used to conduct focus groups. We'd have parents come in and tell us what they might like and we'd pay them $75. We'd sit on the other side of a one-way mirror and do the whole standard thing. I don't want to belittle focus groups because we got very valuable information.

Now, compare that with what we can do at idealab!. Let's say we have a new idea for something—like selling CDs on the Internet. Obviously this has already been done, but let me use it as an example. We'll design a prototype Web site. In 10 days we'll go live. We'll put a field in the Web site where we take credit cards even though we won't yet have the capability to process credit cards, and we won't have any inventory either. But we'll go live and we'll test 10 different sales propositions like CDs at the lowest price, or the top 10 CDs always in stock, or CDs to you in one day, and so on. Customers will come to the site, they'll type in their credit card to get the CD. We'll discard the credit card information. We won't charge them because we don't have that ability yet. Instead, we'll take their order and go to Tower Records. We'll buy the CD and send it out to them for free. So we're losing the money on that CD. But we can fully test the way customers will respond to a specific proposition.

It's unbelievable what kind of feedback you can get from consumers when it's a real test and not just some lame question about their opinion. Everything on the Internet is measurable. Everything is exactly quantifiable. It's like the ultimate direct marketing experiment. That's why it's a great way to take ideas and test them. In a day you can get insights that used to take you a year to acquire.

It is doubtful that there's any place on earth where the wheel of innovation spins faster than at idealab!—and rapid-cycle customer feedback is a major reason why. So ask yourself a question: Is the development team

portfolio

you're using *outside* your company bigger than the one *inside* your company? If not, your wheel of innovation isn't going to spin fast enough to get you to the future first.

Kill the Losers Fast

In the absence of bounded experiments with tightly defined learning objectives, it's all too easy for would-be entrepreneurs to fall in love with a deeply flawed business concept. Again, Bill Gross speaks to this:

> We try and kill a project as fast as possible. We try and do a $10,000 experiment like putting up a temporary Web site. If we don't get the demand that we expected, we try and kill it at that point. If we get any reasonable amount of demand, we'll try and spend $50,000 to take it to the next stage. And then we really try and cut things off at $250,000.
>
> We try to kill many more ideas than we actually go forward with. In fact, over the last three years, we've come up with about 80 ideas where we've spent somewhere between $10,000 and $250,000. We've gone ahead with 24 ideas, the rest we've killed. And of course we see hundreds that we kill before we spend a thing.

Are you getting this?

- Be honest about what you don't know.
- Design tight, short experiments.
- Maximize the ratio of learning over investment.
- Bring your customers inside the tent.
- Love your project but kill it quick if you find unfixable flaws.

of unconventional

THE INNOVATION PORTFOLIO

Think of nascent business designs and early-stage experiments as options on the future. Your company's chance of creating new wealth is directly proportional to the number of ideas it fosters and the number of experiments it starts. So ask yourself, How diverse is your company's portfolio of unconventional strategy options? What percentage of corporate initiatives are aimed at incremental improvement, and how many are testing opportunities for business concept innovation?

The innovation portfolio is actually three distinct portfolios. First is the portfolio of ideas, of credible, but untested, new business concepts. Second is the portfolio of experiments. Ideas that have particular merit get advanced to the portfolio of experiments, where they are validated

strategy options? through low-cost market incursions. Third is the portfolio of new ventures. Experiments that look promising advance to venture status. Here the goal is to begin to scale up the original idea. The "imagine" and "design" phases of the innovation process fill up the first portfolio with ideas. Ideas that advance to the "experiment" and "assess" stages populate the second portfolio, and those ready to be taken to "scale" comprise the third (see the figure "The Innovation Portfolio").

THE INNOVATION PORTFOLIO

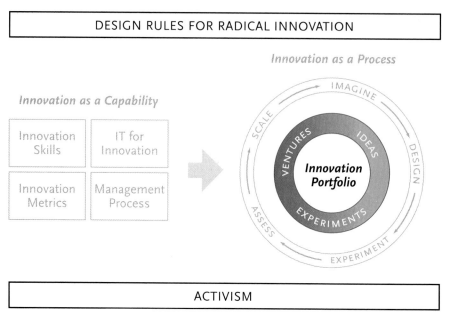

While top management often views the company as a portfolio of businesses, it seldom applies the logic of portfolio investing to investments in business concept experiments. This is particularly surprising when more and more companies are setting up venture funds to invest in a portfolio of upstarts *outside* the company. The logic of portfolio investing is to minimize the risk of the overall portfolio by diversifying your investments. With a diversified portfolio, the risk that the entire portfolio will take a big dive is substantially less than the risk that any single stock will fall through the floor. Yet all too often, executives expect *every* new idea or experiment to yield a bonanza. Such an expectation will invariably make a company overconservative and will quickly drain the portfolio of ideas and the portfolio of experiments of many interesting strategic options.

It is important to distinguish between the risk that a particular idea or experiment doesn't pan out and the risk that the entire innovation portfolio yields a big fat zero. A bias against anything with the slightest hint of downside ensures a company will never find anything with an amazing upside. Spectacular new opportunities seldom start out as 90% sure things. That's why it's important to distinguish an "idea" or an "experiment" from a venture or a fully-fledged business. Perhaps the following analogy will help. In the act of procreation, millions of sperm get "wasted." You need a lot of little swimmers to fertilize an egg. Yet we seldom bemoan the lost sperm. One huge win—a new baby—offsets millions of small failures—dead sperm. Although we can hope for a substantially better ratio of wins to losses than a prospective father, the principle is much the same: you have to be willing to tolerate a lot of small losses for the occasional gigantic win. You don't have to risk big, but you have to risk often.

The risk of the innovation portfolio is further reduced when you remember that it typically sits alongside a portfolio of large, ongoing businesses. Today's businesses are like bonds in an investment portfolio—low yielding and low risk. Too many companies are like timid investors, dumping all their savings into AAA bonds, afraid to invest in the NASDAQ. They may sleep a little better, but they're going to have a meager retirement. There is no way to become a wealth-creating superstar without first building and then investing in the innovation portfolio.

A PORTFOLIO OF IDEAS

The portfolio of ideas is really a "portfolio of possibilities." There are hundreds of half-baked, ill-formed ideas that bump around in the heads

of your colleagues. Most never get articulated. Others exist only as water cooler conversations. Few organizations have attempted to collect and manage nonlinear ideas as part of an explicit portfolio of possibilities. So for the dozen or so that actually work their way up through the usual sclerotic approval channels, there are

hundreds that never escape the heads of eager but isolated entrepreneurs.

This is why companies must create opportunities for the advocates of nonlinear innovation to be heard and a way of cataloging radical, innovative ideas. Bill Gross maintains a spreadsheet with around 1,000 e-commerce-related business concepts. He's constantly reviewing the list: What idea seems ripe right *now*? What ideas might be viable in combination? What ideas have already been done and should be struck off the list? Where would I go in *your* organization to find an inventory of potential new business concepts?

One can easily imagine a number of things a company might do to help fill out its portfolio of ideas.

- Appoint several business development officers (BDOs) to serve as advisors to prospective entrepreneurs. Rather than schmoozing with investment bankers, the BDOs would get rewarded for finding and nurturing internal innovation.

- Ask each member of the executive committee to spend a couple days every month coaching eager, young entrepreneurs drawn from the far reaches of the organization. Each member of the executive committee would be asked to sponsor at least one new idea every quarter.

- Put an "innovation" button on your company's internal home page. Anyone who clicks on it would find a simple form that would allow them to post their idea in a corporatewide, virtual "Ideaspace."

All this is in addition to training people in the basics of business concept innovation.

A PORTFOLIO OF EXPERIMENTS

Ideas that have great upsides, offer the chance for increasing returns, and are sponsored by truly passionate advocates get moved into the portfolio of experiments. Ideas that fail these tests get kicked out of the portfolio or are held back for further development as ideas. The portfolio of experiments contains ideas that have been worked into reasonably coherent versions of a business concept. They are ideas that have begun to attract a constituency.

Few companies make it easy for the advocates of radical innovation to attract sponsors and team members with complementary skills. Why not, for example, let internal innovators post banner ads on the company's intranet as a way of attracting talent and resources? Moreover, most companies don't have an explicit and legitimate designation for experimental-stage businesses or for radical but underdeveloped ideas that could dramatically transform the core business.

Indeed, many large companies have a bias against small experiments. They believe you have to do something BIG to make a noticeable impact on the top line. A typical objection goes something like this: "Sure, we can start a bunch of small experiments, but you have to understand we're a $20 billion company. It takes something pretty big to make a material difference to our shareholders." This helps explain the preference for mega-mergers and bet-the-company investments. Yet the real problem is that senior management too often can't see an oak tree in an acorn. They need to consider, for a moment, the current market capitalization of Yahoo! or Dell or The Home Depot, and then ask themselves, How big were these companies a decade or two ago? Indeed, I recently surveyed the list of

Most experiments won't pay off. But

publicly traded companies in the United States and found 62 companies with a market capitalization greater than $10 billion and current revenues less than $100 million. Most of these companies are less than five years old. In the age of revolution, it's not your revenue line that counts, but the size of the opportunity you have envisioned. The challenge isn't finding that one enormous mega-deal but planting enough acorns to raise the chances of getting an oak tree. Yeah, you can go find an oak tree, uproot it, and try to replant it, but this is a difficult and risky proposition, as any CEO who's ever tried to integrate a large acquisition will tell you. It's the innovation portfolio a CEO needs to worry about, not the queue of investment bankers panting outside the door.

For every 1,000 ideas, perhaps 1 in 10 will have enough merit to be turned into an experiment. So after you've asked yourself whether your company has a portfolio of 1,000 ideas, ask yourself if your organization has a portfolio of 100 ongoing experiments. If it doesn't, and it's a sizable organization, its future is at risk.

A portfolio of new-rules experiments should cover the discontinuities most likely to upend current business models as well as those most likely to spawn entirely new opportunities. For example, a maker of mobile phones in the late 1990s would have wanted to have a few experiments focused on the mobile telephone as a replacement for fixed-line services in large corporations. It would have focused other experiments on the cell phone as a chic fashion accessory or as a requisite in every student's backpack. Other experiments would have addressed the convergence of voice and data and the wireless phone as a way to surf the Net. Others might have explored the convergence of the phone with online games. Yet another set of experiments would have focused on using wireless technology to build a communications capability into everything from household appliances to car engines.

Most experiments won't pay off. But this hardly means they are worthless. After all, your fire insurance wasn't a bad investment last year, even if your house didn't burn down. Bill Gross finds value even in failed experiments:

If you kill an idea soon enough, you can take the knowledge you gain from that experiment and apply it to something else. So we learn something from every idea. We think of every $250,000 spent as a $250,000 class. We want to learn from that class and apply it to another class. And we love killing an idea if we learn something from it.

People come in and pitch us ideas. Sometimes we look at them and we say, "Oh, my gosh, you don't even know what you don't know. The things we've learned just from

this hardly means they are worthless.

*what we've killed could help you immensely." There are so many things we can avoid
now because we've done them once and they didn't work. It's unbelievable.*

A business concept that gets killed rather than scaled up isn't a dead loss.
Every experiment produces learning, which, if captured and shared, can
help a company increase the odds that the *next* radical idea finds its mark.

A PORTFOLIO OF VENTURES

At the experimentation stage, the goal is to identify and reduce market
and technology risk: Does the business concept generate sufficient customer interest? Is it technically feasible? If there's sufficient upside, and no
insurmountable technical hurdles, the idea advances to the venture stage.
At the venture stage learning focuses on the feasibility of the profit model
and the operating model, as opposed to the business concept itself. The
question is not whether the business concept will create new revenue
streams, but whether they can be created economically: Can we manage
the execution risk? Can we avoid the competitive risk that our innovation
will be quickly imitated?

This is also the stage where one begins a serious search for strategic
partners who will share risks and contribute complementary skills. There
are three primary factors to consider when deciding whether to partner
and how many partners to have:

- *Financial commitments*: If scaling requires large, irrevocable financial
  commitments, partners may be needed.
- *Range of skills or assets required*: If a company doesn't have all the critical
  skills in-house, it will need partners.
- *Size of the strategic window*: If the risk of preemption is high, partners may
  be needed to help accelerate market penetration.

At this point, it may well be that the original sponsors have to give way
to venture leaders with business-building experience. With the quality of
the business concept already validated, it is the quality of the venture
team that becomes critical.

This is also the stage where decisions must be made about whether to
reintegrate the innovation into a line unit, set it up as a stand-alone business, license the intellectual property to another company, or spin the
venture off as an independent entity. At least four criteria are key to this
decision:

- The fit between the venture and the company's long-term strategic
  goals. If a venture is clearly tangential to a company's long-term
  aspirations, it should be spun off in order to conserve management's

time for projects that are more congruent with long–term ambitions. If the venture is not spun off, it probably won't get the love and attention it needs to reach its potential.

- The venture's *dependence on firm assets and competencies.* If a venture could benefit enormously from leveraging existing assets and competencies, it probably should not be spun off. If it is spun off, it should be given preferential access to those competencies and assets.

- The possibility that the venture will be a *platform for other ventures.* Some ventures are ends in themselves; others are stepping–stones to other ventures. If a venture promises to open up a broad new opportunity arena, that may be a reason to keep it inside.

- The potential for the venture to dramatically outperform other businesses in the portfolio. Increasingly companies are spinning off ventures that might be undervalued by Wall Street were they to be im-prisoned inside a company with otherwise mediocre performance.

Spin–offs are an increasingly popular way of releasing shareholder value from new ventures and fast–growth businesses that have an enor-mous upside. The newly formed company gains the freedom to build an entrepreneurial culture, can pursue its own strategy, and can use its highly valued equity to make acquisitions and motivate employees via stock options–something that is often critical in attracting scarce talent. This is the logic that has driven Barnes & Noble, Microsoft, and dozens of other companies to spin off their Internet ventures.

More often than not, new ventures will lack a tight fit with the com-pany's long–term goals, will be only partly dependent on the company's existing assets and competencies, and won't be a gateway to a vast array of new opportunities. Hence we shouldn't be surprised if the majority of ventures end up as spin–offs or licensing deals, rather than as new busi-ness units.

Occasionally new business concepts will be closely enough related to the existing business that it doesn't make sense to spin them off entirely. This has been the case at Enron. Enron's success in moving from gas trad-ing to electricity trading to online energy trading to energy outsourcing to bandwidth trading rests on its ability to leverage a largely common set of core competencies. It is interesting to note that while Enron typically gives a new venture its own organization home, it also fills the new venture with individuals who carry Enron's competence "genes." Moreover, once a business reaches critical mass, it is often reintegrated into a preexisting division. This ensures that the new genetic material that has been devel-oped in the experimentation and scaling phases gets the chance to imbue the old business with new ideas.

To say that you can't launch a new business concept inside an old business may be true, but it's also simplistic. A new business may need to borrow competencies, systems, or infrastructure from the rest of the company. Indeed, it is this kind of "borrowing" that has allowed Enron to rapidly scale its new businesses. This is an advantage that an independent start-up simply doesn't have. Later on, the need to present a common face to customers or the opportunity to exploit shared costs may argue for the reintegration of a previously independent business. Listen to Enron's president as he describes Enron's move from trading gas to trading power (electricity):

> *When we decided to go into the power-trading business, we moved the people to a different floor. Once the business got big enough, we combined it with our gas business in a single division because they're building off the same core competencies and using the same systems. We wanted similar contract structures so we wouldn't get risk control problems. If the new business wasn't keying off the same core competencies, we wouldn't have to reintegrate it. Another argument for reintegration is to keep the skills fungible. If a new business stays hived off, you kill the internal market for ideas. The old business doesn't get to learn from the new business.*

Spinning a business off is easy—giving it sufficient independence to grow, while at the same time helping it leverage well-honed competencies,

Think about *spin-ups* as well as spin-outs.

is a much more delicate balancing act. Reintegration is more subtle still. But it is the very ability to export competencies to young units, and then subtly combine units to extract economies, that gives large companies their potential advantage over upstarts.

Sometimes the goal of business concept innovation is not to create entirely new businesses, but to reinvent existing businesses. Too often companies think of internal entrepreneurship as focused solely on new businesses—ones that often lie far outside the company's core. A bigger problem for many companies is how to transform a slowly dying core business. For example, while Xerox's Palo Alto Research Center has spun off a number of successful entrepreneurial companies, Xerox's core business has languished for years with anemic growth. A business incubator that throws off new businesses but leaves the core business to languish will inevitably, and rightly, be regarded as little more than a sideshow.

For that reason, it's important to think about *spin-ups* as well as spin-offs. An idea that has the power to radically improve the economics of an existing business shouldn't be held captive in some new venture division. Instead it should be spun up into a corporatewide initiative. A company that embraces the new innovation agenda should expect to create, as Shell has done, dozens of game-changing ventures *inside* existing businesses—a radical new pricing approach here, an unconventional distribution model over there, and so on.

So while high-potential ventures based on entirely new business concepts should probably be nurtured in a new business incubator, successful ventures with the power to transform the core business should be "spun up" inside those businesses. Simply, there is no single mechanism for going from a venture to a business. Most of Schwab's innovations have been spin-ups rather than spin-offs, reinforcing and reinventing Schwab's core brokerage business. In contrast, GE Capital's popcorn stand experiments often end up as new business units.

Let's recap. To go from a possibility to an experiment, an idea *must* be able to be described as a reasonably coherent business concept—with an attractive value proposition, a credible story around wealth creation potential, and a clear sense of how the various components of the business concept will fit together and be mutually reinforcing. For an experiment to become a venture, it *must* have elicited genuine customer enthusiasm and be technically feasible (at least on a small scale). For a venture to move out of the innovation portfolio and become a business, or be spun up inside an existing business, there *must* be a sound profit model, unimpeachable evidence that it's possible to actually capture wealth, and evidence that the business concept can be scaled up.

Now take a detailed look at your company's various innovation portfolios. How many *ideas* does your company have in its innovation bank? Do you have thousands? How many rule-bashing *experiments* are being conducted across your company right now? Do you have hundreds? How many new *ventures* are being nurtured right now? Do you have dozens? And how many big *new businesses* are being built right now? Can you think of even one or two?

Map the size of each portfolio (see the graph "Mapping Your Innovation Portfolios"), and it will be immediately clear whether or not your company is investing in enough options on the future. Turn the diagram 90 degrees to the right, and you have a funnel. If a company hasn't learned how to fill the top of the funnel, it won't get much out the bottom. To return to our

MAPPING YOUR INNOVATION PORTFOLIOS

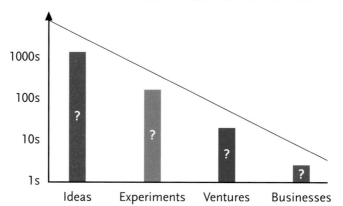

earlier analogy, you have to ask yourself, What's my company's sperm count? You don't get a terrific new business without hundreds of dumb ideas, failed experiments, and aborted ventures.

FROM RADICAL INNOVATION TO CORPORATE STRATEGY

So where does all this leave corporate strategy? Indeed, where does it leave the very concept of a "corporation"? In the age of revolution, will corporate strategy be anything more than the sum of a few dozen, or a few hundred, loosely connected experiments and ventures? Will companies be anything more than a set of bottom-up projects united by shared overhead? Will some combination of internal markets, de-verticalization, value networks, and self-organizing teams reduce the notion of a corporation to disembodied bits of intellectual property floating free in some kind of virtual innovation network? While all these things will undoubtedly make companies less monolithic, they are not going to remove the need for an overarching strategy, nor are they going to entirely do away with the benefits of size and scale.

SIZE STILL MATTERS

In the new economy, size counts for just as much as it did in the old economy. The early winners in the new economy are not will-o'-the-wisp, thin-as-gossamer virtual companies. They may have hundreds of strategic partnerships, but each company is built around a set of core activities and assets where scale is undeniably important. If you look at Microsoft or AOL or Cisco or Amazon.com, you have to believe that there are substantial advantages of scale and scope in the new economy. At one time there were hundreds of carmakers, today there are a handful. So will it be in the new economy. Most Silicon Valley start-ups fail to capture the full benefits of scale and scope. These companies end up as acquisition fodder for companies that have. Mirabilis, Hotmail, Broadcast.com, Netscape, and hundreds of other Internet start-ups have already been swallowed up. More soon will be.

Size will always matter.

Of course it is not size, per se, that counts. Size is the first-order derivative of profit boosters that rely on increasing returns, network effects, and learning effects. Exploit these, and a company will inevitably grow, and smaller, me-too competitors will begin disappearing out the rearview window.

Many among the digerati have been predicting the collapse of large-scale enterprises. They are wrong. Size will always matter. Indeed, at the end of 1999, just 32 companies accounted for half the market capitalization of the S&P 500. An oft-used analogy is the movie industry, where teams of writers, producers, directors, and actors coalesce around a project and then disband when the film is completed. Yet the most enduring fact of the movie business has been the power of the big studios. They are repositories for an enormous amount of project management wisdom.

Despite the occasional "duds," they are skilled story editors, and they have the global reach necessary to market films around the world. Indeed, as every European cultural minister knows, it is the studios that have given Hollywood its global hegemony in the film business. You don't hear Italian or French filmmakers complaining that their colleagues aren't creative enough; you hear them complaining that they can't match the size and scale of American studios. Of course a market of 250 million customers helps, but a market of this size is of no particular advantage unless there are economies of scale in serving such a market.

It is interesting to note that even highly fluid, project-based companies such as Bechtel, Andersen Consulting, and Schlumberger are far, far more than a collection of individual projects. If that were all they were, they wouldn't be multibillion-dollar enterprises.

So, yes, companies may become more like film studios, relying on free agents, raising outside funding for each new venture, and creating short-lived project teams. But somewhere in this brave, new model, size and scale will still matter—because if they don't, you're back to frictionless capitalism where no one has an incentive to invest in something new. On average, companies may shrink. After all, scale and scope advantages apply to activities, not companies per se. But size will be far from irrelevant in the age of revolution.

Indeed, without scale and scope advantages, it is difficult to imagine how a company can enjoy the fruits of radical innovation. Of course when a hot start-up is sold, its founders get a big win. But this just shifts the problem of building scale and scope onto the acquirer—and if the acquirer fails at this, it will never recoup its investment (a common enough occurrence, by the way).

CONSISTENCY COUNTS

You can't build economies of scale and scope without consistency, without doing things over and over in a reasonably consistent way. You can't build difficult-to-imitate competencies without cumulative learning. In turn, it is impossible to achieve consistency and cumulativeness without a degree of coordination across projects or businesses. Consistency requires a set of mutually agreed upon rules about what is "in" and what is "out," what a company is and what it isn't. Lacking some overarching strategy, a company will have a vast greenhouse where thousands of shoots are pushing up through the soil but where few grow big enough to yield a substantial harvest. So innovation is not the *whole* story, but it is the *big* story—because most companies have already figured out the scale and scope thing and now need to start planting new seeds.

INNOVATION IS NOT THE WHOLE STORY, BUT IT IS THE BIG STORY

In the age of revolution, the challenge will be to marry radical innovation with disciplined execution—to merge the efficiency of a Toyota production line with the radical innovation of Silicon Valley, to blend diligence and curiosity. To be a gray-haired revolutionary, a company must be systematic *and* spontaneous, highly focused *and* opportunistic, brutally efficient *and* wildly imaginative.

Oil and water, chalk and cheese, such amalgams are impossible without a new synthesis. Notice that in making an argument for mass and scale, I haven't used words like hierarchy, control, and plan. These are industrial age words. Instead I talk about consistency, cumulativeness, boundaries, and focus. Remember, the goal is "order without careful crafting." So where does this order come from? It must *emerge* from the stream of radical innovation that begins to flow once you make innovation a corporatewide capability.

FINDING STRATEGY

In any stream of ideas, some kind of deeper pattern will be evident. The trick is to look for patterns, for consistency and cumulativeness that will yield advantages of scale and scope *across* ideas, experiments, and ventures. Patterns come in many forms:

- *Allegiance to a standard,* such as Microsoft's allegiance to the Windows operating system, which spawned, both within Microsoft and without, hundreds of small innovations built atop the Windows standard.

- *A widely shared core competence,* such as GE Capital's competence in risk management and deal structuring, based on cumulative learning.

- *A set of values around a brand* that can be applied broadly, as in the case of Virgin and Disney, and thereby yield economies of scope.

- *A common customer set* that is best served in a coordinated way, which is the logic behind Amazon.com's creating a wide variety of "stores within a store" rather than making each store an entirely independent entity.

These patterns provide the *logic for the corporation.* They provide the connective tissue that makes the company more than a collection of stand-alone projects. While there is nothing new in saying that a company must be more than a sum of its parts, what is new is how the summing up gets done. It can't start with some grand pronouncement from on high about "what business we're in." It can't come from a bunch of senior vice presidents working to craft a common mission statement. It certainly shouldn't come as the panicked reaction to demands from stock analysts for a strategy that will hold water. Instead, it has to be filtered out of the stream of innovation that flows from the fertile minds of individuals throughout the organization.

While senior executives can no longer be the sole source of new business concepts, it is their responsibility to look across the patchwork of radical innovation to find the interesting—and wealth-laden—patterns. One set of opportunities will push the company in one direction, allowing it to build one kind of scope or scale advantage; another set of opportunities will push the company in another direction, with another set of potential synergies. At Cisco, it is account management, rather than a particular technology, that turns a myriad of products into customer solutions and provides the dominant logic for what the company gets into and stays out of. Not surprisingly, Cisco finds it much easier to latch onto a new technology than to change its customer focus. (As networking moves into the home, it will be interesting to see if Cisco can win there as big as it has won in Fortune 500 accounts.) In contrast, Microsoft's commitment has been to the Windows standard. Microsoft's innovations—be it Windows CE, Internet Explorer, Microsoft Office, or Windows NT—all exploit a common architecture. Windows-based products are available to a wide range of customers through an almost infinite number of channels. Indeed, Microsoft is as agnostic about channels and customers as Cisco is about technologies.

The examples of Cisco and Microsoft bring home a crucial point. While idea generation should be unbounded, a company is compelled to make choices about where it focuses its energies. Yet it is important that such choices do not rule out the possibility of entirely "unscripted" innovation. That's why every company needs well-functioning internal markets for innovation that funnel resources to nascent ideas and propel them through the experimentation stage. But at some point the most promising experiments will need big injections of capital. It is here that senior management must begin to make choices about which patterns it wants to emphasize and which it wishes to de-emphasize.

Those choices must be based on an unimpeachable and clearly articulated logic—"We will create more wealth by exploiting this particular dimension of scale and relatedness than we will by exploiting some other dimension." Over time, these choices will begin to bias the innovation process. Again, it's not that top management declares some kinds of innovation to be out of bounds. *Nothing* is out of bounds. Instead, would-be revolutionaries come to understand that by exploiting shared assets and

competencies or getting access to a big customer base, they gain scale and scope advantages that give their ideas added momentum. Of course those who want to go off in different directions can still do so, and there will be mechanisms—licensing, spin-offs, and alliances—for capturing wealth out of ideas that don't fit within the emerging corporate strategy. Occasionally those out-of-bounds ideas will be so compelling and valuable that they will force the company to redefine the very essence of its strategy. This has been the case at GE, which no one regards any longer as an "industrial" company. In this sense, top management doesn't so much *make* strategy as *find* strategy.

Of course there are already deep patterns that determine what kinds of strategies people create in your company—I've called these patterns ortho-doxies. But they are the patterns of precedent, not the patterns of possibility. So don't take any of what I've just said as an excuse to simply lock down your current definition of corporate strategy. Remember, corporate strategy must be *distilled from a torrent of innovation.* If you don't yet have a torrent of nonlinear business concepts and weird and wonderful experiments, that's where you need to start. Don't build a dam before you have a stream.

ARE YOU REVOLUTION-READY?

Is your organization ready for the age of revolution? Does it have an irrevocable commitment to building the components of the new innova-tion solution? Is its top management finished "making" strategy and ready to "find" it? To determine this, ask yourself these questions:

- Have individuals been given the training and the tools they need to become business concept innovators?
- Do the metrics in your company focus as much on innovation and wealth creation as on optimization and wealth conservation?
- Does your IT system support a corporatewide electronic marketplace for innovation?
- Has your organization committed itself to systematically redesigning its core management processes to make them more innovation-friendly?
- Does the "wheel of innovation" spin rapidly in your organization, or is it limited by the speed of quarterly and annual processes?
- Do would-be entrepreneurs know how to design experiments around radical ideas?
- Are there formal mechanisms for capturing and monitoring the learning from innovation experiments?
- Does your organization get the very best talent behind the best new ideas, even when those ideas are at an early stage of development?
- Is your organization explicitly managing a portfolio of ideas, a portfolio of experiments, and a portfolio of ventures?
- Is your organization flexible enough to design the right kind of institu-tional home for promising ventures?
- Are you confident that *your* company is in charge of the transformation agenda in its industry?

Don't despair if you answered "no" more often than "yes." There's not one company in a hundred that has fully committed itself to building the new innovation solution. What matters is what *you're* going to do *next.*

Are you ready to commit yourself to the new innovation agenda?

THE NEW INNOVATION AGENDA

Continuous improvement	*and*	Nonlinear innovation
Product and process innovation	*and*	Business concept innovation
"Releasing" wealth	*and*	Creating wealth
Serendipity	*and*	Capability
Visionaries	*and*	Activists
Scientists, workers	*and*	Silicon Valley

Are you ready to start working on the new innovation solution? (See the figure "The Innovation Solution.")

THE INNOVATION SOLUTION

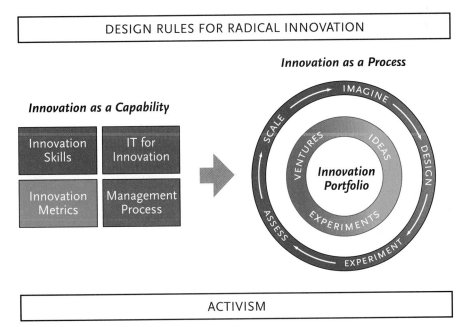

You can start now and get ahead of the curve, or wait and fight a rearguard action. What's it going to be?

ARE *YOU* A REVOLUTIONARY?

It doesn't matter whether you're the big cheese or a cubicle rat. It doesn't matter whether you fly in a Gulfstream V or ride the crosstown bus. It doesn't matter whether you command a legion of minions or only your PalmPilot. All that matters is whether you care enough to start from where you are. So ask yourself, Do you care enough about your integrity to speak the truth and challenge the little lies that jeopardize your company's future? Do you care enough about the future to argue with precedent and stick a thumb in the eye of tradition? Do you care enough about your colleagues to help them get off the treadmill of progress? Do you care so much about the magnificent difference you can make in this world that you're willing to try and change it with your bare heart? Do you care enough about finding meaning and significance in the 80 percent of your life you devote to work that you're ready to start a movement within your company? Do you care enough about the creative impulse that resides in every human breast that you're ready to help everyone be a revolutionary? Do you care enough about doing something so wonderful and unexpected for customers that you're willing to put your comfy job on the line? Go ahead, ask yourself, Do you care enough to lead the revolution?

I began this book with a simple observation—that for the first time in history our heritage is no longer our destiny. Our dreams are no longer fantasies, but possibilities. There isn't a human being who has ever lived who wouldn't want to be alive right now, at this moment so pregnant with promise. Among all your forebears, among the countless generations who had no hope of progress, among all those whose spirits were betrayed by progress, you are the one who now stands on the threshold of a new age—the age of revolution. You are blessed beyond belief. Don't falter. Don't hesitate. You were given this opportunity for a reason. Find it. Lead the revolution.

All that matters is whether you care enough to start from where you are.

Notes

1 The End of Progress

1   Andrew Ross Sorkin, "Internet Stock Fever Spreads to Britain as Freeserve Surges," *The New York Times on the Web*, 27 July 1999, <www.nytimes.com>.

2   Katherine Cavanaugh, "Bandwidth's New Bargaineers," *Technology Review—MIT's Magazine of Innovation*, November/December 1998.

3   Simon Patterson and Gordon Clark, "Net Firms Show How to Balance Risk and Reward," *Sunday Times* (London), 31 October 1999, sec 3.

4   "Competition 2000," an unpublished survey sponsored by MCI and carried out by The Gallup Organization.

5   Gary Hamel and C. K. Prahalad, *Competing for the Future* (Boston: Harvard Business School Press, 1994).

6   "P&G to Slash 15,000 Jobs, Shut 10 Plants," *Wall Street Journal*, 10 June 1999.

7   Alan Cowell, "Drastic Cuts Are in Store for Unilever," *San Jose Mercury News*, 23 February 2000.

8   "ConAgra Products," <www.conagra.com/product.html>.

9   Susan Moran, "The Candyman," *Business 2.0*, June 1999, 66–67.

10 Charles Handy, *The Alchemists* (London: Hutchinson, 1999).

2 Rising Expectations, Diminishing Returns

1   Nikhil Deogun and Steven Lipin, "When the Big Deal Turns Bad," *Wall Street Journal*, 8 December 1999.

2   "Addicted to Mergers?" *Business Week*, 6 December 1999, 85.

3   Strategos calculations.

4   Tish Williams, "WorldCom's Big Bluffer," *Upside Today*, 14 July 1999, <www.upside.com/texis/mvm/daily_tish?id=37649f420>.

5   Jolie Solomon, "When Cool Goes Cold," *Newsweek*, 30 March 1998, 37.

6   John Markoff, "Silicon Valley Accelerates to Web Speed," *International Herald Tribune*, 4 June 1996.

7   *Primetime Network Ratings and Shares*, Nielsen Media Research, 2000.

8   Bill Carter, "As Their Dominance Erodes, Networks Plan Big Changes," *New York Times*, 11 May 1978.

3 Business Concept Innovation

1   Marianne Wilson, "Say Chic—C'est Sephora," *Chain Store Age*, July 1998, 134.

2   Rebecca Quick, "New Web Sites Let Kids Shop, Like, Without Credit Cards," *Wall Street Journal*, 14 June 1999.

3   Neal Templin, "Electronic Kiosk Checks in Guests at More Hotels," *Wall Street Journal*, 16 February 1999.

4   Renee Deger, "Hitting the Jackpot," *The Recorder/Cal Law*, 6 January 2000, <www.lawnewsnetwork.com/stories/A12840-2000Jan5.html>.

5   Kevin Maney, "Media Deal Will Change How Musicians Peddle Their Products," *USA Today*, 19 January 2000.

6   Calmietta Y. Coleman and Ernest Beck, "Retailers from U.S. and Europe Form Internet Supply Exchange," *Wall Street Journal Interactive Edition*, 3 April 2000 <www.interactive.wsj.com/archive>.

7   Peter D. Henig, "And Now, EcoNets," *Red Herring*, February 2000, 96–108.

8   Richard Siklos and Amy Barrett, "The Net-Phone-TV-Cable Monster," *Business Week*, 10 May 1999, 32.

9   "Interview: Gordon Moore, Intel," *PC Magazine*, 25 March 1997, 236.

10 United Rentals, <www.unitedrentals.com> (23 August 1999).

11 Michael A. Hiltzik, *Dealers of Lightning: Xerox PARC and the Dawn of the Computer Age* (New York: HarperBusiness, 1999).

4 BE YOUR OWN SEER

1   "Garbage In, Garbage Out," *The Economist*, 3 June 1995, 70.

2   Fara Warner and Joseph B. White, "New From Japan: Bar Stools on Wheels," *Wall Street Journal*, 25 October 1999.

3   Michael Kavanagh, "Porn Will Continue to Dominate Web Revenue," *Marketing Week*, 27 May 1999, 43.

4   These distinctions are adapted and reprinted from *European Management Journal*, volume 13, Georg von Krogh and Johan Roos, "Conversation Management," page 393, copyright 1995, with permission from Elsevier Science.

5 CORPORATE REBELS

1   Debra E. Meyerson and Maureen A. Scully, "Tempered Radicalism and the Politics of Ambivalence and Change," *Organizational Science* 6, no. 5 (September–October 1995): 585–600.

2   Robert A. Guth, "Inside Sony's Trojan Horse," *Wall Street Journal*, 25 February 2000.

6 GO AHEAD! REVOLT!

1   Saul D. Alinsky, *Rules for Radicals: A Practical Primer for Realistic Radicals* (New York: Vintage Books, 1989).

2   Mary Beth Rogers, *Cold Anger: A Story of Faith and Power Politics* (Denton, TX: University of North Texas Press, 1990), 88.

7 GRAY-HAIRED REVOLUTIONARIES

1   Erick Schonfeld, "Schwab Puts It All Online," *Fortune*, 7 December 1998, 94.

2   Joseph Nocera, "Cooking with Cisco," *Fortune*, 25 December 1995, 114.

3   Glenn Drexhage, "How Cisco Bought Its Way to the Top," *Corporate Finance*, June 1998, 21.

4   Eric Nee, "Interview with John Chambers of Cisco Systems, Inc.," *Upside Magazine*, 30 June 1996, 54.

5   Andrew Kupfer, "The Real King of the Internet," *Fortune*, 7 September 1998, 84.

8 DESIGN RULES FOR INNOVATION

1   M. Mitchell Waldrop, *Complexity: The Emerging Science at the Edge of Order and Chaos* (New York: Simon & Schuster, 1992), 241, 242.

2   Viktor E. Frankl, *Man's Search for Meaning* (New York: Pocket Books, 1984), 17.

3   Tim Stevens, "Breaking Up Is Profitable Too," *Industry Week*, 21 June 1999, 28–34.

4   Matt Krantz, "Online Workers' Windfall Could Flatten Investors," *USA Today*, 26 October 1999.

5   Neal E. Boudette, "How a Software Titan Missed the Internet Revolution," *Wall Street Journal*, 18 January 2000.

9 THE NEW INNOVATION SOLUTION

1   Steve Kerr, "On the Folly of Rewarding A, While Hoping for B," *Academy of Management Journal* 18 (December 1975): 769–783.

PHOTO CREDITS

p. 2—© 2000 Martin Barraud/Stone; p. 5—© 2000 Juan Silva/The Image Bank;
p. 6—© Alexandra Avakian/Contact Press Images/Picture Quest; p. 8—Digital Imagery/
© PhotoDisc, Inc.; p. 9—top: SuperStock; bottom: Digital Imagery/© PhotoDisc, Inc.;
p. 11—© 2000 Zigy Kaluzny/Stone; p. 20—© Charles March/The Image Bank; p. 22—Digital
Imagery/© PhotoDisc, Inc.; p. 26—Digital Imagery/© PhotoDisc, Inc.; p. 27—Underwood Photo
Archives/SuperStock; p. 29—Eyewire; p. 32—© 2000 Euan Myles/Stone; p. 36—Carl Purcell
© The Purcell Team/Picture Quest; p. 38—© Bob Daemmrich/Stock Boston/Picture Quest;
p. 43—Artville/© PhotoDisc, Inc.; p. 46—© Rich Iwasaki/Allstock/Picture Quest;
p. 57—© Eric Meola/The Image Bank; p. 60—Digital Imagery/© PhotoDisc, Inc.; p. 67—© 2000
Laurence Dutton/Stone; pp. 72–73—Artville/PhotoDisc, Inc.; p. 74—Artville/Picture Quest;
p. 81—Artville/Picture Quest; p. 83—© Black Star Publishing Co./Picture Quest; p. 84—© James
Schnepf; p. 89—© Jeffrey L. Rotman/CORBIS; p. 98—Carl Purcell © The Purcell Team/Picture
Quest; p. 104—© 2000 Betsie Van der Meer/Stone; p. 107—© Robert Rathe/Stock Boston/
Picture Quest; p. 109—Digital Imagery/© PhotoDisc, Inc.; p. 116—© Digital Vision/Picture
Quest; p. 118—Bettmann/CORBIS; p. 121—Digital Imagery/© PhotoDisc, Inc.; p. 123—CMCD,
Inc./Picture Quest; p. 125—© 2000 John Lund/Stone; p. 127—© 2000 Steven Weinberg/Stone;
p. 130—© Photri, Inc./The Stock Market; p. 133—Eyewire; p. 134—© Juan Silva/The Image Bank;
p. 137—Digital Imagery/© PhotoDisc, Inc.; p. 138—© SIE Production/The Stock Market;
p. 144—© Lynne Siler/Focus Group International/Picture Quest; p. 146—© Digital Vision/
Picture Quest; pp. 148–49—© Magellan Geographix/Picture Quest; pp. 152–53—CORBIS;
p. 155—Underwood Photo Archives/SuperStock; p. 159—© Tom Campbell/IT Stock
International/Picture Quest; p. 160—© Bob Daemmrich/Stock Boston/Picture Quest;
p. 163—© Segar/Archive Photos; pp. 166–67—© 2000 Mike McQueen/Stone;
pp. 174–75—left to right: Digital Imagery/© PhotoDisc, Inc.; © Photo Sphere Images,
Ltd./Picture Quest; Artville/Picture Quest; © Photo Sphere Images, Ltd./Picture Quest; Digital
Imagery/© PhotoDisc, Inc.; © Photo Sphere Images, Ltd./Picture Quest; p. 183—© 2000 Marc
Carter/Stone; p. 186—© 2000 Reza Estakhrian/Stone; p. 189—Alfred Gescheidt/The Image Bank;
p. 191—© 2000 Nick Dolding/Stone; p. 194—Digital Imagery/© PhotoDisc, Inc.;
p. 195—top: © 2000 Steve Vaccariello/Stone; center: CORBIS; bottom: Digital Imagery/
© PhotoDisc, Inc.; p. 197—© Artville/Picture Quest; pp. 200–201—CMCD, Inc./Picture Quest;
p. 203—© 2000 Reza Estakhrian/Stone; p. 205—© 2000 Mark Harris/Stone;
p. 208—© 2000 Tony Arruza/ Stone; p. 213—© Bettmann/CORBIS; p. 214—CORBIS;
p. 217—© 2000 Stephen Swintek/Stone; p. 221—© 2000 Laurence Monneret/Stone;
p. 222—© Tom Stewart/The Stock Market; p. 227—Artville/Picture Quest; p. 233—© 2000 Tim
Flach/Stone; p. 236—Eyewire; p. 239—© Phyllis Picardi/Stock Boston/Picture Quest;
p. 240—Artville/PhotoDisc, Inc.; p. 242—© Harold Pfeiffer/Allstock/Picture Quest;
p. 245—CORBIS; p. 246—Digital Imagery/© PhotoDisc, Inc.; p. 251—© West Stock, Inc.;
p. 252—Digital Imagery/© PhotoDisc, Inc.; p. 253—© Ray Fisher/Black Star Publishing
Co./Picture Quest; p. 259—© Oliver Strewe/Stone; p. 267—© Gavriel Jean/The Stock Market;
p. 269—© Yoav Levy/Phototake/Picture Quest; p. 272—© 2000 Steve Taylor/Stone;
p. 278—© 2000 Dugald Bremner/Stone; p. 280—© 2000 Bruce Forster/Stone; p. 282—Digital
Imagery/© PhotoDisc, Inc.; p. 285—Digital Imagery/© PhotoDisc, Inc.; p. 288—© Earl Glass/
Stock Boston/Picture Quest; p. 292—Palazzo Ducale, Venice, Italy/Lauros-Giraudon, Paris/
SuperStock; p. 295—Digital Imagery/© PhotoDisc, Inc.; p. 299—CNRI/GJLP/©Phototake/
Picture Quest; p. 304—Eyewire; p. 314—© Jose Azel/Aurora/Picture Quest.

INDEX

ABOUT THE AUTHOR

Gary Hamel is a Founder and Chairman of Strategos, a company dedicated to helping its clients develop revolutionary strategies. He is also Visiting Professor of Strategic and International Management at London Business School.

The Economist calls Hamel "the world's reigning strategy guru." Peter Senge calls him "the most influential thinker on strategy in the Western world." As the author of a multitude of landmark business concepts, he has fundamentally changed the focus and content of strategy in many of the world's most successful companies. The *Journal of Business Strategy* recently ranked Professor Hamel as one of the top 25 business minds of the twentieth century.

His previous book, *Competing for the Future*, has been hailed by *The Economist*, the *Financial Times*, the *Washington Post*, and many other journals as one of the decade's most influential business books, and by *Business Week* as "Best Management Book of the Year." With C. K. Prahalad, Hamel has published seven articles in the *Harvard Business Review*, introducing such breakthrough concepts as strategic intent, core competence, corporate imagination, expeditionary marketing, and strategy as stretch. Hamel's more recent articles, "Strategy as Revolution" and "Bringing Silicon Valley Inside," are already on their way to becoming management classics. His articles have also been published in *Fortune*, the *Wall Street Journal*, MIT's *Sloan Management Review*, and a myriad of other journals. Hamel serves on the board of the Strategic Management Society. He also sits on the board of K.I.D.S. (Kids in a Drug–Free Society).

Hamel has led initiatives within many of the world's leading companies. In his work he helps companies to first imagine and then create the new rules, new businesses, and new industries that will define the industrial landscape of the future.

He resides in Woodside, California.